MASLOW ON MANAGEMENT

ABRAHAM H. MASLOW

with
DEBORAH C. STEPHENS and GARY HEIL

JOHN WILEY & SONS, INC.
New York • Chichester • Weinheim • Brisbane • Singapore • Toronto

Published by John Wiley & Sons, Inc.
Published simultaneously in Canada.

This publication is designed to provide accurate and authoritative information
in regard to the subject matter covered. It is sold with the understanding that the
publisher is not engaged in rendering legal, accounting, or other professional services.
If legal advice or other expert assistance is required, the services of a competent
professional person should be sought.

Library of Congress Cataloging-in-Publication Data:
Maslow, Abraham H. (Abraham Harold)
    Maslow on management / Abraham H. Maslow
        p.   cm.
    Based on: Eupsychian management.
    Includes bibliographical references.
    ISBN 0-471-24780-4 (cloth : alk. paper)
    1. Psychology, Industrial.   2. Maslow, Abraham H. (Abraham
Harold)—Contributions in management.   3. Maslow, Abraham H.
(Abraham Harold)—Diaries.   4. Self-actualization (Psychology)
I. Maslow, Abraham H. (Abraham Harold). Eupsychian management.
II. Center for Innovative Leadership (U.S.)   III. Title.
HF5548.8.M3754   1998
158.7—dc21   98-21068

Printed in the United States of America.

10   9

This book is dedicated to my daughters,
Ann and Ellen.

Contents

Foreword to the New Edition

37 Years Later

It's amazing, isn't it, that a book out-of-print for almost 37 years, a book that just barely sold its first printing and then virtually vanished from view—into oblivion really, without even a whimper—has suddenly burst upon the scene, piquing just about everybody's interest. Intriguing thousands of Maslow fans and thousands of others who mistily remember his name from their undergraduate classes or when phrases like self-actualization or peak experiences or hierarchy of needs come to mind or scroll across their computer screens.

Why the book disappeared still bedevils me. Maybe it was the title. I had implored Abe to use a more reader-friendly title but who was I to challenge the maze of phrases and seductive writing. The original publishers, though, went ballistic but Abe stubbornly held out for, yes, *Eupsychian Management*.

But more likely, it was the times. A rather complacent industrial America, famously supreme since World War II, was not particularly interested in business books, especially by a psychologist who had no business experience to speak of. In addition to that daunting title, Abe writes in a discursive manner—thought pieces, nuggets thrown about, rough drafts, like artists' sketches or finger exercises for the violin.

The entries in this book were transcribed word-for-word from his journals. When Abe first showed his journals to me, I said very forcefully, "you must publish them." He resisted for months, said they were just "works in progress," only drafts, "not academic," "I'm new to this field," and so on. One excuse after another. Finally, reason prevailed. I talked him into publishing his journals and then found a publisher whose editor, I'm sure, didn't truly appreciate the book's meaning, asking me in confidence if English was Abe's second language.

There are sections of the book that are hilariously innocent and other parts which are terrifyingly prescient and penetrating. But there are no neat little formulaic *paradigms*—if you can bear reading that word one more time. Nor are there 19 Rules for Effective *Anything*. What you *will* experience throughout this marvelous book is a genius-at-play with all of his elegant ruminations, a thoughtful writer who throughout his life cultivated a beginner's mind. As he says in the Preface, "A novice can often see things that the expert overlooks."

He takes on and challenges the major management figures of the 1960s who were then writing about the industrial workplace, notably Drucker, McGregor, Rogers, and Likert. Always in a friendly, non-adversarial way, but in a way that you know must have turned those iconic heads. Drucker claims that Abe wrote this book to bring him and McGregor down to earth. I doubt that that was the primary motive, but Abe certainly does question the assumptions of those giants. But as you continue reading, I hope you'll notice some other things as well, many of which I either missed or didn't fully understand 35 years ago.

For example, Abe was one of the earliest figures to realize that, "the industrial situation may serve as the new laboratory for the study of the psycho-dynamics, of high human development, of the ideal ecology for the human being." His prescience was also quite extraordinary. In the last chapter, to take only one example, he foresees, with terrifying accuracy the eventual downfall of the Soviet Union and America's future success because "of the growth-fostering tendencies in industry . . . If the Americans can turn out a better type of human being than the Russians [remember, dear reader, he wrote this at the peak of the Cold War] then this will ultimately do the trick. Americans will simply be more loved, more respected, more trusted, etc., etc."

There are two other things about this book I'd like to mention. One is how politically incorrect he sounds today and how downright courageous Abe has always been. Read his chapter on the Aggridants, where he discusses the dilemma of democracy: what do we do with superior individuals? What do we do with extreme disparities in talent? He tackles issues that everybody ducked in the 1960s and are still ducking today. Abe has always asked the *BIG* questions. This book tries to deal with two major questions or moral edicts throughout but are worth repeating over and over again: "How good a society does human nature permit?" "How good a human nature does society permit?"

Maybe that helps to explain my opening questions: Why has the promise of republication generated such perfervid interest and why did the book so unceremoniously migrate over to the remaindered shelf so soon after publication? The first question is a little easier to answer. The problems organizations face today are far more vexing than the problems they had to address in the 1960s: globalization, intense competitiveness, galloping technology, change/change/change. As to the second question, now that I reread the book, it's very clear. The book raises tremendously threatening questions and Abe always thought that the primary goal of science was "to shove truth down the reluctant throat." Maybe our throats or even our minds are now ready for Maslow's profound medicine.

Abe Maslow requires no explanation or interpretation. He is an open book, knowledgeable by his words and his treasured person. The first sentence in one of Abe's most important books, *Toward a Psychology of Being,* published in 1962:

> There is now emerging over the horizon, a new conception of human sickness and of human health, a psychology that I find so thrilling and full of wonderful possibilities that I yield to the temptation to present it publicly even before it is checked or confirmed, and before it can be called reliable scientific knowledge.

It is all there in that one sentence—a sentence that has sentenced psychology to a new life; that has turned it inside out or more precisely outside in: to gain truth through personal experience, be a "courageous knower."

Science to Abe was a way of life and love—his poetry and debureaucratizing it (or as he would prefer—resacralizing it) was his goal. Abe was a conquistador—a lone one for many years—always advancing with courage and charm like the most seductive crusader.

He wrote in his last book, *The Psychology of Science:*

> The assault troops of science are certainly more necessary to science than its military police. This is so even though they are apt to get much

dirtier and to suffer higher casualties, but somebody has to be the first
one through the mine fields.

Science was his poetry, his religion, his wonder. He wrote, also in his
Psychology of Science:

> Science can be the religion of the nonreligious, the poetry of the non-
> poet, the art of the man who cannot paint, the humor of the serious
> man, and the love making of the inhibited and shy man. Not only does
> science begin in wonder, it also ends in wonder.

I quote lavishly from Abe's own work, because his work was his
life, and to know one is to greet the other. I first got to know Abe—
or encounter him (like many of us) through one of his books. It was
my senior year at Antioch College, and while taking a tutorial with
the then president, Douglas McGregor, he recommended a book on
abnormal psychology written by Maslow and Mittelmann.

It was a breath of fresh air. It was a book that really drew me into
psychology as a calling. I'll never forget in this book, in the fron-
tispiece, there were two panel pictures: one that showed a group of
happy-looking gurgling babies in the maternity room of a children's
hospital—newborn babies—and just beneath that was another panel
showing a group of people—haggard, drawn, and sallow—crowded
into the New York subway hanging on, with the most baleful looks,
to the straps above their heads, and through the windows you could
see these sallow faces. And the caption beneath these two panels was,
"What happened?" And that's the question that Abe spent most of his
life trying to answer.

That was my first encounter with Abe, and my last was in Buffalo
in the spring of 1968, when he was on his way to Columbus, Ohio, to
visit his new granddaughter and celebrate her birth. At that time I conducted a long interview with Abe Maslow from which we made a film.
He said to me at that time, right after the filming of our interview, "I
have to make an important decision." He knew at the time that to
write at all took all the energy he could still muster. He questioned,
"Have I written all the good psychology I can expect to write?" It was
brought to a head by Bill Laughlin's (chairman and CEO of Saga
Foods) marvelous offer to join him in California. He said, "I hesitated
for days and then, with Bertha's approval, I refused all the other offers

from the major universities to go out West and to spend my full time writing." He said, "I am about to cut myself adrift from all external circumstances—no Harvards, no Brandeises, I want to make a last song, sweet and exultant."

Between the first encounter with Maslow and Mittelmann at Antioch and the visit to Buffalo were crowded many lovely times with the Maslows, shimmering, genial, and warm visits, always graced by Bertha's effortless sociability (like the meandering Charles River outside the wooden deck of their Newton home) and her crowded and sumptuous refrigerator. And always Abe—with that incredibly soft, shy, tentative, and gentle voice making the most outrageous remarks. Breakfast with the Maslow family was intellectual nirvana—good and endless food, good and endless talk—where always I had the distinct feeling of gaining energy, of being lifted off my feet.

Franck, a Nobel laureate in physics, once said, "I always know when I hear a good idea because of the feeling of terror which seizes me." In this respect, Abe was a terrorist—a terrorist always bursting through the barricades of conventional wisdom and outdistancing the emplaced cannon.

I always sensed, when with Abe, a childlike spirit of innocence and wonder—always wearing his eyebrows (as Thomas Mann said about Freud) continually raised in a constant expression of awe. Abe wrote, about Aldous Huxley, what I consider to be actually an accurate self-description of Abe Maslow:

> May I mention one more technique that I saw at its best in Aldous Huxley, who was certainly a great man—one who was able to accept his talents and use them to the full. He managed it by perpetually marveling at how interesting and fascinating everything was, by wondering like a youngster at how miraculous things are, by saying frequently, "extraordinary, extraordinary!" He could look out at the world with wide eyes, with unabashed innocence, awe, fascination—which is a kind of admission of smallness, a form of humility—and then proceed calmly and unafraid on the great tasks he set for himself.

During those years, Abe was making history by remaking psychology. So many of the terms, phrases, and concepts now accepted, even into the national vernacular, are Abe's: need hierarchy, self-actualization, peak experiences. And all that went into the Third Force of Psychology as Humanistic Psychology.

Anthony Sutich said recently, "Abraham Maslow is the greatest psychologist since Freud. The second half of this century belongs to him."

If the first half of this century saw modern psychology take the mind and heart out of psychology, then Abe Maslow, under heroic conditions, disinterred them—more burnished than before. He wrote:

> In exchange for Freud, Adler, Jung, Fromm, and Horney, we are offered beautifully executed, precise, elegant experiments which, in at least half the cases, have nothing to do with enduring human problems and which are written primarily for other members of the guild. It is so reminiscent of the lady at the zoo who asked the keeper at the zoo whether the hippopotamus was male or female. "Madam," he replied, "it would seem to me that that would be of interest only to another hippopotamus."

For me—perhaps for all humanistic scholars—Abe's core legacy was to revive the full humanness to science by declaring all of our human experiences capable of study. He wrote, in the final pages of his *Toward a Psychology of Being:*

> All the world, all of experience must be open to study. Nothing, not even the "personal" problems need to be closed off from human investigation. Otherwise, we will force ourselves into the idiotic position that some labor unions have frozen themselves into: where only carpenters may touch only wood. New materials and new methods must then be annoying and even threatening catastrophes rather than opportunities. I remind you also of the primitive tribes who must place everyone in the kinship system. If a newcomer shows up who cannot be placed, there is no way to solve the problem but to kill him. . . .

For Abe—for us—each man's task is to become the best "himself." Joe Doakes must not try to be like Abraham Lincoln or Thomas Jefferson or any other model hero. He must become the best Joe Doakes in the world. This he can do, and only this is necessary or possible. Here he has no competition.

What Abe has done is to make what was religious, mystical, or supernatural natural—to give man ownership over his human potentials rather than have them arrogated by the temporal nonhuman institutions which at times science, business, and the church have been. He quotes Rainier Maria Rilke, who said, "If your everyday life seems poor to you, do not accuse it; accuse yourself; tell yourself you are not poet enough to summon up its riches since to the Creator there is no poverty and no poor or unimportant place."

Two big things that Abe gave to all of us: the art and science of becoming more fully human and the democratization of the soul. For these we will be forever indebted.

WARREN BENNIS
University Professor and Distinguished
Professor of Business Administration,
Marshall School of Business,
University of Southern California

Introduction

This is not about new management tricks or gimmicks or superficial techniques that can be used to manipulate human beings more efficiently. Rather it is a clear confrontation of one basic set of orthodox values by another newer system of values that claims to be both more efficient, and more true. It draws on some of the truly revolutionary consequences of the discovery that human nature has been sold short.

—Abraham Maslow

ABRAHAM MASLOW

What can a set of journal entries that are nearly 37 years old teach us about managing today? We asked ourselves that question when Ann Kaplan, Abe's daughter, approached us with the idea of republishing them. Our answer is that Maslow's ideas about work, self-actualization, and the influence of business in developing "the good society" are some of the most profound thinking we have discovered in nearly 20 years of studying leaders.

We immersed ourselves in Maslow's work: his published books, articles, and personal papers. Although we had always equated Maslow with his hierarchy of needs theory, we discovered in his work a collection of research and wisdom and insights that were decades ahead of its time. His pioneering work in the field of management, creativity, and innovation speaks to us today in a voice that makes current work and thinking appear almost obsolete. Maslow's theories regarding self-actualization and work, customer loyalty, leadership, and the role of uncertainty as a source of creativity, paint a picture of today's digital age that is profound.

The future Maslow describes in his journals is the world we live in today—the digital age. A world in which human potential will be the primary source of competitive advantage in almost every industry, every organization, every institution. Maslow's work makes us question whether we understand the crossroads we have come to. A crossroads, where in our effort to just keep pace, we will need committed, educated, and highly motivated people at all levels; crossroads where compliance or authoritarian means of leadership no longer work; crossroads where the needs of society and the needs of a business are becoming so intertwined that if one entity is dysfunctional the other will suffer the consequences.

Yet, are we prepared to go forward? We speak the language of this new frontier, but have yet to embrace the meaning. We need look no further than our new vernacular for people: intellectual capital, human resources, knowledge workers, and all of the other terms we have invented to disguise the fact that what we are speaking of are people and their untapped potential.

People spend too many hours in organizations and institutions that do not support them in reaching their true potential. We believe this should be as much a driving force as financial management, product development, return on investment, and all of the other indicators we put into place to measure success. Without this force, our successes will be short lived, our plans nothing more than short-term, and our ability to continue to compete in a global world severely restrained. Perhaps it is time we embrace Maslow's words and truly believe that we can create organizations which fully tap the true potential of people.

BUILDING GREAT ORGANIZATIONS

In bringing back the journals of Abraham Maslow, we set out to prove that his theories and ideas were, in fact, possible. Our journey took us to leaders in a wide variety of industries. We asked these leaders to discuss their thoughts on Maslow's words and their own struggles and triumphs in building enlightened organizations.

We would like to thank the numerous leaders who gave their time to read these journals and who allowed us time to explore their thoughts:

- Mort Meyerson, Former Chairman, Perot Systems
- Warren Bennis, University of Southern California
- George McKown, Chairman McKown and De Leeuw
- David Wright, Chief Executive Officer, Amdahl

- Linda Alepin, Chief Executive Officer, Pebblesoft Learning
- Brian Lehnen, Director, Village Enterprise Trust
- Sherri Rose, Former Director, Apple University
- Michael Ray, Stanford Graduate School of Business
- Jackie McGrath, Insight Out Collaborations
- Anne Robinson, Former Chairman and Co-Founder, Windham Hill Records
- Michael Murphy, Co-Founder, Esalen Institute
- Andrew Kay, Founder, KAYPRO Computers
- Tom Kosnik, Professor Engineering and Global Marketing, Stanford University
- Stanford Engineering students in IE 292
- Aspen Ski Company
- Pat O'Donnell, Chief Executive Officer, Aspen Ski Company
- Richard Karesh, Co-author, *Fifth Discipline Handbook;* founder, Learning Org. Dialogue
- Art Kleiner, Co-author *Fifth Discipline Handbook;* Author, *Age of Heretics*
- Allan Webber, Co-Founder, Editor-in-Chief, Fast Company Magazine
- Ken Morris, Co-Founder, PeopleSoft
- Dr. John Popplestone, History of American Psychology at the University of Akron
- Dr. Edward Hoffman, Author, *The Right to Be Human: A Biography of Abraham Maslow*
- Allan Wernick, Attorney at Law, Columbus, Ohio
- Jeanne Glasser, John Wiley & Sons, Inc., for her enthusiastic support of this project

We would like to thank Ann Kaplan and Ellen Maslow for persisting in their efforts to bring their father's work to a new generation of leaders and managers. Their gift to us was significant: Through the process of bringing their father's journals back to life, we ourselves have become better educators, better leaders, better parents, and better human beings.

Deborah C. Stephens
Gary Heil

July 1998
The Center For Innovative Leadership
San Mateo, California

Dr. Abraham H. Maslow in front of his home
Auburndale, Massachusetts circa 1965.

Abraham Maslow:
The Man and His Work

*. . . Sometimes I get the feeling of my writing being a com-
munication to my great-great grandchildren, who, of course
are not yet born. It's a kind of an expression of love for them,
leaving them not money, but in effect affectionate notes, bits
of counsel, lessons I have learned that might help them . . .*

Abraham Maslow left a legacy for all of us. His pioneering
work in the field of humanistic psychology has made an in-
delible imprint on the way we view ourselves, our lives, and
our institutions.

Maslow began his career at Brooklyn College where his unusual
combination of confidence in his subject and personal humility made
him very popular with his students. Many students recalled that it was
his love of psychology and his enthusiasm for the science of psychology that led them to careers in the field.

Maslow left Brooklyn College to become chairman of the Department of Psychology at Brandeis University. He was also president
of the American Psychological Association from 1967 to 1968.

Although Maslow conducted research and studies in a myriad of
areas, he is most remembered for his hierarchy of needs and the concept of self-actualization as the highest motivating force. From his
work, people began to form a more positive framework for human
motivation and human potential. Referred to as the father of humanistic psychology, Maslow broke ranks with the behaviorists and
Freudian aligned practitioners and academics to postulate a much more
enlightened theory about mankind.

A prolific writer, he authored hundreds of articles on topics ranging from creativity, enlightened management techniques, human motivation, and self-actualization. His most popular book, *Toward a*

Psychology of Being was the kind of book passed around from person to person. Described as a book that not only inspires, but changes peoples' lives, it catapulted Maslow into the national spotlight. Terms such as self-actualization and peak experience became household words, integrated into the vernacular of the turbulent 1960s.

Maslow's defining work was perhaps his development of the hierarchy of needs. Maslow believed that human beings aspired to become self-actualizing. He viewed human potential as vastly underestimated and an unexplained territory. The now famous pyramid has come to illustrate his concept:

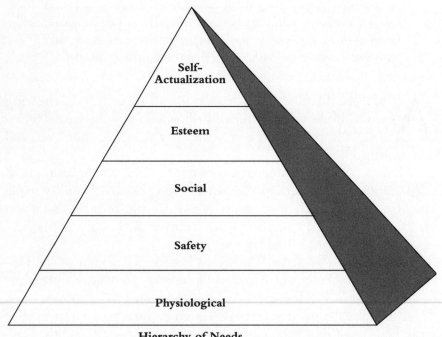

Hierarchy of Needs

In the summer of 1962, Maslow kept a journal while at a factory in southern California. The journal, originally mimeographed, was entitled *Summer Notes*. The journal first appeared in print under the title *Eupsychian Management* and was known mainly to academics and business theorists. It is being republished today under the title *Maslow on Management*.

Abraham Maslow died in June 1970 at Menlo Park, California, at the age of 62.

Preface to the First Edition

I have made no effort to correct mistakes, to second guess anything, to cover up my prejudices, or to appear wiser or more knowledgeable than I was in the summer of 1962.

These journal notes were made during the summer of 1962 when I was a sort of Visiting Fellow at the Non-Linear Systems, Inc. plant in Del Mar, California, at the invitation of Andrew Kay, President.

I came there, for no specific task or purpose, but I became very much interested in what was going on there for various reasons which will be apparent in the journal itself.

This is, however, not at all a study of a particular plant. It was the plant that opened up to me a body of theory and research which was entirely new to me and which set me to thinking and theorizing.

I had never before had any contact with industrial or managerial psychology, so the possibilities for general psychological theory hit me with great force, as I read first the books by Drucker and McGregor[1] that were used as "textbooks" at Non-Linear. I began to understand what Andrew Kay was trying to do there, and I read on voraciously in this fascinating new field of social psychology.

It has been my custom for some years to write to myself in a journal, to think things out on paper, sometimes freely associating and improvising, sometimes writing from previously worked out notes and outlines. This journal, however, was not handwritten as usual, but dictated on a tape recorder because I had available to me *several* excellent secretaries to transcribe the tapes almost immediately. This is something that happens very rarely to a professor. It accounts in part for the unusual amount of manuscript produced.

[1] P. Drucker, *Principles of Management* (New York: Harper & Row, 1954). D. McGregor, *The Human Side of Enterprise* (New York: McGraw-Hill Book Co., Inc., 1960).

These notes were bound together in a mimeographed book without editing, addition, subtraction, or other change, beyond correction of typographical and grammatical errors. They were further edited for the present book, but this was primarily to pull together the scattered memoranda that belong together, to remove some obscenities, to clarify sentences that might be confusing, to fill in references, to make it here and there a little less personal and intimate, etc. I have made no effort to correct mistakes, to second-guess anything, to cover up my prejudices, or to appear wiser or more knowledgeable than I was in the summer of 1962. Nor has much been added or subtracted. That would be in direct contradiction to the point of publishing a journal at all.

These notes should be understood primarily as first impressions and first responses, of a theoretical psychologist taking his first look at a new field of knowledge and realizing that that body of knowledge was of great import for various of his theoretical concerns (and vice versa). I have learned from other such experiences that the novice can often see things that the expert overlooks. All that is necessary is not to be afraid of making mistakes, or of appearing naive.

I have appended my complete bibliography, including reprintings, translations, etc., as much for my own convenience as for the readers'. I want to have it in print *someplace* so that I can refer to it when I need to. Numbers in parentheses in the text refer to the numbers in this bibliography.

Utopian and normative thinking of this sort is not very common these days, and even when it does occur, is by many rejected as being not in the realm of acceptable knowledge, much less in the realm of science. Science, even social and human science, is supposed to be value free, although of course I would maintain that it cannot be (95).[2] Anyway, this journal is a sampling of the kind of normative or ideal social psychology that I've been trying to work up. I've coined the word Eupsychia (81) and defined it as the culture that would be generated by 1,000 self-actualizing people on some sheltered island where they would not be interfered with (57, 79, 81). Then, by contrast with the classical Utopian and Dystopian dreams of fantasies, the questions become quite real; e.g., how good a society does human nature permit? How good a human nature does society permit? How good a society does the nature of society permit? Since we know more about

---

[2] Numbers in parentheses refer to articles listed in Bibliography.

the heights to which human nature can attain, we can now extrapolate to the "higher" forms of interpersonal and social organization which this taller human nature makes possible in principle. We might, if we wished, call this simply "planning." Or we might get more flossy and call it the History of the Future, or use the newly coined word "cyber-cultural." But I prefer the word "eupsychian" as implying *only real possibility and improvability* rather than certainty, prophesy, inevitability, necessary progress, perfectibility, or confident predictions of the future. I am quite aware of the possibility that all mankind may be wiped out. But it is also possible that it *won't* be wiped out. Thinking about the future and even trying to bring it about is, therefore, still a good idea. In an age of rapid automation, it is even a necessary task.

But the word, Eupsychia, can also be taken in other ways. It can mean "moving toward psychological health" or "healthward." It can imply the actions taken to foster and encourage such a movement, whether by a psychotherapist or a teacher. It can refer to the mental or social conditions which make health more likely. Or it can be taken as an ideal limit; i.e., the far goals of therapy, education, or work.

Since this journal was first written in 1962,[3] Non-Linear Systems has had to weather a contracting demand for its products along with increased competition for this contracting market. Because this journal was not a description of this one firm, I have not had to change my mind about any of the principles set forth in it. But it is worthwhile to reiterate here what is stressed in the journal again and again, that these principles hold *primarily for good conditions, rather than for stormy weather.* The parallel contrast in the motivational life of a single person is between growth motivation and defensive motivation (homeostasis, safety motivation, the reduction of pains and losses, etc.). The healthy individual can be expected to be flexible and realistic; i.e., able to shift from growth to defense as circumstances may demand. The interesting theoretical extrapolation to an organization would be to expect it, also, to be flexibly able to shift from fair weather efficiency to foul weather efficiency whenever this became necessary. It appears to me that just about this has in fact happened and is happening at Non-Linear, although of course this should be demonstrated by research.

---

[3] And distributed as a mimeographed book entitled *Summer Notes on Social Psychology of Industry and Management.*

The Attitude of
Self-Actualizing People to
Duty, Work, Mission

This is the simplest way of saying that proper management of the work lives of human beings, of the way in which they earn their living, can improve them and improve the world and in this sense be a utopian or revolutionary technique.

We can learn from self-actualizing people what the ideal attitude toward work might be under the most favorable circumstances. These highly evolved individuals assimilate their work into the identity into the self, i.e., work actually becomes part of the self part of the individual's definition of himself. Work can be psychotherapeutic, psychogogic (making well people grow toward self-actualization). This of course is a circular relationship to some extent, i.e., given fairly o.k. people to begin with, in a fairly good organization, then work tends to improve the people. This tends to improve the industry, which in turn tends to improve the people involved, and so it goes. This is the simplest way of saying that proper management of the work lives of human beings, of the way in which they earn their living, can improve them and improve the world and in this sense be a utopian or revolutionary technique.

I gave up long ago the possibility of improving the world or the whole human species via individual psychotherapy. This is impracticable. As a matter of fact it is impossible quantitatively. (Especially in view of the fact that so many people are not suitable for individual psychotherapy.) Then I turned for my utopian purposes (81)* to

*Numbers in parentheses refer to articles listed in Bibliography.

1

education as a way of reaching the whole human species. I then thought of the lessons from individual psychotherapy as essentially research data, the most important usefulness of which was application to the eupsychian improvement of educational institutions so that they could make people better en masse. Only recently has it dawned on me that as important as education perhaps even more important is the work life of the individual since everybody works. If the lessons of psychology, of individual psychotherapy, of social psychology, etc., can be applied to man's economic life, then my hope is that this too can be given a enlightened direction, thereby tending to influence in principle all human beings.

It is quite clear that this is possible. My first contact with the management literature and with enlightened management policy indicates that management has already in its most advanced forms taken an enlightened, as well as a synergic, direction. Many people seem to have discovered, simply in terms of improved production, improved quality control, improved labor relations, improved management of creative personnel, that the Third Force kind of psychology works.

For instance, the intuitive conclusions that Peter Drucker has arrived at about human nature parallel very closely the conclusions of the Third Force psychologists (86, Preface). He has come to his conclusions simply by observation of industrial and management situations, and apparently he knows nothing of scientific psychology or of clinical psychology or of professional social psychology. [The fact that Drucker comes to approximately the same understanding of human nature that Carl Rogers has achieved, or Erich Fromm, is a most remarkable validation of the hope that the industrial situation may serve as the new laboratory for the study of psychodynamics, of high human development, of ideal ecology for the human being.] This is very different from my own mistake, which I fell into automatically, of regarding industrial psychology as the unthinking application of scientific psychological knowledge. But it's nothing of the sort. It is a *source* of knowledge, replacing the laboratory, often far more useful than the laboratory.

Of course the opposite is also true or at least can be more true than Drucker realizes. There are rich gold mines of research data that the industrial psychologist and the management theorist can use and can apply to the economic situation. My guess is that Drucker and his colleagues took a quick look at what passes for scientific psychology and gave it up at once. It is obviously true that the rats and the pigeons

THIRD FORCE PSYCHOLOGY

I think it significant that in more than a quarter of a century since Maslow's death, there has been no sign of a decline in his reputation, whereas Freud's and Jung's are heavily bullet scarred. This, I believe is because there is a sense in which Maslow has still not come into his own. His significance lies in the future and will become apparent in the 21st century.

—*Colin Wilson*

Abraham Maslow is often referred to as the father of Third Force Psychology. The Third Force (also referred to as humanistic psychology) was a body of knowledge and theories separate from the behaviorist and Freudian movements. Throughout much of his life, Maslow argued for a new philosophy of humanity to help recognize and develop the human capacity for compassion, creativity, ethics, love, spirituality, and other uniquely human traits. Yet, Dr. Maslow considered himself first and foremost a scientist. He did not spew forth this new approach in psychology without much thought, rigorous testing, hypothesizing, and debate. Thus, his work has powerfully affected managerial theory, organizational development, education, health care, and science as well as psychology.

Maslow deplored the cynicism and dark images that surrounded the concept of human nature. He became quite certain that the classic Freudian or neo-Freudian approaches to human nature were inadequate. Perhaps his most famous quote sums up the concept of Third Force Psychology:

A musician must make music, and artist must paint, a poet must write, if he is to be ultimately at peace with himself. What a man can be, he must be. This need we may call self-actualization. . . . It refers to man's desire for self-fulfillment, namely to the tendency for him to become actually in what he is potentially: to become everything that one is capable of becoming. . . .

and the conditioned reflexes and the nonsense syllables are of no earthly use in any complex human situation, but in throwing out the nonsense in psychology they also threw out the gold nuggets of which there are also plenty.

Insofar as my own effort is concerned, it has in any case always been an ethical one, an attempt to wed science with humanistic and ethical goals, with efforts to improve individual people and the society as a whole. For me industrial psychology opens up a whole new horizon; for me it means a new source of data, very rich data. Also it represents for me a whole set of validations of hypotheses and theories that I have based on purely clinical data. Furthermore it represents to me a new kind of life-laboratory, with going-on researches where I can confidently expect to learn much about the standard problems of classical psychology, e.g., learning, motivation, emotion, thinking, acting, etc.

(This is part of my answer to Dick Farson's question, "Why are you so hopped up about all of this stuff? What are you looking for? What do you hope to get out of it? What do you hope to put into it?" What this amounts to is that I see another path for enlightened thinking.)

One advantage that the industrial situation has over individual psychotherapy as a path of personal growth is that it offers the homonomous[1] as well as the autonomous gratifications. Psychotherapy tends to focus too exclusively on the development of the individual, the self, the identity, etc. I have thought of creative education and now also of creative management as not only doing this for the individual but also developing him via the community, the team, the group, the organization—which is just as legitimate a path of personal growth as the autonomous paths. Of course, this is especially important for those who are not available for symbolic psychotherapy, psychoanalysis, insight therapy, etc. This holds true especially for the feeble-minded and for those reduced to the concrete, who are now mostly beyond the reach of Freudian-style therapy. The good community, the good organization, the good team can help these people where the individual therapist often is helpless.

---

[1] A. Angyal, *Neurosis and Treatment* (John Wiley & Sons, Inc., 1965).

Additional Notes on Self-Actualization, Work, Duty, Mission

To do some idiotic job very well is certainly not real achievement. I like my phrasing, "what is not worth doing is not worth doing well."

After talking recently with various students and professors who "wanted to work with me" on self-actualization, I discovered that I was very suspicious of most of them and rather discouraging, tending to expect little from them. This is a consequence of long experience with multitudes of starry-eyed dilettantes—big talkers, great planners, tremendously enthusiastic—who come to nothing as soon as a little hard work is required. So I have been speaking to these individuals in a pretty blunt and tough and nonencouraging way. I have spoken about dilettantes, for instance (as contrasted with workers and doers), and indicated my contempt for them. I have mentioned how often I have tested people with these fancy aspirations simply by giving them a rather dull but important and worthwhile job to do. Nineteen out of twenty fail the test. I have learned not only to give this test but to brush them aside completely if they don't pass it. I have preached to them about joining the "League of Responsible Citizens" and down with the free-loaders, hangers-on, mere talkers, the permanent passive students who study forever with no results. The test for any person is—that is you want to find out whether he's an apple tree or not—Does He Bear Apples? Does He Bear Fruit? That's the way you tell the difference between fruitfulness and sterility, between talkers and doers, between the people who change the world and the people who are helpless in it.

An Interview with Anne Robinson

Anne Robinson co-founded Windham Hill Records in her garage with little capital investment, but a compelling vision of what could be. She blended her love of music with her love for design and graphics to produce records which turned the music industry upside down. In a business where success is measured in weeks, many of Windham Hill's first records are still selling today, 23 years after their introduction.

Your experience as an entrepreneur in the music industry more or less demonstrates Maslow's observation that "the novice can often see things that the expert overlooks. All that is necessary is not to be afraid of making mistakes or appearing naive."

Because we didn't know the record business, we broke a lot of the rules.

Maslow said, "self-actualization is hard work, that it involves a calling to service from the external, day-to-day world, not only a yearning from within."

Yes, he spoke the truth. One is always in the process of becoming. You never finish if you are really living your life. You are always taking in information and new experiences and synthesizing them into your work and into your philosophy.

My experience with Windham Hill was that we seemingly came out of nowhere. Yet we had been working at it nonstop for about six or seven years. There were a couple of years where we had no competition. The industry thought we were the Alpha and the Omega. Yet, at the same time, we knew that someone was going to come along and improve upon our vision, imitate or copy our concept. We also knew that people would grow tired of us because they move on to other things.

The music that we produced evoked intense personal and philosophical responses in people, ranging from complete bliss and adoration to complete distaste. I had to find where I fit with all of this. When you're making a product and you are presenting something that is personal and elicits such a personal response from people, it goes to the core of your being. For me to be good at what I was doing, I had to be emotionally involved in all aspects of the business. Otherwise, it would not have been my truth. I would have felt as though I was simply manipulating consumers of music. The music was not about manipulation.

You mentioned that people interpreted your work in ways you never intended. How did you deal with that?

Well, sometimes you deal very well and sometimes you don't. You create through your work a product or concept and people respond in ways you never imagined. People take your work and make it into something else, perhaps in ways you never intended or may disagree with. I had to work hard on reconciling the two.

Our work tended to spark an intellectual and emotional response. For every person who hated our music, it meant for me that they actually had listened to the music and thought enough about it to make a judgment that they hated it. In contrast, there were other people we reached who were surprised by their response. For example, I received a letter from a member of the Hell's Angels. If I recall, he started the letter out by saying, "I'm a Hell's Angel. I'm not supposed to like this kind of music but I really do!"

In the role that I played at Windham Hill, I was happy to have opened the door for people, played a role in awakening something within them. I think there are enormous numbers of people who go through life asleep. Frankly, on a certain level, I don't care where they get the stimulation that knocks them out of their sleep; the goal is to help them awaken. I think Maslow, through his work, opened a door for many people.

It's hard to have your ideas twisted seemingly by someone who uses words differently or has a different goal or a purpose you never intended. Yet, at the same time, you have to say, "My God, you're awake, you're thinking"; and that has made my work worth it.

Maslow said that introspection full time in a cave all by one's self someplace was an approach to self actualization which he had never seen work for anybody, that the quality all of his self-actualizing subjects shared was that they were motivated by some great and important job.

You can say you are a scientist or you can say you are a business person but if you are truly committed to what you are doing, there's a point where it becomes your emotional passion and then you don't have that distance. You are always being tested to your very core. "Did I do my research correctly? When I listened to this music with my ears, did I allow my heart to listen also? Is there an integrity to all of what I am doing?" I think the strength of what Dr. Maslow did was that he tested his scientific theories against his inner belief system. It wasn't just A and B equal C. It was much more than that. It was, "I see this and I believe it."

At Windham Hill, one of your trademarks was the number of employees who worked with great passion and commitment. The culture you created there has been studied at Harvard and written up in business books and articles. How were you able to create this incredibly productive environment?

(continued)

I think it was a combination of the work and my strong belief that if I worked to create an environment where people felt empowered, they would bring to their work the very best they had to give. When a company grows large, as happened at Windham Hill, there comes a point where you have to hope that you've hired people who have a vision and integrity that compliments your own.

In looking back, I also think that employees sensed that we were doing something different from the rest of the industry. They sensed that our products had meaning to people. I felt strongly about making a product that had lasting value. I think our employees took real pride in that belief. The product reflected our values. I think our employees, as well as our distributors and suppliers, bought into our business philosophy.

The true struggle for me was after merging with BMG Records. I had quarter-to-quarter projections to make and a bottom line to meet. Yet I realized I needed to work hard at keeping the same value system within the organization or the end product would suffer.

Another point that has been coming up is the talk about personal salvation. For instance, at the Santa Rosa existential meetings there was much of this kind of talk, and I remember exploding in a kind of irritation and indicating my disrespect for such salvation seekers. This was on the grounds that they were selfish and did nothing for others and for the world. Besides, they were psychologically stupid and psychologically incorrect because seeking for personal salvation is *anyway* the wrong road to personal salvation. The only real path, one that I talked about in my public lecture there, was the path set forth in the Japanese movie "Ikiru," i.e., salvation via hard work and total commitment to doing well the job that fate or personal destiny calls you to do, or any important job that "calls for" doing.

I remember citing various "heroes," people who had attained not only personal salvation but the complete respect and love of everybody who knew them; all of them were good workers and responsible people, and furthermore all of them were as happy as was possible for them to be in their circumstances. This business of self-actualization via a commitment to an important job and to worthwhile work could also be said, then, to be the path to human happiness (by contrast with the direct attack or the direct search for happiness—happiness is an epiphenomenon, a by-product, something not to be sought directly but an indirect reward for virtue). The other way—of seeking for personal salvation—just doesn't work for anybody I have *ever* seen—that is the introspection, the full-time-in-a-cave all by one's self some place. This may work for people in India and Japan—I won't deny that—but I have never seen it work for anybody in all my experience in the United States. The only happy people I know are the ones who are working well at something they consider important. Also, I have pointed out in my lecture and in my previous writings that this was universal truth for all my self-actualizing subjects. They were metamotivated by metaneeds (B-values) (89) expressed in their devotion to, dedication to, and identification with some great and important job. This was true for every single case.

Or I can put this very bluntly: Salvation Is a By-Product of Self-Actualizing Work and Self-Actualizing Duty. (The trouble with most of these youngsters who have been after me is that it seems they have in the back of their heads some notion of self-actualization as a kind of lightning stroke which will hit them on the head suddenly without their doing anything about it. They all seem to want to wait passively for it to happen without any effort on their part. Furthermore, I think that practically all of them have tended unconsciously to define self-actualization in terms of the getting rid of all inhibitions and controls in favor of complete spontaneity and impulsivity. My impatience has been largely because of this, I guess, that they had no stubbornness, no persistence, no frustration tolerance, etc.,—apparently just these qualities they consider as the opposite of self-actualization. Maybe this is what I should talk about more specifically.)

One thing about this whole business is that self-actualization work transcends the self without trying to, and achieves the kind of loss of self-awareness and of self-consciousness that the easterners, the Japanese and Chinese and so on, keep on trying to attain. S-A work is simultaneously a seeking and fulfilling of the self *and* also an achieving of the selflessness which is the ultimate expression of *real* self. It resolves the dichotomy between selfish and unselfish. Also between inner and outer—because the cause for which one works in S-A work is introjected and becomes part of the self so that the world and the self are no longer different. The inner and the outer world fuse and become one and the same. The same is true for the subject-object dichotomy.

A talk that we had with an artist at Big Sur Hot Springs—a real artist, a real worker, a real achiever—was very illuminating on this point. He kept on pressing Bertha (my wife) to get to work on her sculpture, and he kept on waving aside all her defenses and her explanations and excuses, all of which were flossy and high-toned. "The only way to be an artist is to work, work, and work." He stressed discipline, labor, sweat. One phrase that he repeated again and again was "Make a pile of chips." "Do something with your wood or your stone or your clay and then if it's lousy throw it away. This is better than doing nothing." He said that he would not take on any apprentice in his ceramics work who wasn't willing to work for years at the craft itself, at the details, the materials. His good-by to Bertha was, "Make a pile of chips." He urged her to get to work right after breakfast like a plumber who has to do a day's work and who has a foreman who will fire him if he doesn't turn out a good day's work. "Act as if you have to earn a living thereby." The guy was clearly an eccentric and talked a lot of wild words—and yet he *had* to be taken seriously because there were his products—the proofs that his words were not merely words.

(Bertha had a very good research idea when we talked about this conversation: The hypothesis is that the creative person loves his tools and his materials, and this can be tested.)

(A good question: Why do people *not* create or work? Rather than, Why *do* they create? Everyone has the motivation to create and to work, every child, every adult. This can be assumed. What has to be explained are the inhibitions, the blocks, etc. What stops these motivations which are there in everyone?)

(Side idea: About D-motivated creators [60], I have always attributed this to special talent alone, i.e., to special genius of some sort which has nothing to do with the health of the personality. Now I think I must add just plain hard work, for one thing, and for another, just plain nerve, e.g., like someone who arbitrarily defines himself as an artist in a nervy and arrogant way and therefore *is* an artist. Because he treats himself like an artist, everybody tends to also.)

If you take into yourself something important from the world, then you yourself become important thereby. You have made yourself important thereby, as important as that which you have introjected and assimilated to yourself. At once, it matters if you die, or if you are sick, or if you can't work, etc. Then you must take care of yourself,

SELLING PEOPLE SHORT

> . . . each of us is born with certain innate needs to experience higher values; just as we are born physiologically with the need for zinc or magnesium in our diet. So, this argument is definitely saying that our higher needs and motivations are biologically rooted. Every human being has the instinctive need for the highest values of beauty, truth, and justice, and so on. If we can accept this notion, then the key question isn't "what fosters creativity?" But it is why in God's name isn't everyone creative?
>
> —*Abraham Maslow*

> Learning, creativity, fairness, responsibility, and justice come naturally to people according to Maslow's theories. Why is it that we often design organizations as if people naturally shirk responsibility, do only what is required, resist learning, and can't be trusted to do the right thing?
>
> Yet, most of us would argue that we believe in the potential of people and that people are our most important organizational assets. If that is the case, why then do we frequently design organizations to satisfy our need for control and not to maximize the contributions of people?

> . . . For centuries human nature has been sold short.
>
> —*Abraham Maslow*

you must respect yourself, you have to get plenty of rest, not smoke or drink too much, etc. You can no longer commit suicide—that would be too selfish. It would be a loss for the world. You are needed, useful. This is the easiest way to feel needed. Mothers with babies do not commit suicide as easily as nonmothers. People in the concentration camps who had some important mission in life, some duty to live for or some other people to live for tended to stay alive. It was the other ones who gave up and sank into apathy and died without resistance.

This is an easy medicine for self-esteem: Become a part of something important. Be able to say, "We of the United Nations. . . ." or "We physicians. . . ." When you can say, "We psychologists have proven that. . . ." you thereby participate in the glory, the pleasure, and the pride of all psychologists any place.

This identification with important causes, or important jobs, this identifying with them and taking them into the self thereby enlarging the self and making it important, this is a way of overcoming also actual existential human shortcomings e.g., shortcomings in I.Q., in talent, in skill, etc. For instance, science is a social institution, with division of labor and colleaguehood *and* exploitation of characterological differences—this is a technique for making uncreative people creative, for enabling unintelligent men to be intelligent, for enabling small men to be big, for permitting limited men to be eternal and cosmic. *Any* scientist must be treated with a certain respect, no matter how minor a contributor he may be—because he is a member of a huge enterprise and he demands respect by participation in this enterprise. He represents it, so to speak. He is an ambassador. (This makes a good example also: The ambassador from a great country is treated differently from the ambassador from some dopey or inefficient or ineffective or corrupt country—even though they are both individual human beings with individual human shortcomings.)

The same is true for a single soldier who is a member of a huge victorious army by contrast with a single soldier who is a member of a defeated army. So all the scientists and intellectuals and philosophers, etc., even though they are limited figures taken singly, taken collectively they are very important. They represent a victorious army, they are revolutionizing society; they are preparing the new world; they are constructing Eupsychia. So they become heroes by participation in heroic enterprises. They have found a way for small men to make themselves big. And since there exists in the world only small men (in various degrees) perhaps some form of participation in, or identification with, a worthwhile cause may be essential for any human being to feel a healthy and strong self-esteem. (That's why working in a "good" company [prestige, good product, etc.] is good for the self-esteem.)

This is all related to my thinking on "Responsibility as a Response to the Objective Requirements of the Situation." "Requirements" equals that which "calls for" an appropriate response, that which has "demand-character," which rests so heavily on the self-perceived constitution or temperament or destiny of the perceiver. That is, it is that which *he* feels impelled to make right, to correct; it is the burden that fits *his* shoulders, the crooked picture on the wall that *he* of all people in the world has to straighten. To some extent this is like a recognition of one's self out there in the world. Under ideal conditions there *would* be isomorphism, a mutual selection between the person and his

Why Do People Not Create or Innovate?

The key question isn't "what fosters creativity?" But it is why in God's name isn't everyone creative? Where was the human potential lost? How was it crippled? I think therefore a good question might be not why do people create? but why do people not create or innovate? We have got to abandon that sense of amazement in the face of creativity, as if it were a miracle if anybody created anything.

—Abraham Maslow

Throughout corporate boardrooms around the world, leadership teams and consultants are attempting to manage for creativity and innovation. Yet, if we believe, as Maslow did, that it is human nature to create and innovate, our search for the answers takes us down a very different path.

Perhaps we should begin to seek out the creativity and innovation killers in our organizations instead of trying to fix the people within? One step in the right direction might be to ask, "Why do people not create or innovate in the current environment? The question reminds us of a story told about Peter Drucker, the legendary author and tireless teacher. He was speaking to a group of senior level executives and he asked them to raise their hands if there was a lot of "dead wood" in their companies. Many in the audience raised their hands. He then responded, "Were the people dead wood when you interviewed them and decided to hire them or did they become dead wood?"

Sam Stern, an education professor at Oregon State University and an expert on creativity thinks that the main task of an organization is not to squelch creativity in its employees. The U.S. Forest Service and its suggestion system may well be a good example. If a U.S. Forest Service employee wished to suggest an improvement, a new service or process improvement, each was required to complete a four-page suggestion form for every idea. In one region, with 2500 employees, there were only 252 ideas submitted over a four-year period. Stern calculated this to be one idea per person every 40 years!

The U.S. Forest Service changed its system. Now, anyone with an idea simply submits a brief description via e-mail to the appropriate management. If there is no response within 30 days, the employee can act on the idea as long as it is legal. During the first year under the new procedure, employees sent in 6000 ideas! By asking the question, "why do people not create and innovate," one may be able to uncover procedures, policies, and mindsets that inhibit creativity and innovation.

Source: Interview: *Seattle Post-Intelligencer,* Sam Stern, Author, *How Innovation and Improvement Actually Happen,* Berrett Koehler Publishers, 1997, and Peter Drucker quote: *Inc.* Magazine Conference and Products Producer Kevin Gilligan as told to Deborah Stephens 2/9/98.

S-A work (his cause, responsibility, call, vocation, task, etc.) That is, each task would "call for" just that one person in the world most uniquely suited to deal with it, like a key and a lock, and that one person would then feel the call most strongly and would reverberate to it, be tuned to its wave length, and so be responsive to its call. There is an interaction, a mutual suitability, like a good marriage or like a good friendship, like being designed for each other.

What happens then to the one who denies this unique responsibility? who doesn't listen to his call-note? or who can't hear at all any more? Here we can certainly talk about intrinsic guilt, or intrinsic unsuitability, like a dog trying to walk on his hind legs, or a poet trying to be a good businessman, or a businessman trying to be a poet. It just doesn't fit; it doesn't suit; it doesn't belong. One must respond to one's fate or one's destiny or pay a heavy price. One must yield to it; one must surrender to it. One must permit one's self to be chosen.

This is all very Taoistic. It's good to stress this because responsibility and work are seen unconsciously under the terms of Douglas McGregor's Theory X, as duty, as picking up a burden reluctantly because forced to do so by some external morality, some "should" or "ought" which is seen as different from natural inclination, different from free choice through delight or through tasting good. Under ideal conditions—that is, of healthy selfishness, of deepest, most primitive animal spontaneity and free choice, of listening to one's own impulse voices—one embraces one's fate as eagerly and happily, as one picks one's wife. The yielding (surrender, trusting response receptivity) is here the same as in the embrace of the two people who belong together. The polarity between activity and passivity is here transcended and resolved just as it is in the love embrace or in the sexual act when this is ideal. So also is the will-trust dichotomy resolved. So also the difference between the Western and the Eastern. So also the dichotomy between free will and being determined. (One can embrace one's determinants—but even that statement is too dichotomous. Better said—one can recognize that what *appear* to be one's determinants out there in the world are really one's self which seems to be out there, which appear to be different from the self because of imperfect perception and imperfect fusion. It's a kind of self-love, or a kind of embracing one's own nature. Those things that belong together melt into each other and enjoy that melting, preferring it to being separated.)

THE GREAT DEBATES: DOUGLAS MCGREGOR AND ABRAHAM MASLOW

Douglas McGregor wrote *The Human Side of Enterprise* in 1960. He quickly became known as the father of Theory X and Theory Y—theories of managerial leadership that portrayed managers as authoritarian (Theory X) or as collaborative and trustful of people (Theory Y). In outlining Theory Y, McGregor clearly subscribed to Maslow's view of human nature. In fact, McGregor used much of Maslow's research on the hierarchy of motivation to develop his assumptions of the Theory Y manager.

Andrew Kay (see pages 116–120 for interview with Andrew Kay) introduced Douglas McGregor and Abraham Maslow in 1960. Kay told us he was visiting the Maslow family in Boston when he realized that Maslow and McGregor had never met. Kay couldn't believe the men hadn't met face to face, yet had corresponded with one another on the issues of enlightened management for nearly a year. Kay said, "I looked at Abe and told him to find his coat and get in the car" and off we went to McGregor's office at MIT.

That day the great debates began. Both men died imploring every leader to look into the mirror and question their assumptions. Their questions, a half century old, still seem a great place to begin:

1. Do you believe that people are trustworthy?

2. Do you believe that people seek responsibility and accountability?

3. Do you believe that people seek meaning in their work?

4. Do you believe that people naturally want to learn?

5. Do you believe that people don't resist change but they resist being changed?

6. Do you believe that people prefer work to being idle?

Our answers to these questions affect everything that we do. We've asked groups of executives these questions. Surprisingly, we've found that many of us have never really taken the time to analyze our assumptions about people.

We often recommend that managers and leaders spend time in groups discussing the questions mentioned above. Debate and dialogue over the answers should be encouraged. Perhaps organizations should state their assumptions about people for everyone to read and discuss. We feel they are as important as mission statements and corporate values.

(So, Letting-Go [rather than self-control] equals Spontaneity and is a *kind* of activity, which is not other than, which is not separated from, which is not different from passivity.)

So—to recognize one's responsibility or one's work out there is like a love relationship, a recognition of a belongingness, a *Zusammenhang;* it has many of the paradoxical or dichotomy-transcending qualities of sexual intercourse and love embracing, of two becoming one perfectly. This also reminds me of C. Daly King[1] and his notion of "paradic design" which equals a recognition of suitability and belongingness and normality and rightness through the recognition of the intention or fate implied by the design.

Applying this whole notion to the relationship between a person and his work destiny is difficult and subtle, but not much more so than applying this principle to the relationships between the two people who should get married as compared to two people who obviously should not get married. One personality can be seen to fit with another personality in this same paradic design.

If work is introjected into the self (I guess it always is, more or less, even when one tries to prevent it), then the relationship between self-esteem and work is closer than I had thought. Especially healthy and stable self-esteem (the feeling of worth, pride, influence, importance, etc.) rests on good, worthy work to be introjected, thereby becoming part of the self. Maybe more of our contemporary malaise is due to introjection of nonprideful, robotized, broken-down-into-easy-bits kind of work than I had thought. The more I think about it, the more difficult I find it to *conceive* of feeling proud of myself, self-loving and self-respecting, if I were working, for example, in some chewing gum factory, or a phony advertising agency, or in some factory that turned out shoddy furniture. I've written so far of "real achievement" as a basis for solid self-esteem, but I guess this is too general and needs more spelling out. Real achievement means inevitably a worthy and virtuous task. To do some idiotic job very well is certainly *not* real achievement. I like my phrasing, "What is not worth doing is not worth doing well." (39)

---

[1] C. D. King, "The Meaning of Normal," *Yale Journal of Biology and Medicine,* 1945, *17,* 493–501.

Self-Actualized Duty

Every age but ours has had its model, its ideal. All of these have been given up by our culture; the saint, the hero, the gentleman, the knight, the mystic . . . Perhaps we shall soon be able to use as our guide and model the fully growing and self-fulfilling human being. The one whom all potentialities are coming to full development, the one whose inner nature expresses itself freely . . .

A t the point where the S–A job is assimilated into the identity or into the self by introjection, then such work can be therapeutic and self-therapeutic. This is because the work or the task out there which has become part of the self can be worked on, attacked, struggled with, improved, corrected in a way that the person cannot do directly with his own inner self. That is to say, his inner problems can be projected out into the world as outer problems where he can then work with them far more easily and with less anxiety, less repression than he could by direct introspection. As a matter of fact this may be one main unconscious reason for projecting an inner problem into the outer world i.e., just so that it can be worked on with less anxiety. I think probably the best examples here and the most easily acceptable ones are, first, the artist (certainly everybody will agree that he does exactly this with his inner problems, putting them on his canvasses), and second, many intellectual workers who do about the same thing when they select some problems to work with which are really projections of their own inner problems, even though they don't recognize them as such.

Different Management Principles at Different Levels in the Hierarchy

Each new invention, each new discovery creates turmoil behind the lines. The people who have settled down comfortably are shaken and disturbed out of their comfort. It is clear then that any great discovery, any new invention . . . anything which will require a reorganization of the conquered territory will not easily be accepted . . .

Where we have fairly evolved human beings able to grow, eager to grow, then Peter Drucker's management principles seem to be fine. They will work, but only at the top of the hierarchy of human development. They assume ideally a person who has been satisfied in his basic needs in the past, while he was growing up, and who is now being satisfied in his life situation. He was and now is safety-need gratified (not anxious, not fearful). He was and is belongingness-need satisfied (he does not feel alienated, ostracized, orphaned, outside the group; he fits into the family, the team, the society; he is not an unwelcome intruder). He was and is love-need gratified (he has enough friends and enough good ones, a reasonable family life; he feels worthy of being loved and wanted and able to give love—this means much more than romantic love, especially in the industrial situation). He was and is respect-need gratified (he feels respect-worthy, needed, important, etc.; he feels he gets enough praise and expects to get whatever praise and reward he deserves). He was and is self-esteem-need satisfied. (As a matter of fact this doesn't happen often enough in our society; most people on unconscious levels do not have enough feelings of self-love, self-respect. But in any case, the

American citizen is far better off here let's say than the Mexican citizen is.)

In addition, the American citizen can feel that his curiosities, his needs for information, for knowledge, were and are satisfied or at least are capable of being satisfied, if he wants them to be. That is, he has had education, etc.

But now we can also ask what would be the proper principles of management for a person who is *not* satisfied in these various ways? How about the people who are fixated at the safety-need level, who feel perpetually afraid, who feel the possibilities of catastrophe, for instance, of unemployment, etc. What would management be like with people who could not identify with each other, who were suspicious of each other, who hated each other—let's say as seems to be the case among the different classes in France, Germany, Italy, etc., at least much more so than in the United States?

Clearly, different principles of management would apply to these different kinds of motivational levels. We don't have any great need to work out management principles for the lower levels in the motivation hierarchy. My main purpose here is to keep on making more explicit the high level of personal development that is unconsciously being assumed.

Enlightened Economics
and Management

*Assume that everyone prefers to be a prime mover rather than
a passive helper, a tool, a cork tossed about on the waves.*

These assumptions underlie Enlightened Management Policy.
Look into Drucker, Likert, McGregor, Argyris, *et al.*

1. *Assume everyone is to be trusted.*

This does not assume that everyone in the world is to be trusted—
that no one is to be mistrusted, etc. It definitely assumes the reality of
individual differences. It assumes that the people selected for the particular plant are a fairly evolved type of person, relatively mature, relatively healthy, relatively decent. By definition it also assumes good
environmental conditions. Better spell these out below.

2. *Assume everyone is to be informed as completely as possible of as many
facts and truths as possible;* i.e., everything relevant to the situation.

There is the clear assumption in enlightened management that
people need to know, that knowing is good for them, that the truth,
the facts, and honesty tend to be curative, healing, to taste good, to be
familiar, etc. See *The Need to Know and the Fear of Knowing* (93).

3. *Assume in all your people the impulse to achieve;* assume that they
are for good workmanship, are against wasting time and inefficiency,
and want to do a good job, etc.

This is the place for a discussion of the Gestalt motivations. Also
look up Veblen's *Instinct of Workmanship*. Add notes on the impulse to

perfection and the impulse to improve the imperfect. Remember again that this impulse is either absent or very weak in a fairly large proportion of the human species but that we are selecting for our organizations those people who have a reasonable amount of this impulse. Point out that all fairly healthy people will have such impulses. To avoid any unreal, Pollyannish, or overoptimistic outlook, point out the classes of people who don't have such an impulse or don't have much of it, e.g., the crushed, the hopeless, the beaten, people reduced to the concrete, anxiety-ridden, fearful, demented people, the psychopaths, the totally unaesthetic, the dilapidated, and so on.

4. *Assume that there is no dominance-subordination hierarchy in the jungle sense or authoritarian sense* (or "baboon" sense). The dominance is of the "chimpanzee" sort, older-brotherly, responsible, affectionate, etc. (20, 78).

Where the jungle view of the world prevails, enlightened management is practically impossible (33). If all people are divided into hammers and anvils, lambs and wolves, etc., then brotherhood, sharing of goals, identification with team objectives becomes difficult, limited, or impossible. There must be an ability to identify with a fairly wide circle of human beings, ideally with the whole human species. The ultimate authoritarian can identify with nobody or perhaps at best with his own blood family. It follows that this is another principle of selection of personnel for the enlightened organization. Authoritarians must be excluded or they must be converted.

5. *Assume that everyone will have the same ultimate managerial objectives and will identify with them no matter where they are in the organization or in the hierarchy.*

What is necessarily implied here is the replacement of polarizing and dichotomizing by the principle of hierarchy-integration. Use as an example for instance Piaget's little Genevan boy who could understand that one was Genevan or Swiss but couldn't understand that one could be both until he grew up a little more and realized that one could integrate with the other, include the other.[1] Perhaps we could

---

[1] Quoted with other relevant examples in G. Allport, "Normative Compatibility in the Light of Social Science." In A. H. Maslow (Ed.), *New Knowledge in Human Values* (New York: Harper & Bros., 1959).

also talk about the general semanticist and his multivalued logic and his two-value logic. I suppose we will have to work out here a little bit of the psychodynamics of teamwork, of identification with the team or the organization, e.g., "I'd die for dear old Rutgers." Or one could try to work on the example of an army, in which perfect patriotism exists as well as knowledge of all the facts, and in which each one has the same ultimate goal of victory that everybody else has, and therefore uses himself and his own peculiar capacities in the best possible way toward this ultimate goal of victory, even if it means self-sacrifice. Certainly this is problem-centered rather than ego-centered; i.e., one asks, "What is best for the solution of the problem or the effectuation of the goal rather than what is best for my ego, or my own person?"

6. *Enlightened economics must assume good will among all the members of the organization rather than rivalry or jealousy.*

Here use the example of sibling rivalry as a kind of evil or a psychopathology arising out of perfectly good but immature impulses, i.e., the child who wants the love of his mother but is not mature enough to recognize that she can give love to more than one. Such a child may bang his little infant brother on the head, not out of intrinsic hostility, but because it looks as if this little one is siphoning off the mother's love altogether. Observe that the two- or three-year-old child would be dangerous to his own newborn sibling but not to any other infant. That is, he is not against infants in general but only the one who will steal his mother's love. Of course, eventually we all grow out of this immaturity and recognize that Mama can love us all, but this takes a fairly high psychological development. So the growing out of sibling rivalry in any team or organization must also demand this fairly high level of personal maturity.

6a. *Synergy is also assumed.*

Synergy can be defined as the resolution of the dichotomy between selfishness and unselfishness, or between selfishness and altruism. We normally assume that the more one has the less the other has. The selfish person has less altruism than the unselfish person, but this need not to be so under the correct institutional and social arrangements. It is possible to set up organizations so that when I am pursuing my own self-interest, I automatically benefit everyone else, whether I mean to or not. Under the same arrangement, when I try to be altruistic and philanthropic, I cannot help benefiting myself or advancing my own self-interest.

For instance, among my Blackfoot Indians the "giveaway" was such a synergic institution. The way in which the Blackfoot could attain prestige, respect, status, love, etc., from everybody and in his own eyes as well, was by being very generous during the Sun Dance ceremony; and so it was that the Blackfoot Indian might work hard and save and borrow for a whole year so that he would have a pile of blankets and food, etc., to give away to the public at the Sun Dance ceremony in early summer. The rich man is defined there as one who is very generous or who has given away a good deal. After such a giveaway he might not have a nickel in his pockets, but he is defined as a very wealthy man. He benefits by winning the respect and love of everyone, by proving how much he is able to gather by his own efforts and intelligence, by how clever he is; he can get rich again so to speak. The people most respected in this tribe are the people who have given away most.

How does he get along, how does he survive after giving away everything? He has such prestige that he is eagerly sought out by everyone in the tribe. They fight for his presence. He bestows a great honor upon the family whose hospitality he accepts. He is regarded as so wise that to have him at the fireplace where he can teach the children is regarded as a great blessing. In this way he benefits and everyone benefits from his skill, his intelligence, his hard work, his generosity. For a Blackfoot Indian to discover a gold mine would make everyone in the tribe happy because everyone would share the benefit from it. Whereas in the modern society, finding a gold mine is the surest way of alienating many people, even those who are close to us.

If I wished to destroy someone I can think of no better way of doing it than to give him a million dollars suddenly. Only a strong and wise person could use this wealth to advantage. Many persons would undoubtedly lose their friends, family, and everything else in the process of inevitably losing the million dollars also.

Enlightened economics must assume as a prerequisite synergic institutions set up in such a way that what benefits one benefits all. What is good for General Motors is then good for the U.S., what is good for the U.S. is then good for the world, what is good for me is

SYNERGY IS ANYTHING BUT SIMPLE

Maslow defined synergy as a culture in which what is beneficial for the individual is beneficial for everyone. High synergy cultures are secure, benevolent, and high in morale. Low synergy cultures are insecure, in conflict, and low in morale.

The concept of synergy became increasingly more important to Maslow's organizational theories as he saw too many business cultures in which one's success could only occur at the expense of others. Yet, during his summer at Non-Linear Systems, Maslow witnessed first-hand, a high synergy work environment. The environment Andy Kay and his colleagues had worked hard to create reminded Maslow of his field work with the Blackfoot Indians.

Much of what Maslow believed about synergy came from his study of the Blackfoot Indians whose culture was unmistakably synergistic. He found the Blackfoot culture stood in stark contrast to that of a modern organization. For example:

- An emphasis on generosity was the highest virtue of the tribe. Accumulating assets or knowledge received scant praise. Giving assets, knowledge, and property away was what brought one true prestige and security within the tribe.
- Through extensive testing, Maslow discovered that the Indian tribe suffered less from self-doubt and self-consciousness than did people from more competitive environments and ways of life. It was as if each tribe member knew his or her strengths and weaknesses. Weaknesses were not ostracized but accepted as a normal part of the human condition.
- There was a strong emphasis on personal responsibility within the tribe which began with the very young. Parents encouraged their children, at a very young age, to do things for themselves in the context of a very loving and supportive environment.
- The needs of the tribe as a whole were effortlessly combined with the needs of the individual tribe members.
- The tribe tended not to have general leaders with general power but rather they had different leaders for different functions. Thus the one best suited to lead the Sun Dance was not expected to lead the representation of the tribe to the government. Each leader was chosen for a particular job based on the needs of that job.

Leaders often comment on the need to create synergistic organizations where teamwork flourishes. We speak about the necessity to align organizational goals with personal goals. Based upon what we've learned from Maslow's work in synergistic cultures, have we underestimated the challenge?

then good for everyone else, etc. This gives a very powerful instrument of classification and of choice for every social institution. Which institutional arrangements tend toward synergy? Which point away from it? According to Drucker, enlightened economics points toward the enhancement of synergic good management principles, although he is not very conscious of it. Since this is so, I had better expound it at greater length separately.

7. *Assume that the individuals involved are healthy enough.*

What this means quantitatively is hard to know at this point. At least they cannot be psychopaths, schizophrenics, paranoids, brain injured, feeble-minded, addicts, and so on.

8. *Assume that the organization is healthy enough,* whatever this means.

There *must* be criteria for a healthy organization. I don't know what they are or if anybody has listed them, but it is imperative to do this if it hasn't already been done. Certainly, such principles will overlap with the criteria for personal psychologicl health, but also just as certainly they will not be altogether the same. Organizations are different from persons in some respects. Find out about this.

9. *Assume the "Ability to Admire"* (to be objective and detached), in a special sense, i.e., to be purely objective not only about other people's capacities and skills, but also about one's own.

This means particularly that there must be little or no Nietzschean resentment, no hatred of self, no hostility to the "B-values," no hostility to truth, beauty, goodness, justice, law, order, etc., or at least no more than the irreducible minimum inevitable in human nature. (This is one form of cognition of the objective facts and of respect for them.) Given the ideal situation in which everyone is wise and all-powerful in a godlike way and without any selfish ego whatsoever, then this would be easy. Then I could freely say that Smith had better be chosen for the job because he was best for the job or more skillful than I, without feeling any pang of envy, hurt, inferiority, or whatever. Of course *in practice* this is impossible because human beings cannot achieve this perfection except in small areas of life, but at least it is the limit toward which enlightened management tends to approach. At least there must be more of this rather than less. Objectivity of this sort must be enhanced rather than damaged, to the extent that human nature permits. To see with clear eyes, objectively, that which is hurtful to our own self-esteem is extremely difficult, and yet, after all, it is possible to some extent. We know, from countless experiences in psychotherapy, that countless numbers of people have learned to see in themselves that which crushed their own self-esteem and then proceeded to profit thereby.

10. *We must assume that the people in organizations are not fixated at the safety-need level.*

That is they must be relatively anxiety-free, they must not be fear-ridden, they must have enough courage to overcome their fears, they must be able to go ahead in the face of uncertainty, etc. This can be quantified at this point. (See Chapter 4, "Defense and Growth," in my *Toward a Psychology of Being*[2]—use the details and examples from this chapter.) Point out that there is a kind of simple statement of the psychodynamics of enlightened management as contrasted with authoritarian management, i.e., that the simple dialectic between fear and courage, or between regression or progression will approximately do the trick. On the whole, where fear reigns, enlightened management is not possible. In this and in may other places, Drucker reveals his lack of awareness or knowledge of psychopathology, of evil, weakness, bad impulses, etc. There are many people in the world, especially outside of the United States, for whom Drucker's management principles will simply not work at all. So also for the human relations stuff and for the personnel stuff. They forget that there are many people in the world for whom those principles will fail, people who are too sick to function in an enlightened world. Point out also Drucker's lack of use or awareness of the problems of individual differences.

11. *Assume an active trend to self-actualization*—freedom to effectuate one's own ideas, to select one's own friends and one's own kind of people, to "grow," to try things out, to make experiments and mistakes, etc.

[2] A. H. Maslow, *Toward a Psychology of Being* (Princeton, NJ: D. Van Nostrand & Co., 1961).

This follows the same principle that psychotherapy or growth are conceptually impossible unless we assume such an abstract variable. We must assume the will to health or to grow, etc. This can be seen concretely rather than abstractly in the Carl Rogers kind of data from psychotherapy.[3]

12. *Assume that everyone can enjoy good teamwork, friendship, good group spirit, good group homonomy, good belongingness, and group love.*

Beware of stressing only the pleasures of autonomy, of actualization of the individual self. Not enough attention has been given to the pleasures of being in a love community with which one can identify, not enough studies yet of the *esprit de corps*. Talk about identification with the group, the kind of pride that a high school boy can have in his own school's basketball team or the increased self-esteem that a college student will have from the heightened prestige of his college. Or that a member of the Adams family will have simply from being a member of the Adams family, even if he doesn't amount to very much himself.

13. *Assume hostility to be primarily reactive rather than character-based,* i.e., that it will be for good, objective, present, here-now reasons and that it is therefore valuable rather than evil, and that it is therefore not to be stifled and discouraged. (Phrased in this way it comes close to being simply honesty.)

Certainly this freedom to express reactive hostility will make for increased honesty and an improved situation rather than for the kind of permanent strain which comes when justified resentments and irritations cannot be expressed openly. For instance, the same thing is true with a good manager; the better the manager, the more freedom people will feel to express irritation, disagreement, etc. The same has now been empirically proven for the relation between the psychotherapist and his patient. It is far better for them both to be honest rather than to conceal. Too much character-based hostility, i.e., transference, carried over from the past, reactions to symbols, displaced hostility, etc., must make good, objective, interpersonal relations difficult or impossible. If I am the boss and someone reacts to a normal order as

[3] C. Rogers, *On Becoming a Person* (Boston: Houghton Mifflin Co., 1961).

if I were his father who is going to spank him, and if he cannot tell the difference, then good relations are very difficult.

14. *Assume that people can take it,* that they are tough, stronger than most people give them credit for.

One can easily enough find the limits for each individual and how much he can take and not take. Certainly the strain should not be constant, but people can benefit from being stretched and strained and challenged once in a while at least. As a matter of fact, they *must* be stretched and strained once in a while in order not to get slack and bored. It makes life in all its aspects more interesting if one works at concert pitch, at one's highest level once in a while. Furthermore, we can assume that many people *want* to take it, to be stretched and challenged.

15. *Enlightened management assumes that people are improvable.*

This does not mean that they are *perfectable.* Furthermore, it does not exclude their having the vision or hope of perfection. All it says is that people can be better than they are by a little bit at least.

16. *Assume that everyone prefers to feel important, needed, useful, successful, proud, respected, rather than unimportant, interchangeable, anonymous, wasted, unused, expendable, disrespected.*

This is simply the assertion that esteem needs and self-esteem needs are universal and instinctoid (96).

17. *That everyone prefers or perhaps even needs to love his boss (rather than to hate him), and that everyone prefers to respect his boss (rather than to disrespect him),* is an assumption that Drucker overlooks. Here respect is probably prepotent over loving—that is, while we prefer to respect and to love our boss, if we can choose only one of these, most of us would choose to respect the boss and not love him, rather than to love him and not respect him.

This can be worked out more in the Freudian style and also in the relation to the data available on dominance–subordination relationships. Ultimately the whole thing will have to be generalized in a universal theory of the interrelations between the strong and the weak, along with a clarifying discussion of the advantages of being strong and of being weak, and the disadvantages of being strong and weak—most especially in the relations between males and females, between adults and children, and also in the employer and employee, leader and led situations (78). The dynamics of fearing the boss or the strong one, the advantages and disadvantages of fearing, also have to be worked out. So also do the dynamics of the Strong Man have to be worked out more and especially the question of how all the people around the Strong Man react to him and are affected by him.

18. *Assume that everyone dislikes fearing anyone (more than he likes fearing anyone), but that he prefers fearing the boss to despising the boss.*

We may not like the strong men, e.g., DeGaulle, Kennedy, Napoleon, T. Roosevelt, etc., but we can't help respecting them, and in a pinch preferring them, trusting them. Certainly this is a universal testimony in the life and death situation in war. The tough and hard but capable leader may be hated, but he is much preferred to the soft and tender weaker leader who may be more lovable but who may also bring about one's death.

19. *Enlightened management assumes everyone prefers to be a prime mover rather than a passive helper,* a tool, a cork tossed about on the waves.

Drucker talks much about "responsibility" and the liking for responsibility and cites all sorts of industrial investigations that show that people function better when they get responsibility. This is certainly true but only for the more mature, more healthy person, just the kind of person whom Drucker assumes throughout. But point out that this kind of person is not universal. There are still plenty of people, even in the U.S. and certainly in many other countries of the world, who are frightened to death, who much prefer to be dependent and slavish and who don't want to make up their own minds. Refer to the many studies of the authoritarian character. Refer to the speech of the Grand Inquisitor in *The Brothers Karamazov.* It is clear that we must be more conscious than Drucker that this is a prerequisite, an assumption, a selection out of particular kinds of people (65).

INTERVIEW WITH MORT MEYERSON

Mort Meyerson, former chairman and chief executive officer of Perot Systems and former vice chairman of EDS, has an enviable track record. Under his leadership, EDS was taken public and became a leading company in its industry. The same scenario seems to be playing itself out at Perot Systems. Meyerson and his team have increased revenues nearly 40 percent each year since his tenure. Transformed by what he has learned about the current world of work, Meyerson has implemented many enlightened management techniques at Perot Systems.

Perhaps Meyerson is most famous, not for his corporate accomplishments, but for being courageous enough to admit and smart enough to know, that the ways of the past will no longer work in today's world.

We first learned of Meyerson from a cover story in a popular business magazine (*FAST COMPANY,* April/May 1996). The article was one Meyerson wrote entitled "Everything I Thought I Knew About Leadership Was Wrong." The article struck a chord with readers when he asked questions such as, "To get rich do you have to be miserable? To be successful do you have to punish your customers? Can we create a more human organization?" The article attracted hundreds of letters. His printed words gave birth to a new kind of corporate hero, a role Meyerson reluctantly plays. Yet play it he does, because he knows it is the right thing to do.

His approach to the reinvention of Perot Systems incorporates what Dr. Maslow wrote many years ago. Maslow stated that, "I must help these corporate types to understand that it is well to treat working people as if they were high type Theory Y human beings not only because of the Golden Rule and not only because of the Bible or religious precepts or anything like that, but also because this is the path to success of any kind whatsoever, including financial success."

We had the opportunity to discuss some of Dr. Maslow's thinking on management and leadership with Meyerson in his Dallas headquarters.

You have commented that Maslow's proposed assumptions for the healthy organization are so close to what you believe that you found it almost eerie. Now that you have had the opportunity to read more of the journals, what do you think of these ideas?

I think the book is stunning. Everyone has certainly heard of Abraham Maslow and his hierarchy of needs. Yet, the papers he wrote that summer and the basic thoughts contained therein were not 1950s thinking. The thoughts were 1990s thinking or even twenty-first century thinking. Much of the work is obtuse, but when you bring it all together—especially the 36 points—one realizes that his thoughts are really clear and pertinent to today. It is fascinating to me or stunning. If you review Maslow's work and study the context from which he was writing and remember what the world looked like and the time in which he was writing, I think you may understand why I use the word stunning. He was so far ahead of his time that there is a discontinuity from conventional wisdom of his time.

Yet, for many years, we have had a body of knowledge from the likes of Abraham Maslow, Douglas McGregor, Warren Bennis, and others who predicted the importance of the human side of enterprise. Why were we unable to listen?

Peter Drucker's work has also shown us many of the same points as Maslow. I think these ideas are so radical it will take us decades to fully understand—if we are ever able to own these ideas. They are counter-intuitive. Everything we do in life has a certain set of unspoken assumptions of the underlying ways things work. Maslow's work is counter-intuitive to the body of knowledge of business. The underlying assumptions of how business is done is that our main focus is to make a profit, or in today's words, to increase shareholder value.

Most human beings deal in analytical material easier than they deal with non-analytical material. Therefore, metrics is a vehicle to measure and get comfortable. Accounting has become the way we measure business to find out whether we are indeed making a profit or doing well. Most of these metrics are easy and quantifiable. From this body of knowledge, we have developed management by objectives. Business is built upon assumptions of analytical and metric-oriented work.

I think that most males are more comfortable in the world of metrics and measurements than they are in a psychological or feeling world. For now, males dominate the leadership of business and enterprise worldwide. I think the Native American males were a special group of people who were comfortable in dealing with the spiritual, the more psychological, the emotional, the more human world. The language of business has been tied to things that were easier for males to deal with. Males also tend to be more comfortable in hierarchical organizations.

Yet, there was a time when there were less hierarchical dominated organizations. We had tribal organizations. We have forgotten what it was like to be in nonhierarchical organizations. We tend to think that big organizations have been in existence forever, but they have not. So Dr. Maslow's journals are counter-intuitive to us not only in the United States, but around the world. Each company has its own national culture and business culture.

(continued)

The article you wrote regarding your own transformation in leadership was quite similar to what Maslow wrote about. In your article, you questioned some of the core elements and thoughts of business. Why do you think there was such intense interest and response to your article?

In retrospect, I think the piece that I wrote had a more universal appeal than the business story I was telling. When I started getting letters from priests and ministers, I knew that something greater was at work here. However, I urge you to be wary of being ethnocentric about these ideas and concepts. I live in both worlds and as I have tried to develop the concepts that Dr. Maslow was writing about and that I have been talking about in my own company, the more I know this is not a movement whose time has come. These are but a tiny speck of the number of people who are intuitively trying to hear the music while they are reciting the words and dance of business.

The main body of business is not listening to this type of information. They think it is poppycock and soft-headed thinking and maybe the stuff of revolutions. Let me give you an example that illustrates my point. I gave a talk at MIT on this general subject and at the end of my talk a man from the audience approached me. When he was within six inches of my face, he screamed something to the effect that I was going to be the reason why Western civilization and American free enterprise were going to be destroyed. He viewed my speech not as a point of discussion, but as an attack on free enterprise, on the American way of life, on profit motives, and on Western society. I thought that was a bit much!

The encounter was interesting in that it unleashed all of these emotions. From a psychological standpoint, it was very clear to me that the man was not discussing any of the subjects we were talking about. He was talking about himself. If this were an isolated incident and it had happened only once, I wouldn't have mentioned it. Most people do not yell at me or scream at me. They will speak to me on the same issues, almost backing into the subject, particularly if I have any kind of power or position in the situation. People inside of our company or board members come at the same issue obliquely, but they say the same thing as the man at the MIT gathering, just less violently.

I had one board member ask me why I wasting my time on these people issues. I said, "What business are we in?" As I see it, we are in the business of forming teams of people to do things for companies that create value for them. Without our people, we have no business. We don't make anything tangible.

He said, "I know that, but you are dealing in this soft stuff. People don't even want the creativity, the freedom, and the things that you are trying to give them. They aren't trying to find meaning in their work. People just want to come to work, do their job, and have a clear understanding of what's expected from them. They want to be paid fairly and that is all that they want."

I said, "You couldn't have stated more clearly everything that I don't believe about people and work. It's just plain wrong. Those reasons are not the only reason people come to work. People also come to work because it is community, because it is family, because work is an important part of their identity, and because they are trying to do something for their families. The money meets their needs, but it is not an exchange of service for money. It is much more powerful than that. If you only deal on the level of a fair exchange of work for money, you are missing the whole essence of what is happening in the work place."

In this continuing dialogue with the board member, I said, "The question is do I say to our associates 'This is what needs to be done' so it is clear to the person? Do I say 'If you choose to do it then I will reward you in the following way?' Or do I say, 'Let us create value for our customer. Let us create an environment which is good for our people and watch what will happen'? I predict that what will happen in the last scenario will be ten times more powerful than if I tell employees what to do. Under the board member's scenario, we are limited by what is inside my head and my experiences. If we follow the latter scheme I have outlined, I am able to tap into the experiences, the creativity, and the power of everyone in the organization.

Maslow spoke about the line between business and community being so tightly aligned that it's impossible to separate them. You have stated that one of the most controversial values, which was narrowly approved in your organization, spoke to the corporation's commitment to the community. You have said it was also the one you argued most heatedly for. Can you tell us that experience?

One of the more difficult areas to discuss in the early days of Perot Systems was the value of community relations. The reason is related to what I said earlier. A community contribution is not directly in the path toward profits and is not analytical or easily measured. We cannot say that if we contribute one hundred thousand dollars to the community, we will get two hundred thousand dollars back. Yet, I am intuitively convinced we will get more value back than we put into the effort.

During the discussions, the people in the room were predominately male and much more comfortable with the measurements or the metrics of a given situation. Think of the situation in this way; if it is a stretch to put the customer first (and it is in many organizations), then it is a

(continued)

huge stretch to put the idea of the importance of community on the table for discussion!

If we do not deal with the whole employee or the life of the employee then we are dealing only with part of the power or creativity of the person. Isn't that what Maslow said also?

Although the payback to the company is not easily measured, we can measure the productivity of employees. For example, in Dallas, some of the cultural organizations were having trouble developing a database and they could not get enough computers together for the task. We gathered together a number of volunteers who were interested in the arts and we facilitated the whole process for these organizations.

Although we cannot measure how our efforts paid off in business for Perot Systems, we could measure how the people in our company felt about their contribution. They felt more connected to their community through their contribution and they felt better as human beings. The connection with the cultural groups or the arts—the side of our community that speaks to the soul—affected them. Thus, they were better people and were better contributors to Perot Systems. Plus, we helped make our community a better place.

However, if business does not take on this type of endeavor, who is going to? Government cannot possibly do all that needs to be done. Churches cannot do it all. The nonprofit organizations can only do so much. Businesses are the most efficient organizations on earth, so far. Because they are so efficient, if businesses do not put on their agendas to work on issues of community, the environment, family life, and the broader aspect of who and what their employee is, then we will lose the ability to produce a better whole life for the individual. That is important, because people do not work just for a paycheck.

It is obvious to me that you have to work on all of these issues. It is also obvious that businesses have an obligation beyond just making a profit. I do not say this must be done for philosophical reasons. Ultimately, I tie it back to the fact that it is in the company's best interest. The question is how does an organization get there? That is the basic argument.

Are you measuring these activities in your organization? The activities and the organizational issues we have discussed so far?

We are trying, but it is very difficult. One can do attitude surveys but I do not believe people give full information in those surveys. The board member, who is my antagonist, said to me, "How are you going to know if this stuff works?" I said, "Well, it's simple. Our customers will tell us they are delighted by our service. They will say that we are creating value for them greater than they could create for themselves. We will be paid extraordinary amounts of money for those services. Our employees will be better people, more satisfied, will raise their families better. They will have a more productive life and will have a soul. People like me will know that it works. However, in the short term, it won't be the metrics which tell us this works. It will be the metrics and intuitive feelings. If we are the most respected, most successful computer service firm 50 years from now, then we will begin to know. We will be networked together, produce great service and be rewarded for it with happy people and delighted customers."

Dr. Maslow stated that the problem for the accountants is to work out some way of putting on the balance sheet the human assets of the organization. Would you agree?

I am pretty sure you are asking the wrong question. The assumption is one of giving credence to the underlying idea that one has to measure it to create any value. I'm just not convinced we have to measure it. We have to start by trusting that it will work and that later, it will show up.

It will show up in customer attitudes, employee attitudes, employee productivity. It will show up eventually, but I am not sure we can measure the connection. Also, some people will feel that the concept of putting human assets on the balance sheet is too close to what was done when slaves were considered to be owned and therefore an asset.

Can you only be successful in a privately held company with this approach?

No, you can do it in a public company.

Yet, we hear that the pressures from Wall Street and the short termism endemic in public companies prevents organizations from doing some of the things we have discussed.

Wall Street is not the problem. If you tell Wall Street what you are going to do, even if it's different, they will give you a year or two to be successful. It would be hard, in that time frame, but not impossible. Quantitative versus qualitative thinking is the problem. The mindset is the problem. Wall Street is just a bunch of people trying to make money based upon a mass psychology of markets.

Business people like to say it's Wall Street because they say they need the ability to think long-term. I heard that same argument 10 years ago from the Japanese. They were telling me they had a better system because they could think longer term. Japan did not have the quarter-to-quarter Wall Street pressures which they believed contributed to their superiority. It appeared

(continued)

that they were superior 10 years ago. Now, it appears that they did not know what the hell they were doing and the bubble burst! They artificially inflated real estate, colluded with banks, did criminal things, and misled the public shareholder. I do not accept, at first blush, the Wall Street argument.

My suspicion is that the phrase "without Wall Street and the quarter-to-quarter earnings pressures everything would be okay" is not true. If Wall Street all of a sudden went to three-year rolling growth levels, I don't think it would materially change our organizations or the mindsets for some period of time.

You stated that during the change process, Perot Systems was becoming a company where the larger issues of life were as important as the demands of profit-and-loss performance. You also have spoken of your personal transformation after leaving EDS. Will you tell us about that transformation?

I don't think the business can be transformed unless the leader and leadership is transforming. This type of change cannot come from the bottom up. It is a leadership issue. It must resonate with the leader. I still get one to five e-mails per week on that article I wrote. One out of five reads, "I work for so-an-so company. We have great potential and wonderful people. We can really make a difference. I've talked to the head of HR and he doesn't get this people stuff. I've been trying to figure out how I can convince the CEO." The themes of the letters are always around the issue of "how do I get them to understand?"

My message is always the same. I tell them that they have an obligation to make sure that the ideas are understood and that they have been heard. I also advise that if one happens to be bold, one can put these ideas on the table. However, it is very important that one really believes in the ideas. I caution anyone not to start down this path unless one really believes because you will probably find yourself out of the company or organization. One has to be willing to have that scenario happen before they start with the ideas. If you are willing, you have an obligation to the company and to the people around you to make an attempt. If you reach the point where you simply can't convince the people, then you have to make a decision about what you are going to do. My recommendation is to leave the company and go find a company where you can convince or where they are already convinced. You will not be successful with the power of one to convince. The power of one will not work inside the company organization. The only time the power of one works is with the aggregation of customers. Employees are not customers.

Maslow described the process of self-actualization through work. What are your comments about self-actualization and work?

I don't think self-actualization comes from work or from that environment. I think the mixture of work involvement along with personal work and spiritual work leads to self-actualization. However, I understand Maslow's thoughts along those lines. I believe he saw businesses as very efficient institutions that could facilitate the role of healthier people, more self-actualized people. Unfortunately, there are a lot of flakes and gurus and New Age people in this arena. They latch onto a theme that appeals to people, moves people, and strikes at the chord for the search for meaning in life. These types of people take advantage of the situation. Perhaps their influence taints it for the mainstream of business.

20. *Assume a tendency to improve things, to straighten the crooked picture on the wall, to clean up the dirty mess, to put things right, make things better, to do things better.*

Actually we do not know very much about this; there is a beginning of scientific knowledge in the work of the Gestalt psychologists on closure and *pragnanz*. I have observed this often enough in healthy people—I have called them the Gestalt motivations—but I have no idea nor does anyone else how strong these tendencies are or even if they exist at all in less healthy, less intelligent, less evolved human beings. In any case it must be pointed out that Drucker is assuming that this exists in all the people that he talks about, and it seems pretty clearly true a priori that he is right in making this assumption as a prerequisite for success in the enlightened economics situation.

21. *Assume that growth occurs through delight and through boredom.* That is, that the parallel with children's growth is fairly sound.

The child who is not anxiety-ridden seeks for novelty, has curiosity, manipulates and explores things, enjoys new things; but then sooner or later becomes bored with them and seeks for still newer and more worthy "higher" things or activities. See Chapter 4 "Defense and Growth" in my *Toward a Psychology of Being*.[4] It is a fairly safe assumption that a prerequisite for enlightened management is a delight

---

[4] *Op. cit.*

in novelty, in new challenges, new activities, variety, in activities that are not too easy, but all of these become sooner or later familiar and therefore become uninteresting and even boring, so that the search then begins anew for additional variety and novelty, work at a higher level of skill.

22. *Assume preference for being a whole person and not a part, not a thing or an implement, or tool, or "hand."* A person prefers to use all his capacities, to flex all his muscles and resents being treated as just a part of the person.

Use here my examples on resistance to being rubricized in Chapter 9 in my *Toward a Psychology of Being* book.[5] For instance, the resistance of the woman, at least the highly developed woman, to being *only* a sexual object, or the resistance of the laborer to being *only* a hand, or a set of muscles or a strong back, or the resistance of the waiter in the restaurant to being *only* a bringer of dishes, etc.

23. *Assume the preference for working rather than being idle.*

Drucker is certainly right in this assumption, but it needs more qualification than he gives it. For instance, most people prefer no work at all to meaningless work, or wasted work, or made work. Furthermore, there are certainly individual differences here in preferences for kind of work, e.g., intellectual, muscular, etc. We must stress also the differences between the pleasures in the processes of working and in the goals or ends of work. Furthermore, in any full discussion, ultimately we shall have to talk about the resolution of the dichotomy between work and play. The ultimate implication in the Drucker kind of management, whether or not he has spelled it out, must be that work is enjoyed, is even fascinating, is even loved. In self-actualizing people, the work they do might better be called "mission," "calling," "duty," "vocation," in the priest's sense. This mission in life is actually so identified with the self that it becomes as much a part of the worker as his liver or lungs. For the truly fortunate worker, the ideally enlightened worker, to take away work (mission in life) would be almost equivalent to killing him. The truly professional worker would be an example. A clarifying

---

[5] *Ibid.*

discussion of the semantics of work is absolutely necessary at this point because of the typically implied notion in our society, perhaps throughout the world, that labor is unpleasant by definition and that enjoying yourself means lying in the sun and doing nothing. Point out that to force people not to work is as cruel a punishment as could be devised.

24. *All human beings prefer meaningful work to meaningless work.*

This is much like stressing the high human need for a system of values, a system of understanding the world and of making sense out of it. This comes very close to the religious quest in the humanistic sense (102). If work is meaningless, then life comes close to being meaningless. Perhaps here also is the place to point out that no matter how menial the chores—the dishwashing and the test-tube cleaning, all become meaningful or meaningless by virtue of their participation or lack of participation in a meaningful or important or loved goal. For instance, cleaning up baby diapers is repulsive work in itself, but it can be very lovingly done, it can be a beautiful thing for a mother who loves her baby. Washing the dishes can be the most meaningless chore or it can be a symbolic act of love for one's family and can therefore take on great dignity and can even become a sacred activity, etc. This can all be applied to the organization. I can use here my case of a woman who developed an anhedonia (loss of zest and pleasure in life) because she had a job as personnel manager in a chewing gum factory and simply couldn't get excited about chewing gum. She might have enjoyed very much exactly the same kind of work in a more meaningful (to her) factory (93).

25. *Assume the preference for personhood, uniqueness as a person, identity (in contrast to being anonymous or interchangeable).*

Drucker has many examples from industrial situations.

26. *We must make the assumption that the person is courageous enough for enlightened processes.*

This does not mean that he lacks fears, but rather that he can conquer them or go ahead in spite of them. He has stress-tolerance. He knows creative insecurity. He can endure anxiety.

27. *We must make the specific assumptions of nonpsychopathy* (a person must have a conscience, must be able to feel shame, embarrassment, sadness, etc.).

He must be able to identify with other human beings and to know what they feel like. We must also assume a minimum of paranoia, i.e., of suspicion, of grandiosity, of persecution feelings.

28. *We must assume the wisdom and the efficacy of self-choice.*

Drucker mentions this once or twice, but doesn't spell it out. Actually it is an almost basic assumption for enlightened management people to find out what they are best at by finding out what they like most. This assumes that what one likes, what one prefers, what one chooses, is a wise choice. We must spell this out very carefully, especially because there is some evidence to the contrary. This principle of the wisdom of self-choice is on the whole true, but it is especially true for healthy individuals and much less true for neurotic and psychotic people. As a matter of fact, neurosis may also be defined as the loss of the ability to choose wisely, i.e., in accordance with one's true needs. We also know that habit interferes with wise self-choice. So also does continual frustration, so also do lots of other things. To make the brash assumption that self-choice is also wise for every person under every circumstance is in contradiction to the facts. Again we are confronted with the necessity which Drucker overlooks of selecting and choosing and screening the people for whom enlightened management principles will work. Again we find that they tend to be relatively healthy and strong people, relatively nice and good and virtuous people.

29. *We must assume that everyone likes to be justly and fairly appreciated, preferably in public.*

Our false notions of modesty and humility stand in the way here. The Plains Indians are far more realistic about this. They assume that everyone likes to boast about his accomplishments and likes to hear others praise his accomplishments. This must be realistic, just, and fair. To be praised for what one does not deserve or to have one's accomplishment unduly exaggerated can actually be guilt-producing.

30. *We must assume the defense and growth dialectic for all these positive trends that we have already listed above.* What this means specifically is that every time we talk about a good trend in human nature, we must assume that there is also a counter trend.

For instance, it is perfectly true that almost every human being has a tendency to grow toward self-actualization; but *it is just as true* that every human being has a trend toward regression, toward fear of growth, toward *not* wanting self-actualization. Certainly, every person has some courage; but just as certainly, every person has some fear also. It is true that everybody loves the truth; it is also true that everybody fears the truth. These opposite trends always form a balance and relate to each other in a dialectical way. The question is, which is the strongest in the particular person at the particular time under the particular circumstances?

31. *Assume that everyone but especially the more developed persons prefer responsibility to dependency and passivity most of the time.*

Certainly it is true that this tendency to prefer responsibility and maturity lessens when the person is weak, frightened, or sick or depressed, etc. Another point is that it must be set at the right level so that he can manage it well. Too much responsibility can crush the person just as too little responsibility can make him flabby. Responsibility put upon a child's shoulders too early in life can make him or her anxious and tense forever after. Therefore we must take into account pace, level, etc.

32. *The general assumption is that people will get more pleasure out of loving than they will out of hating* (although the pleasures of hating are real and should not be overlooked).

Or it can be said in another way that for fairly well-developed people, the pleasures of loving, of friendship, of teamwork, of being a part of a well-functioning organization, that these pleasures are real and strong and furthermore are greater than the pleasures of disruption, destruction, antagonism, etc. We must remember that for people who are *not* highly developed, i.e., for deeply neurotic or psychotic people, there is the fair number of instances in which the pleasures of hatred and of destruction are greater than the pleasures of friendship and affection.

33. *Assume that fairly well-developed people would rather create than destroy.* The pleasures of creating something are greater than the pleasures of destroying something.

Although the latter pleasures actually do exist and must not be overlooked, especially since they can be rather strong in poorly developed people, e.g., neurotics, immature people, acting out and impulsive people who have not learned enough controls, psychopaths, etc.

34. *Assume that fairly well-developed people would rather be interested than be bored.*

This can be said more strongly, i.e., practically all people hate being bored.

35. *We must ultimately assume at the highest theoretical levels of enlightened management theory, a preference or a tendency to identify with more and more of the world, moving toward the ultimate of mysticism, a fusion with the world, or peak experience, cosmic consciousness, etc.*

This is in contrast with increasing alienation from the world. This will need discussion eventually, but is not necessary now.

36. *Finally we shall have to work out the assumption of the metamotives and the metapathologies,* of the yearning for the "B-values," i.e., truth, beauty, justice, perfection, and so on.

The Neglect of Individual Differences in Management Policy

It seems that the core of my outlook—at least so far as management is concerned—is the notion that everything springs from the individual's own character structure, that is, whether it is essentially democratic or authoritarian. It is also my firm conviction that the empowered management approach is the difference between people leading active lives rather than existing as helpless pawns. . . .

The general principles that Drucker and others talk about are for the most part far *too* general. Certainly managing women is different from managing men. So also do the people who are fixated at the safety-need level or who are stuck at the love level, etc. This point becomes clearer if we ask about the possibility of applying Drucker's principles in Colombia, Iran, Syria, and South Africa. There are many places in the world where only authoritarian management, cracking the whip over fearful people, can work. Authoritarian characters confronted with human relations principles of management based on all sorts of beneficent and benevolent assumptions would consider the manager certainly weak in the head and at the very least sentimental, unrealistic, etc.

Frequently it turns out that the profoundly authoritarian person has to be broken a little before he can assimilate kindness and generosity. Some people have to be frightened before they will take seriously any orders or suggestions. The studies of the German character during the war, for instance, indicate that the very definition of a teacher, professor, manager, foreman, all had intrinsically built in the assumption of toughness, sternness, even harshness. For instance, in one study the teachers who were not harsh were sneered at by the young children themselves and were considered to be bad teachers, therefore not worth paying attention to. Discipline is impossible for such teachers until they play the role as the authoritarian children expect (33).

Apparently I have put together two criticisms of Drucker here and combined them. One was the point that he slurs the necessity for selecting the right kind of individuals for his management principles to work; the other criticism was that he neglects the presence of evil, of psychopathology, of general nastiness in some people (22, 51).

The Balance of the Forces toward Growth and Regression

Shall we accentuate the positive? Absolutely yes—but under the conditions where this is objectively called for, where it will in fact work. . . .

Another thing that has to be said very clearly and made far more conscious than it now is in the management literature is that Drucker and the other theorists are assuming good conditions and good luck, good fortune. It is perfectly true that these assumptions are valid in the United States at this time. It is just as true that they are probably not valid or at least not as valid in other countries and would not be valid in the United States if there were some kind of atomic catastrophe, for instance. We will be more realistic as scientists if we phrase the question in a more sober, a more realistic, way. For instance, what do we mean by "good conditions" and "bad conditions," what forces, what changes in our society could change the dynamic balance toward regression instead of toward growth? What would simple economic scarcity do, for instance?

It is after all conceivable that if a fair proportion of the American population were killed, the whole structure would fall apart since it is so delicately balanced, and we might suddenly change from a complex industrial society to a jungle, hunting society. Obviously, Drucker's principles then would not apply. To trust people then, to assume that they were honest, to assume good will, to assume philanthropy, altruism, would be insane. Certainly I would not assume it under such circumstances, even though I *do* assume all of these things under present circumstances. The higher life and the higher kind of human being which Drucker has been assuming certainly does exist now. Historically, the American citizen is a relatively high type—especially American women, who are far more advanced than the women of most of the rest of the world. But this higher life rests upon the prior gratification of the lower basic needs, e.g., safety needs which are now satisfied, belongingness needs which are now satisfied, and so on. But supposing that these basic need gratifications were removed or threatened or put into short supply. Then the high superstructure of health psychology (eupsychology) would collapse.

Another point is that Drucker is assuming a high proportion of synergic laws and organizations. I think this assumption is quite correct and realistic. But would it be under catastrophic circumstances? Would people not be set against each other under conditions of scarcity of food, for instance. We have already seen a little of this in the turmoil over individual fallout shelters. Who is to die and who is to be saved? If ten people can be saved out of a thousand, I would certainly like to be one of those ten, but so would every one of the thousand like to be one of the saved. Who decides? My guess is that under conditions of disorganization it would be decided by force, maybe individual, maybe collective.

Anything that increases fear or anxiety tips the dynamic balance between regression and growth back toward regression and away from growth. So also does loss or separation or bereavement. So also does change of any kind have its two-sided effects, and its dynamic balance, i.e., everybody loves change and everybody fears change. The particular working out of the balance so as to favor loving change more than fearing it rests on fairly good conditions in the world. Such conditions now actually exist for fortunate people in good economic situations, in good organizations. But just to make the point clearer, Drucker's management principles do not apply for most American Negroes, who certainly do not live under good psychological conditions. It is quite clear that we can expect that if they did live under fortunate and good psychological conditions in a good economic situation that then they would respond in the ways already outlined. But again we have to say, as Drucker does not, that this must be explicit. We must be conscious that we are fortunate, that we are graced, or we shall not be as realistic and as flexible and as responsive to changes in the objective situation as we must continue to be in a world in process, a world in flux. Conditions are good today; therefore we can use good management principles. Tomorrow conditions may be rotten; it will be suicidal if we hang onto "good management principles," which are good only under good conditions, which must not be believed to be good for all eternity, for any circumstances.

Still other things need emphasizing. One is the importance of communication. There are good communications and there are bad communications at all levels, as the general semanticists would point out. I would think that it would be profitable for Drucker to include the principles of general semantics in his principles of management.

Perhaps another way of saying much of the above is this: Shall we accentuate the positive? Absolutely yes—but under the conditions where this is objectively called for, i.e., where it will in fact work. To be realistic we must also accentuate the negative in whatever proportion is realistically and objectively called for by the existing facts.

Memorandum on the Goals and Directives of Enlightened Management and of Organizational Theory

. . . It's really fantastic that one book after another will make a pious statement about this new development and about organizational theory and management theory all resting on a new knowledge and a new conception of human nature and especially of motivation, and then proceed to say nothing whatsoever about values and purposes except in some vague way that any high school senior could match. . . .

The theoretical situation in enlightened management is one respect at least very much like the situation in psychotherapy: an awful lot of people are doing an awful lot of things and doing a lot of talking, and they don't have the courage to delineate carefully the goals, the purposes, the far aims of all that they are doing. It's as if they were afraid to talk of values and purposes in the hope again of conforming with nineteenth-century science. But the whole thing makes hardly any sense if the far goals of enlightened enterprise and enlightened organization, enlightened groups, are examined. Just as it's possible to say bluntly and unmistakably that the purpose or the far goal of all psychotherapy is growth toward self-actualization and toward the metamotivational state which applies in self-actualization, so also can we say that this is the function of any good society; so also is it the function of any good educational system.

48

And now I think it necessary to add that it is also the far goal of any enlightened work enterprise, just as it is the far goal of all the semitherapeutic groups like the T-groups, the sensitivity training groups, the leadership groups, and so on. This is also true for organizational theory in general. It's really fantastic that one book after another will make a pious statement about this new development and about organizational theory and management theory all resting on a knew knowledge and a new conception of human nature and especially of motivation, and then proceed to say nothing whatsoever about values and purposes except in some vague way that any high school senior could match. The same thing is true for the higher aspect of motivational theory, namely the far goals or metamotivations or B-values which draw the more healthy person on, and which, to say it in another way, are the motivating forces in the self-actualizing person.

It's perfectly true that we can forget about the far goals in our discussions and think only about the immediate goals of an enterprise—that is, to make a profit, to be a healthy organism, to have some insurance for the future, etc., etc. But this is not enough. The managers of any enterprise want it to continue, and they don't mean for two or three years, they mean for fifty years or a hundred years. And not only do they want it to continue for a hundred years (which makes necessary, then, the profoundest discussion of human motives and human far goals), but they would also like their organism, the group or the enterprise, or the organization to grow in a healthy way. So frequently I get the impression that they are still dealing with an extension of the corner grocery store, or a slight enlargement of it, or perhaps a slight modification of the Henry Ford kind of situation.

I've seen very few of these managers or writers on organizational theory who have the courage to think in far terms, in broad-range terms, in utopian terms, in value terms. Generally they feel they're being hard-headed if they use as the criteria of management success or of healthy organization the criteria of smaller labor turnover or less absenteeism or better morale or more profit or the like. But in so doing they neglect the whole eupsychian growth and self-actualization and personal development side of the enlightened enterprise.

I suspect that they are afraid that this latter is a kind of a priori moralism, that it is brought in only because some particular person has a moralistic character and would like it to be that way on an a priori basis. But it can so easily be shown that if the long run is taken into consideration, hard-headedness and tough-mindedness and profits and all the rest of it absolutely require considerable attention to what we might call personal development and what could also be called the training of the proper managers, the training of workers, the changing of the organizational atmosphere. All of this involves just about the same kind of goals that we would have to talk about in psychotherapy or in the analysis of our educational system, or in the analysis of a good political democracy.

It seems very clear to me that in an enterprise, if everybody concerned is absolutely clear about the goals and directives and far purposes of the organization, practically all other questions then become simple technical questions of fitting means to the ends. But it is also true that to the extent that these far goals are confused or conflicting or ambivalent or only partially understood, then all the discussion of techniques and methods and means in the world will be of little use. I must try to work out as clear a statement as I can of not only the near goals but the far goals and far aspiration level of an enlightened business. And I must stress that I can stick entirely, if I wish, to the question of profits as a validation, if only I am permitted to point all this discussion toward the long run, that is, take into account a whole century rather than three or four or five years. This is so because practically all the utopian and eupsychian and ethical and moral recommendations that must be made for such an enterprise will improve everything in the situation; *and this includes profits.* I must stress with these people that this is a path to financial and economic success. That, for instance, it is well to treat working people as if they were high-type Theory "Y" human beings, not only because of the Declaration of Independence and not only because of the Golden Rule and not only because of the Bible or religious precepts or anything like that, but also because this is the path to success of any kind whatsoever, including financial success.

IT'S PROFITABLE AND THE RIGHT THING TO DO . . .

. . . I must stress with these people that this is the path to financial and economic success. That it is well to treat working people as if they were high-type Theory Y human beings not only because of the Declaration of Independence and not only because of the Golden Rule and not only because of the Bible or religious precepts or anything like that, but also because this is the path to success of any kind whatsoever, including financial success . . .

—Abraham Maslow

Dr. Maslow never undertook the scientific and measurable work he had planned to prove that enlightened management would lead to financial and economic success. Today, people are just beginning to build processes to measure the financial successes attributed to enlightened management practices.

Columbia University has been tracking the relationship between human resource practices and economic indicators since 1986. Collaborative partners in this research have included the Alfred P. Sloan Foundation, Carnegie Mellon University, and The World Bank. Two of the studies in this collaboration have produced evidence that is quite compelling. The first study, led by David Lewin, covered 495 organizations and reached the following conclusions:

- Companies that share profits and gains with employees have significantly better financial performance than those who don't.

- Companies that share information broadly and that have broad programs of employee involvement (the researchers define involvement as areas of intellectual participation) perform significantly better than companies that are run autocratically.

- Flexible work design (flexible hours, rotation, and job enlargement), is significantly related to financial success.

- Training and development have a positive effect on business financial performance.

- Two-thirds of the bottom line impact was due to the combined effect of group economic participation, intellectual participation, flexible job design, and training and development.

As if Lewin anticipated the skepticism of the findings, he and his team went a step further, using statistical techniques to identify casual

(continued)

relationships between human resource practices and bottom-line performance. Thus, the conclusions listed demonstrate that not only do such practices affect bottom-line performance but actually help to cause it.

The 1990 Brookings Institution conference on pay and productivity also demonstrated Maslow's words in its investigation of the relationship between pay and bottom line performance. When all of the results were in, Conference chairman Alan S. Blinder concluded from the data that "changing the way workers are treated may boost productivity more than changing the way they are paid. Worker participation apparently helps make alternative compensation plans like profit sharing, gain sharing, and employee stock ownership plans work better and also has beneficial effects of its own. This theme, which was totally unexpected when I organized the conference, runs strongly through all papers."

No doubt during the next decade we will undertake and conclude the various correlations between the treatment of workers and people's effect upon performance and profit. It seems that for some, it won't be the right thing to do unless it is the most profitable thing to do. Yet, perhaps the most important debate has just begun to take place: the true purpose of business and work in an enlightened society. We add to the debate with a thought provoking quote:

> *The purpose of a business firm is not simply to make a profit, but is to be found in its very existence as a community of persons who in various ways are endeavoring to satisfy their basic needs and who form a particular group at the service of the whole of society. Profit is a regulator of the life of a business, but it is not the only one; other human and moral factors must also be considered, which in the long term are at least equally important for the life of a business.*
> —Pope J. Paul II in "The Hundredth Year: An Essay"

Sources:

The Age of Participation by Patricia McLagan and Christo Nel; Berrett-Koehler Publishers, 1995.

"Financial Dimensions of Workforce Management," March 1989 (Paper presented at Instructional Systems Association Conference).

Paying for Productivity: A Look at the Evidence; Alan S. Blinder, Brookings Institution, Washington, DC, 1990.

Regressive Forces

. . . I have no doubt that the conformist standard of practice which has worked in large organizations absolutely needs modification and revision. We'll have to find a way of permitting people to be individualistic in an organization. . . . We've got to face it.

S ince enlightened management depends on all sorts of preconditions in order to make itself possible, we must be very careful about these conditions, not only the ones which make progression possible but also the ones that make regression more likely. The forces which tend to make for regression are, for instance: scarcity of goods (not enough to go around); cessation of prepotent basic need gratifications (or threat to these gratifications); antisynergic organization or laws; anything that increases fear or anxiety; loss or separation of any kind for the person leading to grief or bereavement; change of any kind for those people who are prone to anxiety or to fear; bad communications of various kinds; suspicion; denial in the sense of denial of truth; dishonesty, untruth, lying, vulgarization of the truth, confusion of the lines between truth and falsehood; loss of any of the basic need gratifications in the world, e.g., freedom, self-esteem, status, respect, love objects, being loved, belonging, safety, physiological needs, value systems, truth, beauty, etc.

This all relates to the problem of hitting a suitable balance in management theory between positive and negative forces. Certainly it is OK to accentuate the positive today much more than was done twenty or thirty years ago. But it is also necessary to accentuate the negative, perhaps even before accentuating the positive. How much should each be accentuated? Just as much as the reality of the situation, just as much as the law of the situation, requires.

It is also desirable to underscore the occasional possibility that good enlightened conditions may produce in some people a regressive effect, that is to say, a bad effect. It is necessary to stress this to preclude disillusionment. The fact is that a certain proportion of the population cannot take responsibility well and are frightened by freedom, which tends to throw them into anxiety, etc. This has been noticed often enough by the clinicians, but the management people apparently are not used to thinking this way yet. The fact is that an unstructured situation, a free situation, a situation in which people are thrown back on their own resources will sometimes show their lack of resources. Some then fall into apathy or laxity or inertia or mistrust or anxiety or depression, and so on. They may get by in the ordinary authoritarian, conventional structure situation, but in the free and open and self-responsible situation, they discover that they are, e.g., not really interested in working, or that they mistrust their intelligence, or that they may become overwhelmed by depression which they have been strongly repressing, etc. What this means for organization theorists is that in all their calculations in moving over to the newer style of management, they should assume that a certain proportion—as yet unknown—will not respond well to good conditions.

For instance, one kind of ordinarily concealed tendency is permitted to come out clearly in the freedom situation and this is the masochistic or self-defeating tendency. Perhaps I should add here also what has been observed by plenty of others that where you try to move over from a strictly authoritarian managerial style to a more participative style, the first consequence of lifting the rigid restrictions of authority may well be some chaos, some release of hostility, some destructiveness, and the like. Authoritarians *may* be converted and retrained, but this is apt to take some time, and they are apt to go through a transitional period of taking advantage of what they consider to be the weakness of the managers. This, too, can breed disillusionment in some people who are not prepared for this transitional period of disappointment, and lead to a quick change back to authoritarian management.

Notes on Self-Esteem
in the Work Situation

. . . Where you try to move over from a strictly authoritar-
ian managerial style to a more participative style, the first
consequence of lifting the rigid restrictions of authority may
well be some chaos, some release of hostility, some destruc-
tiveness, and the like. . . .

I f we expand and enrich our understanding of the self-esteem level of motivation, then I think we can clarify and crystallize much which is only half-conscious or groping in the management literature. Everybody seems to be aware at some level of consciousness of the fact that authoritarian management outrages the dignity of the worker. He then fights back in order to restore his dignity and self-esteem,

Human beings avoid	To be a nothing (Rather than a something)	A ludicrous figure regulated by others (Like an object, to be treated like a physical object rather than like a person; to be rubricized, like an example rather than as unique)
Being manipulated	Unappreciated	Given orders
Dominated	Not respected	Forced
Pushed around	Not feared	Screwed (used, exploited)
Determined by others	Not taken seriously	Controlled
To be misunderstood	Laughed at	Helpless
		Compliant
		Deferent
		An interchangeable man

actively with hostility and vandalism and the like, or passively as a slave does, with all sorts of underhanded, sly and secretly vicious countermeasures. These reactions are puzzling to the dominator, but on the whole they are easily enough understood, and they make very real psychological sense, if they are understood as attempts to maintain one's dignity under conditions of domination or of disrespect.

Now, one approach to this is to pick out all the words from the literature, generally from the remarks of the dominated people about the way in which they view their own situations negatively. That is, it is like asking what is it they dislike, what are they avoiding, what makes them feel a loss of self-esteem.

What they are seeking for positively is:

To be a prime mover.

Self-determination.

To have control over one's own fate.

To determine one's movements.

To be able to plan and carry out and to succeed.

To expect success.

To like responsibility or at any rate to assume it willingly, especially for one's self.

To be active rather than passive.

To be a person rather than a thing.

To experience one's self as the maker of one's own decisions.

Autonomy.

Initiative.

Self-starting.

To have others acknowledge one's capabilities fairly.

The difference between the need for esteem (from others) and the need for self-esteem should be made very clear in the final write-up. Make the differentiation sharply, clearly, and unmistakably. Reputation or prestige or applause are very nice, and are for children and adolescents even absolutely necessary before real self-esteem can be built up. Or to say it the other way about, one of the necessary foundations for self-esteem is respect and applause from other people, especially in the younger years. Ultimately, real self-esteem rests upon all the things

INTERVIEW WITH SHERRI ROSE

The problem of management in any organization can then be approached in a new way: how to set up social conditions so that the goals of the individual merge with the goals of the organization.

—Abraham Maslow

A concept Maslow recommended nearly 37 years ago is currently in vogue in corporate America. Aligning personal goals with organizational goals is something many firms are attempting to integrate into their organizations. We interviewed Sherri Rose, former director of Apple University (Apple Computer) to discuss the alignment of corporate goals with organizational goals. In the forefront of corporate America's attempt to create learning organizations, Rose helped create one of the most progressive corporate universities in the country. In her work, she continually struggled with the intricate balancing act of such alignment. Now a consultant to corporations, we talked with Rose about Maslow's concept.

Dr. Maslow refers to organizing work as a way of helping people align their personal goals with the goals of the organization or corporation. As you read the journals, you can see his thought process about this concept unfolding. Today, one of the most popular topics in organizations is the concept of aligning personal goals with organizational goals. Do you think this connection is possible?

Yes. I absolutely think it is possible. I've seen it done on a small scale with teams. We speak of them as high performing teams. In fact, what I have read from Maslow's writing, was certainly similar to our concept of high performing teams. I don't think you can have a team that performs well unless people feel that their beliefs and values are manifest in their work.

Can you give us an example?

At Apple University, we had to be very focused in terms of our people and financial resources. Apple was a global company and we needed to focus our attention on creating management information and training resources via the internet to reach Apple employees in real time. In our work group, we did everything we could do with our combined skills and our places within the organization to create something as quickly as possible. Our values were aligned. We each had a commitment to provide Apple employees with information quickly. We all believed in that goal. So, I had administration people working on the registration side. I had

(continued)

development consultants collecting information and the technical people were completely focused on their tasks. We were all committed to the end product no matter what our title or responsibility. It was a very creative and exciting time because we all believed in the value we were creating and providing.

At the same time we had fun. We supported one another and we didn't burn each other out with the responsibilities or the tasks. Looking back, I realize that we respected one another. We respected individual's limits and boundaries. We also celebrated our accomplishments along the way. We were very much aware that people needed to be appreciated and cared about for their contributions.

Where do organizations go wrong in attempting to align personal goals with corporate goals?

Maslow implies that you can take this approach because it is the right thing to do or you can take this approach as a manipulative strategy. I think one of the ways in which we get into trouble in this alignment is by not listening carefully enough to what team members really want to do. I never really believed in that management theory of whatever you would like to accomplish is fine with me. However, before setting the vision or the goal, I always tried to listen carefully to uncover what people were really excited about. What pieces of work did they love? What pieces did they hate? I always tried to move work projects around so that people could work in the areas they loved. There were many times, however, when I needed to go to people and say the team needs this work from you even though it is not something you would prefer to do. Yet, I always tried to manage the alignment: putting people in the right positions where they could excel with work they loved.

There are times when this alignment just does not work. For example, I remember a trainer telling me she did not want to train anymore. I said I have three trainers left and you don't want to train. I don't think this is an option. However, it really struck me that in order for her to be successful, I was going to need to figure our a way that she could grow in other areas and still train. It is always a real balancing act. Sometimes you are forced to tell people "no." Yet, I also think that in those situations you need to be very clear on why you've come to that decision. You also must figure out a way to help the person you've said no to grow in the direction of their interests.

Maslow told us years ago that there would come a time when people pursued higher level needs rather than money. You spent ten years at Apple Computer in the midst of Silicon Valley where companies struggle to keep talented people. When you talk about helping people grow in the direction of their interests, isn't this similar to what Maslow was speaking of?

Yes. However, it is difficult to generalize because you have people just entering the workforce who have different needs from people who have been in the workforce for a while. You also have people who have financial burdens of one kind or another during various stages of their lives where money is important. As one's career moves up the corporate ladder, the sense of financial security takes a back seat to other needs. In this scenario, I think Maslow was right. In fact, he was so right it makes me think he was much more of a prophet or futurist than a psychologist!

Once people have a sense of security, once they are no longer hungry, all they want to do, no matter what job or level, is to learn and grow. Perhaps my judgment is clouded because I've spent most of my career in this Valley surrounded by people like this. However, when people come here to work, they take on very high levels of risk. For example, some of the highest mortgages in the United States are right here. The pace of change and work is frantic and a common denominator which I've found with employees in this Valley is their inherent need to be challenged and to grow. I refer to it as a culture of challenge junkies looking to change the world with a piece of technology or an idea. When the core financial step has been taken care of, the biggest challenge is to continually keep employees' personal interests, their need for growth, aligned with the needs of the company.

So, would you say that Maslow's theories of aligning personal goals with corporate goals have become a reality?

Let me begin by saying that old ideas have a way of making a comeback! I think that the person who has been at the forefront of this thinking is Peter Senge. He has done a wonderful job of capturing what we are discussing within the context of "shared vision." This is a starting point. Who would say that aligning personal goals with organizational goals is a bad idea? Who could argue with the notion that people should be able to grow and to learn and to self-actualize in their work? The concepts are so important and so basic to our needs as people that leaders tend to grab on to the theory. However, making it a reality is a whole different ballgame. My fear is that more people are paying lip service to the concept than making it a reality. What we're talking about is some of the hardest work in the organization. You really have to analyze and agonize over how work is done, how people are aligned, how they feel about work, how they feel about the organization, etc. Then you have to take the steps—the difficult

(continued)

steps of bringing the concept into reality. If you begin this path of aligning personal goals with organizational goals and you don't fully commit, I am afraid it will result in cynicism and failure.

It is important to remember that corporations are a large collection of human beings connecting with each other. It is all very personal. We are people talking to people—human beings sitting next to one another trying to accomplish a goal. When the alignment we speak of works, the human part of the organization is very well connected. This also changes the role of the leader. The leader has to believe in these concepts. It has to be dripping from his or her pores or people will know (and they always do) that it is nothing more than talk.

And the charisma of the leader is not what it's about. The stirring speech is not what it's about. The beautifully written mission statement is not what it's about. It sounds trite, but it's leading by example, meaning what you say, standing for something, and being willing to take action when what the company stands for is violated.

How does this concept of the leader you have described fit with the alignment of personal and organizational goals?

If alignment really exists throughout the organization, when the company runs into hardship, you don't have to look to that one visionary leader for the strategy or the answers. In the world we live in today, it is almost ludicrous for us to believe that the answers or the direction or the vision will come from the leader.

Can you give us an example?

Let me first say that what intrigues me is that if we really used Maslow's construct—the hierarchy of needs in our organizations as we all say we do, we would know that in a crisis situation there would be two areas we would focus on first. They are the security levels of Maslow's pyramid. For example, if you have a company in turmoil, I think the leadership would need to take steps to make sure the company could survive. These steps involve cost cutting. They involve getting employees to focus on short-term projects that will help the financial picture, such as writing new software, forging alliances and partnerships, things of that nature. However, you have to realize that those actions threaten the basic security of employees. So it is important to trim the fat and stop the financial bleeding. But it is also important to realize that those exact steps, on an organizational level, create uncertainty, fear, and a threat to the security of people. Yet, you need those people to be performing at a higher level in the hierarchy of needs or you stand no chance of surviving in the long term.

I think you can successfully take this step in times of crisis as long as people within the organization know the vision. The vision is so important, that if people understand the big picture, they will bleed with you. They will sacrifice, work harder, and even create in times of great uncertainty. However, if you lose the alignment and the vision of the company, people begin to question why they are continuing to work in an organization with such insecurity. For example, while I was at Apple numerous people on the outside would say to me "Are you crazy? What are you doing? You should be looking for another job. It's only a matter of time before you are laid off. Who knows what they are going to do with your salary." Yet, I was so involved in the Internet training program that I knew I would stay as long as I was able to continue to learn and to contribute. I also still believed in the vision of the company. In the beginning, it was the tiniest culture in the Valley. It inspired an entire computer industry. That vision allowed people to know the direction of the company, where their departments were going, how their work made a contribution to the end goal. Near the end of my tenure with Apple, I would say that people did not leave Apple because they were afraid for their paychecks; they left because they no longer knew the vision of the company. How powerful is vision? When Steve Jobs came back, even Wall Street responded with a 2 percent increase in the stock price. Why? The company was still bleeding but he embodied the original vision. That is how powerful these concepts can be.

mentioned above, on a feeling of dignity, of controlling one's own life, and of being one's own boss. (Let's call this "dignity.") And then work out more carefully the interrelationship between dignity and self-esteem and the whole topic of real achievement, real skill, real mastery (by contrast with applause that may be undeserved). One has to *deserve* applause, prestige, medals, and fame, or at very deep unconscious levels, they can actually be hurtful and produce guilt; all sorts of psychopathogenic processes may start from undeserved applause.

Also, I think it will be extremely instructive to many people to expand considerably on the ways in which outraged dignity protects itself. Look up again John Dollard's *Caste and Class in a Southern Town,*[1]

---

[1] New Haven: Yale University Press, 1935.

and other writings in which it is shown how the Afro-American, stepped upon and submerged, not being able to fight back physically, forced to swallow his rage, can yet strike back in all sorts of passive ways which can be very effective.

For instance, expand on the notion of pseudostupidity (and then pick out parallels in the industrial situation). The same for lethargy and laziness. The same for impulse freedom (which can be not only a form of self-assertion, but also a means of striking back at the oppressor). Do the same for the ways in which slaves, exploited people, oppressed minorities, and so on will fight back by fooling the oppressor secretly and then laughing at him, this too is a kind of retaliation psychodynamics which rests in the need for self-esteem. The same for passivity.

I think I can use in this context some of the examples that I've used in my *Need to Know and the Fear of Knowing* (93). I think we could teach managers and supervisors, not to mention professors of business management and industrial consultants and so on, that so many of these responses in workers, responses which they despise, which produce anger, may have been made by the worker just *in order to* produce that anger; maybe that was the *purpose* of it; maybe it was a striking back. In any case, if these psychodynamics are more readily recognized, then they can be taken for the valuable indicators that they are, just as a thermometer is very useful as an indicator of fever and of hidden sickness someplace. When these passive, sneaky, underhanded, behind-the-back retaliations come, they come out of anger, anger generally about being exploited or dominated or being treated in an undignified way.

And now I would ask the question, "How can any human being help but be insulted by being treated as an interchangeable part, as simply a cog in a machine, as no more than an appurtenance to an assembly line (an appurtenance less good than a good machine)? There *is* no other human, reasonable, intelligible way to respond to this kind of profound cutting off of half of one's growth possibilities than by getting angry or resentful or struggling to get out of the situation.

If I ask the managers or bosses or professors about what they would do in a similar situation, i.e., how they would feel if they were put into some kind of position in which they weren't treated as persons, in which their names weren't known, but in which they were given a number of some sort and in which they were treated not as unique but absolutely as interchangeable, their answer usually implies that they wouldn't resent it; they would work hard and work themselves out of that situation. That is, they would look for a promotion of some sort. They would regard this kind of work as a means to an end.

But this is an evasion of my question because then I would ask them, "Suppose you had to do this for the rest of your life? Suppose there were no promotions possible? Supposing this were the end of the road?" Then I think these upper-level people would see the situation in a different way. My own expectation is that this more forceful, more decisive type would probably be the *most* hostile, most revolutionary, most vandalistic, much more so than the average worker now who has gotten used to the whole idea of living that way for the rest of his life and who will commit only partial vandalisms and be only partially hostile. I suspect that all these "time-study" people and the "scientific management" people and the upper-class people in general who expect that the lower-class people will accept calmly, quietly, peacefully, and without protest the status of slavery and of anonymity and of interchangeability which is being dished out to them, that these very same bosses put into similar situations would start a revolution or a civil war almost immediately.

Such realizations would quickly force a change in the philosophy of managers. Partly this would be because they could identify with, and have intuitions of, and deeply understand and experience the feelings of, a human being put into an interchangeable mechanistic situation. The manager who shudders at the thought of being in such a situation would have more sympathy for the reactions of the person whom fate has forced for the time being into this mechanistic situation. He would understand, for instance, what the situation was if he meditated upon the fact that feeble-minded girls find themselves quite comfortable in these mechanistic and repetitive industrial situations. Should he ask that all people react like feeble-minded people?

Then I think also that this kind of psychodynamic understanding of self-esteem and of dignity would make a great difference in the industrial situation because the feeling of dignity, of respect and of self-respect are *so easy to give!* It costs little or nothing, it's a matter of an attitude, a deep-lying sympathy and understanding which can express itself almost automatically in various ways that can be quite satisfying, since they save the dignity of the person in the unfortunate situation.

Being in an unfortunate situation, or working hard in a mechanistic situation is itself quite tolerable, as we know, if the goals are good and are shared, and if also being in this situation is not threatening to the self-esteem of the person. But the situation can very easily be made unthreatening to the self-esteem in all sorts of simple and easy ways which the case histories in the management literature show by the dozens. I think here of careful and detailed case histories like those in M. Dalton's *Men Who Manage.*[2] One could make a good demonstration of the role of self-esteem in the industrial life simply by going through Dalton's book with this particular fine-tooth comb, i.e., to pick out every instance in the whole book that has to do with the searching for self-esteem, with responses to threats to self-esteem, with retaliations, with self-healing efforts to restore wounded self-esteem, etc.

The more I think of this, the more I think it would pay to put this in the widest psychological context. I think it would pay to make a theoretical generalization from the responses of all exploited or minority groups of various kinds to construct a general abstract theory of responses to domination. I think I could do this by pulling together what I've already written about the relationships between the strong and the weak, between masculinity and femininity (where they are seen as mutually exploitative or rivalrous), between dominance and subordination, between adults and children, between the exploiter and the exploitee, between the general population and our despised minorities of various sorts, between the whites and Afro-Americans, especially in pre-Civil War days, but also more recently.

Perhaps the history of the relations between men and women in the patriarchal cultures would be as illustrative as anything. The ways in which women have responded to being dominated, exploited, and used without dignity and without respect in the past, these ways of retaliation have generally been seen as character traits, and have added up to a definition of femininity in the particular culture and in the particular time. For instance, reading in the Turkish or Arabic literature where women were treated as nothings, just as pieces of property, and nobody ever dreamed of using the word dignity with regard to them, the ways in which Turkish or Arabic men in the last couple of centuries characterized femininity, the feminine soul, the feminine character, adds up to practically all those forms of secret retaliation

[2] New York: John Wiley & Sons, 1959

that we can find in the Negro slaves in the southern plantations, or in "typical" Negro behavior in the South perhaps thirty or forty years ago, where there was no possibility for them to retaliate openly with hostility. The techniques by which a child who is afraid of his parents and who is dominated by them (perhaps we should better say terrorized), manages to get along again comes very close to being the same as the list of characteristics of femininity in a patriarchal situation, or the Negro character in a slavery situation.

I think the point would be made unmistakably and clearly by such a juxtaposition, and with the clear possibility of making a general abstract theory of the relations between domination and subordination, not only for all human beings but even across the species lines. That is, this response of workers to domination and consequent loss of dignity, can be seen as a profoundly normal biologically rooted self-protection, and therefore can be seen itself as a symptom of human dignity. This comes out at the other end of the horn finally from the way in which most people today will see these responses of the outraged worker who is being stepped upon and who is defending himself, precisely as evidence of how low human nature is, how little it can be trusted, how worthless people are, how little they amount to. It is precisely these reactions which *I* can see as respectworthy which make other people lose all their respect for the worker.

The fact that slaves will revolt if not openly then covertly makes *me* proud of the human species; but I can understand quite well that it would make a slave owner or an exploiter or a dominator get very angry and contemptuous. I have seen this happen often in the individual clinical situation: The exploiter comes to take for granted the exploitee almost as a kind of character. This is very subtle and very hard to say, but it's also quite real. The wolf expects that the lamb will continue to behave like a lamb. If suddenly the lamb turns around and bites the wolf, then I can understand that the wolf would get not only surprised but also get very indignant. Lambs aren't supposed to behave that way. Lambs must lie quietly and get eaten up. Just so I have seen human wolves get very angry when their victims finally turn around and strike back.

Or another example that I have observed and which is usable in this situation is the very frequent conversation that one is apt to hear among older people who are wealthy and who always have been wealthy. The standard topic of conversation is how good the servants used to be and how bad they are now. Throughout this kind of conversation I have never detected the slightest doubt that God made it this way, i.e., that these people assumed that it was absolutely just that they should be ladies and gentlemen and that servants should be servants. They never doubted for a moment that loyalty to the master in the servant was a very desirable and just and fair thing. Their indignation when the servants have an opportunity to become unexploited, to give up being slavish, is the kind of indignation I have spoken of above that the queenly wife might show when suddenly the slave of a husband revolted.

"This is not right, this is not becoming," they might say. "This is very ugly and dirty and very depressing. People shouldn't be that way."

What all these people are describing is really the good and well-adjusted slave who likes being a slave and is very well adjusted and adapted to that situation, and whose hostility has either disappeared or has been repressed so profoundly that there is just no surface indication of it anymore at all. But in a democratic society this is exactly the kind of person who should make us depressed instead of glad; this is the kind of person who is an argument *against* the higher possibilities of human nature, of creativeness, of growth, of self-actualization. Just in the same way as a neurosis can be seen either as a sign of sin and evil and human weakness and degradation on the one hand, or can be seen with deeper understanding and insight, as a frightened person's indirect struggle toward health, growth, and self-actualization, just so is the whole of the foregoing applicable to the response of the worker in a bad industrial situation. He may show his anger at being dehumanized in all sorts of sneaky ways, but these are essentially testimonials to his fear rather than to his lack of growth possibilities. The hostility shows that he wants to grow out of that situation. Or to say this in another way, the response of outrage when dignity is attacked is itself a validation of the human being's need for dignity.

The research questions then are: "How can we avoid the organizational situations which cut human dignity and make it less possible? In those situations which are unavoidable in industry, as with assembly lines, how can we decontaminate these so as to retain the dignity of the worker and his self-esteem as much as possible in spite of the circumstances?"

Management as a
Psychological Experiment

*. . . Accountants must try to figure out some way of turning
into balance sheet terms the intangible personnel values that
come from improving the people of the organization . . . .*

There are enough data available, and enough industrial experiences, and also enough clinical-psychological data on human motivations, to warrant taking a chance on the experiment of Theory Y type of management. And yet it is well to keep in mind always that this will be a kind of a pilot experiment for the simple reason that the data which justify this experiment are definitely not final data, not clearly convincing beyond a shadow of a doubt. There is still plenty of room for doubt, as is evidenced by the fact that many academic people and many managers still do, in fact, doubt the validity of the whole line of thinking involved, and this is not entirely arbitrary. They do bring up evidence, experience, data against the new kind of management. We must certainly agree that there is plenty of doubt, and that the whole business is an experiment, and we must also be very aware of the fact that we need lots of data, lots of answers to a lot of questions yet to come.

For instance, the whole philosophy of this new kind of management may be taken as an expression of faith in the goodness of human beings, in trustworthiness, in enjoyment of efficiency, of knowledge, of respect, etc. But the truth is that we don't really have exact and quantitative information on the proportion of the human population which does in fact have some kind of feeling for workmanship, some kind of desire for all the facts and all the truth, some sort of desire for efficiency over inefficiency, etc. We know certainly that some individual human beings have these needs, and we know a little about the conditions under which these needs will appear, but we don't have any mass surveys of large populations that would give us some quantitative indication of just how many people prefer to have somebody else do their thinking for them, for instance. We don't know the answers to the question: What proportion of the population is irreversibly authoritarian?

These are all crucial kinds of information that we would need in order to be absolutely certain about enlightened management policy. We don't know how many people or what proportion of the working population would actually prefer to participate in management decisions, and how many would prefer not to have anything to do with them. What proportion of the population take a job as simply any old kind of a job which they must do in order to earn a living, while their interests are very definitely centered outside of the job.

An example is the woman who works only because she has to support her children. It's perfectly true that she'll prefer a nice and pleasant job to a rotten job, but just how does she define rotten job? How much involvement does she really want in the enterprise if the center of her life is definitely in her children rather than in her job? What proportion of the population prefer authoritarian bosses, prefer to be told what to do, don't want to bother thinking, etc.? What proportion of the population is reduced to the concrete and so finds planning for the future totally incomprehensible and boring? How many people prefer honesty and how strongly do they prefer it to dishonesty, how strong a tendency is there in people against being thieves? We know very little about physical inertia or psychic inertia. How lazy are people and under what circumstances and what makes them not lazy? We just don't know.

All of this then is an experiment (because of inadequate final data) in just about the same way that political democracy is an experiment which is based upon a scientifically unproven assumption: namely that human beings like to participate in their own fate, that given sufficient information they will make wise decisions about their own lives, and that they prefer freedom to being bossed, that they prefer to have a say in everything which affects their future, etc. None of these assumptions have been adequately enough proven so that we would call it scientific fact in about the same way that we would label biological fact scientific. We have to know more about these psychological factors

THEORY X AND THEORY Y: WHERE DO YOU FIT?

Nearly 38 years ago, Douglas McGregor set forth a new foundation for humanistic management. In his book, *The Human Side of Enterprise,* he argued that how well an organization performs is directly proportional to its success at unleashing human potential.

McGregor coined the terms Theory X and Theory Y as sets of assumptions we hold about people. Much of his thoughts about Theory X and Y were based upon Abraham Maslow's hierarchy of needs theory. Many say that McGregor's work brought fame to Maslow's theories. Throughout Maslow's journals, he refers to Douglas McGregor.

We have found that the essence of McGregor's work is sometimes lost in the translation. Theory X and Y are not management styles but our assumptions. Those assumptions play a large role in the development of our management styles.

In McGregor's own words: "the key question for top management is what are your assumptions (implicit as well as explicit) about the most effective way to manage people? The assumptions management holds about controlling its human resources determines the whole character of the enterprise."

So we ask, do you believe:

1. The average person, would prefer not to work than to work? That managers and organizations must control, direct, and ensure adequate effort from the average person? The average employee prefers direction and seeks security above all else in a job? The average employee holds no internal ambition or need for greatness?

2. For the average person, work is as natural and desired as rest or play; most people will exercise self-control, display self-initiative, and actively seek responsibility when they feel committed to a set of objectives; commitment comes primarily not from fear but from rewards, especially intangible rewards like the feeling of achievement and self-actualization; the average person has significant untapped capacity for creativity and ingenuity.

Number 1 corresponds with what McGregor coined Theory X and number 2 describes Theory Y. According to management consultant and author Jim Collins (*Built to Last*) "Theory X management still dominates most organizations. Many managers and entrepreneurs still hold hidden assumptions that people cannot be fully trusted, need to be 'checked up on,' need 'motivation,' or don't really like to work all that hard. Fear, distrust, coercion, carrot-and-stick management, and authoritarianism are alive and

(continued)

well in the 1990s. And it's not just limited to big old companies; many entrepreneurs rule their kingdoms with a Theory X iron fist, too."

How does Theory X play itself out in organizations? The best example we could find was from Douglas McGregor himself. We include a passage from one of his speeches in 1954:

> "I sat in a meeting a few weeks ago with a group of office department heads in a small company in Cambridge. They were considering the problem of getting people to arrive on time in the morning. What interested me was the way the conversation went in that group. One man said the solution was to install time clocks. Someone else said to take a little book and put it in a prominent place on a desk at the front of each department and require anybody who came in after the starting hour to sign his name in a book along with the hour of his arrival. Another man suggested that in his department he could arrange a turnstile at the door to the office in such a way that anybody coming in after 8:30 would ring a bell which could be heard within the whole department. These were serious suggestions made by a group of supervisors who in general were doing a good job. They thought of the problem entirely in terms of the gadgets they could use to solve it. What they did not think of were the attitudes and the backgrounds they were bringing to bear on the problem. I saw in the discussion, although never expressed, feelings of this kind: Coming to work on time is something that people won't do voluntarily. Those attitudes and convictions, always below the surface and never brought out into the open, were what was responsible for the suggestions they made for solving the problem.*

The challenge then, for those of us who concur with Maslow and McGregor's theories lies not in motivating people but in building an environment where motivated people are willing to make a maximum contribution. Perhaps a first step is to analyze the policies and procedures of our organizations. They speak volumes regarding our assumptions about people.

---

* Douglas McGregor's speech to Management Forum E.I. dupont de Nemors Co., 1954.

than we do. Because this is so, we ought to again be very aware, very conscious, of the fact that these are articles of faith rather than articles of final knowledge, or perhaps better said that they are articles of faith with some grounding in fact though not yet enough to convince people who are characterologically against these articles of faith.

I suppose that the ultimate test of scientific fact is that those people who are by temperament and character unsympathetic to the conclusion must accept it as a fact anyway. We will know that our knowledge of the authoritarian character structure is truly scientific final fact when an average authoritarian character will be able to read the information on the subject and then regard his own authoritarian character as undesirable or sick or pathological and will go about trying to get rid of it. Just so long as an authoritarian character can wave aside all the evidence which indicates that he is sick, just so long are those facts not sufficient, not final enough.

After all, if we take the whole thing from Douglas McGregor's point of view of a contrast between a Theory X view of human nature, a good deal of the evidence upon which he bases his conclusions comes from my researches and my papers on motivations, self-actualization, etc. But I of all people should know just how shaky this is as a final foundation. My work on motivations came from the clinic, from a study of neurotic people. The carry-over of this theory to the industrial situation has some support from industrial studies, but certainly I would like to see a lot more studies of this kind before feeling finally convinced that this carry-over from the study of neurosis to the study of labor in factories is legitimate.

The same thing is true of my studies of self-actualizing people—there is only this one study of mine available (57). There were many things wrong with the sampling, so many in fact that it must be considered to be, in the classical sense anyway, a bad or poor or inadequate experiment. I am quite willing to concede this—as a matter of fact, I am eager to concede it—because I'm a little worried about this stuff which I consider to be tentative being swallowed whole by all sorts of enthusiastic people, who really should be a little more tentative, in the way that I am. The experiment needs repeating and checking—it needs working over in other societies—it needs a lot of things which it doesn't yet have. The main support of this theory—and, of course, there's plenty of this support—has come mostly from psychotherapists like Rogers and Fromm.

MASLOW'S THEORY Z

. . . finally I call attention to the question of "levels of pay" and kinds of pay. What is crucially important is the fact itself that there are many kinds of pay other than money pay, that money as such steadily recedes in importance with increasing affluence and with increasing maturity of character, while higher forms of pay (meta pay) steadily *increase* in importance. Furthermore, even where money pay continues to *seem* to be important, it is often so not in its own literal, concrete character, but rather as a symbol for status, success, self-esteem with which to win love, admiration, and respect . . . .

—*Abraham Maslow, personal paper on Theory Z*

In 1968, Abraham Maslow hoped to break new ground in the field of management theory with Theory Z. *"The United States is changing into a managerial society"* he stated. Convinced that a humanistic approach in the workplace was beginning to arise, Maslow began to collect job advertisements as a way of tracking this new phenomena in the American workplace. In studying the advertisements written to attract professional, administrative, or executive employees, Maslow noted not only money but what he termed "the higher needs." The higher needs were reflected in job advertisements that noted friendly coworkers, pleasant surroundings, responsibility, freedom and autonomy, a chance to put one's ideas into action, a company of which one can be proud, a chance to make a difference.

Theory Z presupposed that people, once having reached a level of economic security, would strive for a life steeped in values, a work life where the person would be able to create and produce. Although Maslow died before finishing his work with Theory Z, we see evidence today that his theory was several decades ahead of its time.

The March 1998 cover story in *Fortune* magazine is but one example of Maslow's Theory Z in action. Entitled *Yo Corporate America—I'm the New Organization Man*, the article depicted the wants and needs of the new "gold collar worker." Expecting to be well paid, this generation also believes they are entitled to a job "that's fun, a job that's cool, a job that lets them discover who they really are." "*Work is not about paying the rent anymore—it's about self-fulfillment,*" summarized the *Fortune* reporter after an indepth study of the employment situation in America. Richard Barton, the 30-year-old head of Microsoft's Expedia brought Theory Z to life when he said, *"Work is not work. It's a hobby you happen to get paid for."*

This, of course, leaves the problem of carry-over from the therapeutic situation to the industrial situation still open to testing. It needs to be validated as a legitimate carry-over. I may say also that my paper on the need for knowledge (93), on curiosity in the human being, is also practically the only thing of its kind, and while I trust it and believe my own conclusions, I am still willing to admit like a cautious scientist that it ought to be checked by other people before being taken as final. As we become aware of the probable errors of the data, we must underscore the necessity for more research and more research and more research. Smugness and certainty tend to stop research rather than to stimulate it.

On the other hand, of course, I should make clear that the evidence upon which Theory X management is based is practically nil; that there is even less evidence for Theory X than there is for Theory Y. It rests entirely on habit and tradition. It's no use saying that it rests on long experience, as most of its proponents would say, because this experience is a kind of self, or at least *can* be a kind of self-fulfilling prophecy. That is to say that the people who support Theory X on nonscientific grounds then proceed to use it as a management philosophy, which brings about just that behavior in the workers which Theory X would predict. But with this kind of Theory X treatment of workers, no other kind of behavior would be possible as a result.

To sum this up I would say that there is insufficient grounding for a firm and final trust in Theory Y management philosophy; but then I would hastily add that there is even less firm evidence for Theory X. If one adds up all the researches that have actually been done under scientific auspices and in the industrial situation itself, practically all of them come out on the side of one or another version of Theory Y; practically none of them come out in favor of Theory X philosophy except in small and detailed and specific special circumstances.

The same is true for the studies of the authoritarian personality. These also come out generally in favor of the democratic personality. And yet there are a few specific special instances in which it is better to have an authoritarian personality, in which the authoritarian will get better results. For instance, an authoritarian personality will get better results for a transitional period as a teacher with authoritarian students than will a democratic and permissive Theory Y kind of teacher. This is the same order of evidence which indicates that practically *any* human being, however sick, can be used some place in a complex industrial civilization. I think, for instance, of Bob Holt's demonstration of the adaptive value even of the paranoid character; he showed that such people tend to make better detectives than do normal people—or at least that they do as well.

Another point here comes from my reading of the chapter by Scoutten in the book edited by Mason Haire called *Organization Theory in Industrial Practice*. Scoutten brings to mind that as soon as we take into account such factors as the long-range health of the business (instead of merely short-range health), the duties to a democratic society, the need in an individualized situation for pretty highly developed human beings as workers and managers, etc., etc., *then* the necessity for Theory Y management becomes greater and greater. He speaks of production and sales as the only functions, the only goals, of the company with which he is connected, the Maytag Company. Everything else he considers unnecessary or subsidiary to these two functions. But it should be pointed out that this is a kind of isolated or encapsulated view of the situation, i.e., as if this company had no relationship with the community, the environment, or the society, nor any debt to it. He takes an awful lot for granted in a situation like this, including a democratic society with high levels of education, with great respect for law and property, etc., etc. He leaves these things out entirely. If you include them, then it becomes obvious also that the company or the enterprise has to give certain things to the society as well as receive certain things from the society, and this makes a different picture altogether. The picture that Scoutten gives of an enterprise might work perfectly well in a fascist economy, but it would not work at all if it were taken seriously in our democratic society, where any enterprise—as a matter of fact, any individual—has also its obligations to the whole society.

(At this point there should be a reference to my memorandum on the patriot, and on the enlightened industrialist as a patriot.)

More should be said on the relations between the enterprise and the society, especially if we take into account the ways to keep the organization healthy over a period of a hundred years. It then becomes most obvious about the mutual ties between the enterprise and the society—for one thing the healthy organization will need a steady supply of fairly well-matured and well-educated personalities (it cannot use delinquents, criminals, cynical kids, spoiled and indulged kids, hostile people, warmongers, destroyers, vandals, etc., but exactly these people are the products of a poor society). This is very much like saying that a poor society cannot support healthy enterprises, in the long run at least. (Although it probably is true that some kinds of products can be well made in the authoritarian society or the authoritarian enterprise, or under conditions of fear and starvation. I really should find out what kinds of exports for instance, can come from Spain today, or how good are Negro workers in South Africa? What kind of production do they have?)

It is also true that the healthy enterprise cannot function at all well under conditions of riots and civil war, of epidemics, of sabotage and murder, of class warfare, or caste warfare. The culture itself has to be healthy for this reason as well. Also there cannot be conditions of corruption, political corruption, nor can there be religious corruption or religious domination. The enterprise must be free to develop itself in all ways which do not interfere with the goodness and the health of the society. This means also that there ought not to be too much political domination either.

In effect any company that restricts its goals purely to its own profits, its own production, and its own sales is getting a kind of a free ride from me and other taxpayers. I help pay for the schools and the police departments and the fire departments and the health departments and everything else in order to keep the society healthy, which in turn supplies high-level workers and managers to such companies at little expense to them. I feel that they should, in order to be fair, make more returns to the society than they are making—that is, in terms of producing good citizens, people who because of their good work situation can themselves be benevolent, charitable, kind, altruistic, etc., etc., in the community.

I am impressed again with the necessity, however difficult the job may be, of working out some kind of moral or ethical accounting scheme. Under such a scheme tax credits would be given to the company that helps to improve the whole society, that helps to improve the local population, and helps to improve the democracy by helping to create more democratic individuals. Some sort of tax penalty should be assessed against enterprises that undo the effects of a political democracy, of good schools, etc., etc., and that make their people more paranoid, more hostile, more nasty, more malevolent, more destructive, ect. This is like sabotage against the whole society. And they should be made to pay for it.

INTERVIEW WITH GEORGE McCOWN

The problem for the accountants is to work out some way of putting on the balance sheet the human assets of the organization: that is the amount of synergy, the degree of education of all the workers in the organization, the amount of time and money and effort that has been invested in getting good informal work groups to work together well, like a basketball team. To put it briefly, all the human assets which are not seen on the balance sheet effect the long term welfare of the business . . . .

—Abraham Maslow

3000 Sand Hill Road in Menlo Park, California, is synonymous with power, prestige, and the art of the deal. Home to the venture capitalists, this address houses the people who fuel a large portion of America's economy through funding, acquisitions, and buyouts of companies. Always in search of the next profitable business, Sand Hill Road has become a legend in the archives of corporate American history. In the midst of this financial mecca sits George McCown, who with his partner, David De Leeuw, founded McCown and De Leeuw & Co in 1984. The firm is a private venture banking firm that invests in high quality ventures in partnership with management. Yet, as we discovered, their goal is simply to build great companies where people can self-actualize.

★ ★ ★

You work in an industry where the concept of building great companies that make a difference is scarce. Wouldn't you agree?

I think a lot of people would say that our industry, which is generally defined as being private equity, would not come quickly to mind. If we define our industry, there would be three or four subsegments. The largest is what we call management buy-outs. That business in the last year has raised well over $50 billion of new capital from institutions and wealthy families. Ten billion was in venture capital, thirty some billion were in buyouts. When David De Leeuw and I started our company 15 years ago, the ratio was reversed. The amount of money that went into venture capital was larger than it was in buyouts. It was really not a well recognized industry at the time we started. Yet if we go back to its foundation, our work is about building good and prosperous businesses.

What I have learned from my experiences in the venture community as well as my work as a manager in corporate America is something we describe as "the wrong owner syndrome." When there is a wrong owner, it's like having the wrong boss. It has a massive impact on the organization. The "wrong owner syndrome" can be found in private and publicly held companies.

In my own experience, what became interesting to me was undertaking a plan to "save these companies." Whether it was dissecting and spinning off a number of parts and pieces, I noticed frequently those assets, when turned back into the hands of the employees, magically turned into these flowering businesses. The people were happy and excited. Things we couldn't make work at all because of past policies and procedures magically became terrific companies in the hands of an entrepreneurial environment with adequate financing where the single focus of the enterprise was the business as opposed to being spread across a number of businesses or egos.

I have been a part of large divisions inside of large companies and know firsthand how you had to fight for new ideas. Our business is about setting up the right owner, becoming the right owner, usually in partnership with management. In fact always in partnership with management. Whether it's in the management that exists or the management that we find and put into the situation, we attempt to provide a completely focused and congruent set of objectives so that everybody is lined up, everybody is on the same side of the table.

So, what we've done is create a place where the various pieces and parts can truly be separate and focused and everybody can be lined up. What we have also tried to do is to create a set of conditions within the companies we acquire where people can self-actualize and create.

How does McCown and De Leeuw & Co. build great companies?

What we are in the process of doing right now in our society and around the world, as capitalism essentially has swept the world, is (at least some of us are beginning to try) to redefine a value system that will align our actions in the marketplace with core values of a good society. And Maslow touches on many of them as you go through this journal. He's such a pioneer. He's so willing to think a new thought, to make the intuitive leaps, and then go back to see if he can test it.

Let's talk about vision. It is each individual's mental picture of what that organization could be like in its highest and best self-actualized mode. To best understand what I mean let me describe it as the thing that you think about that gives you joy. My picture will look a little different than your picture. It's that thing which touches our highest and best part. It's the part that is inspirational and aspirational. It touches in each of us what we refer to at McCown and De Leeuw as our noble goal. Our noble goal is that part of us which is connected to everybody else and everything else in the world.

(continued)

Through our discussions, we identified great companies. The ones we were most proud of. Companies that made us feel energized when we thought about them. They made differences in the industries they were in. They were companies that attracted the best employees. They were companies that the communities wanted to have in their town. They were the companies that vendors fought over to have their business. They were the companies that customers wanted to do business with. They were the companies where shareholders loved being shareholders.

We concluded that we wanted to define what making a difference was through the idea of the stakeholders' circle. That is we wanted to build companies that took into account and tried to balance over time, as appropriate, all the interests of these folks. Today, we have done just that and where we have satisfied the stakeholders' circle, we have demonstrated exceptional financial performance.

How do you implement these goals?

We find companies that are undergoing change in an industry that is growing and where we can go in and buy a platform company with a management team. We then provide the resources and the strategies and our systems of thinking that are necessary to create a peak-performing organization. An organization that is self-actualized because the people in it are self-actualized is when it's really fun. That's when you get the fantastic results. That's when people get up in the morning and *want* to go to work.

When we implemented our pyramid, there was still something missing. We weren't working together here at McCown and De Leeuw. We were still operating in what I'll call this "ego system." The ego system has a lot of characteristics and one of them is tremendous competition between people. How can you build a team when the fundamental precept is to compete with each other? But that's really what we tend to do in organizations. It's why teams don't work very well. They become internally competitive and we don't understand why they're that way, we just think that's the way it is. What we are missing is that we don't know that there's another way of being. We may suspect it, and a few of us, in particular those who have had a strong spiritual practice in their life know that there's something better than that. We undertook a very long process with each member of our firm to find that better way.

Tell me about the people who come to work here. I saw your partners in the lobby. I've read their backgrounds. They are an impressive group with credentials from the excellent schools and experience with blue chip firms. I'm also told that your internships are among the most coveted from the best schools.

Our partners came because they wanted to build companies as opposed to simply doing financial transactions. This is one of the major differences between us and most of the people in our industry. The goal of building great organizations has fundamentally transformed our organization. There's no question. We can't go back. This stuff of which we speak isn't easy. It's the toughest and hardest thing to do, but once you've headed down the path, you can't go back. So, in walking our talk and in undertaking the very things which prevented us internally from being synergistic, we have been transformed in the process. After all, we can't bring these transformational qualities to the companies we acquire if they are not present within McCown and De Leeuw. We are so much more effective today.

How does that strategy to build great organizations play itself out with the financial community?

When we were out fund raising this last time to replenish the coffers, which is something we do regularly in this business, we discussed this issue. We discussed how are we going to say something like that to some hard-nosed guy in Wall Street. Well, we came to a conclusion. It was that those people are people, too. They have an innate need to strive for self-actualization. They have noble goals. They know what it's like to work in crummy organizations as compared to great organizations. So we come in and we ignite them! The result? We raised nearly twice the amount of money we had targeted. Our goal was to raise $400 million. That's my answer to Wall Street.

Maslow stated in his journals that organizations with enlightened management could create a better society. Your goals of self-actualized people and self-actualized companies seem to fit with his theory. Would you agree?

I am firmly committed to the proposition that business has a central role to play in the transformation that is going on in the world. Probably a bigger role than any other single institution. Business people have never had that role. They've always had a big role, but not in terms of creating a good society. We must understand that role and we have to raise our consciousness. We have to make the choice as to whether or not we are going to individually and collectively accept the responsibility for creating the kinds of outcomes that contribute to forming good human beings. Outcomes that we would like to leave as our legacy for our children and grandchildren and the many generations to come. That's a new idea for business and the question is, are we going to accept it? Business is where the rubber meets the road—where people spend most of their lives going to work. We and the not-for-profits have a much greater role to play in shaping the good society than any institution I can think of.

Partly it must be put up to the accountants to try to figure out some way of turning into balance sheet terms the intangible personnel values that come from improving the personality level of the workers, making them more cooperative, better workers, less destructive, etc. It does cost money to hire this kind of personnel; it costs money to train and teach them and to build them into a good team, and there are all sorts of other costs involved in making the enterprise attractive to this kind of worker and this kind of engineer, etc. All these real expenditures of money and effort ought somehow to be translated into accounting terms so that the greater value of the enterprise that contributes to the improvement of the whole society can somehow be put on the balance sheets. We all know that such a company for instance, is a better credit risk and lending banks will take this into account. So will investors. The only ones who don't take these things into account are the accountants.

Enlightened Management as a Form of Patriotism

All the experiments on enlightened management and humanistic supervision can be seen from this point of view that in a brotherhood situation of this sort, every person is transformed into a partner rather than an employee.

I t is a question of how to communicate to people who are either ignorant or skeptical or antagonistic to the new principles of management which are based on an understanding of the higher as well as the lower possibilities in human nature. It is a question of how to teach and to communicate what the ultimate goals of this kind of management are. I have thought that I would say this in different ways to different kinds of people, depending on their values and what they consider most important.

For instance, to the patriotic American (that is in the original and in the correct sense, not in the sense of these DAR or American Legions, John Birchers or whoever—we must take this word patriot back from the people who have misused it and give it its original meaning), it would be impressive to point out that the new kind of management is a form of patriotism and love of country and love of Americans applied to the industrial and to the work situation. If democratic, political philosophy means anything at all, then enlightened management can be considered under the head of democratic philosophy applied to the work situation. Stress can also be placed on the contributions that an enlightened enterprise makes in terms of more democratic citizens, or more philanthropic citizens, of less destructive citizens, etc.

In a still larger sense it can be said this way that democracy needs absolutely for its very existence people who can think for themselves, make their own judgments, and finally, who can vote for themselves—

that is, who can rule themselves and help to rule their own country. Authoritarian enterprises do just the opposite of this; democracies do exactly just this. The best way to destroy democratic society would be by way of not only political authoritarianism but of industrial authoritarianism, which is anti-democratic in the deepest sense. Therefore, any man who really wants to help his country, who is devoted to it, and who would sacrifice for it and take upon his own shoulders the responsibility for its improvement, must, if he is to be logical, carry this whole philosophy into his work life. This means the new forms of industry and management.

So far as people are concerned to take religion very seriously, something parallel also is possible. Enlightened management is one way of taking religion seriously, profoundly, deeply, and earnestly. Of course, for those who define religion just as going to a particular building on Sunday and hearing a particular kind of formula repeated, this is all irrelevant. But for those who define religion not necessarily in terms of the supernatural, or ceremonies, or rituals, or dogmas, but in terms of deep concern with the problems of the human species, with the problems of ethics, of the relationship to nature, of the future of man, etc., then this kind of philosophy translated into the work life, turns out to be very much like the new style of management and of organization. It would have been said a few years ago when these things could be said without blushing, that enlightened management was a way of limited human beings trying the best way they could to produce the good life on earth or to make a heavenly society on earth.

For the social psychologists and social theorists, this new philosophy is an improvement on the old utopias and on utopian thinking in general. The trouble with all the utopias of the past, or at least most of them, is that they have tended to be flights from a complicated civilization, in effect trying to run away from it rather than trying to help it or cure it in any way. But of course, we cannot run away from industrialization and from the complexity of society. If we all took seriously a go-back-to-the-farm kind of philosophy, three quarters of the human species would die in a year or two. The Brook Farm kind of utopia will never again be possible so long as industrialization remains. Going back to the farm may be all right for a few selected people, but it certainly is not feasible for the whole human species. We will have to use factories instead of running away from them. Therefore, the social psychological thinking of enlightened management can be

SPIRITUALITY IN THE WORKPLACE

Enlightened management is one way of taking religion seriously, profoundly, deeply, and earnestly. Of course, for those who define religion just as going to a particular building on Sunday and hearing a particular kind of formula repeated, this is all irrelevant. But for those who define religion not necessarily in terms of the supernatural, or ceremonies, or rituals, but in terms of deep concern with the problems of human beings, with the problems of ethics, of the future of man, then this kind of philosophy, translated into the work life, turns out to be very much like the new style of management and of organization.

—*Abraham Maslow*

Ten years ago, few would have planned a business conference around spirituality much less write a book on the topic. Yet today, religion, in the form of "spirituality in the workplace" is taking on greater significance. Corporate retreats run by spiritual guru, Deepak Chopra, who blends Eastern and Western mysticism with the American dream, are sold out two years in advance. Best-selling books, with titles such as *Leading with Soul, Chicken Soup for the Soul at Work, The Seven Habits of Highly Effective People, Jesus as CEO,* and *The Hungry Spirit,* fly off bookstore shelves.

Yet, if we study Dr. Maslow's words, perhaps "work" itself has inspired our renewed interest in spirituality. Organizations everywhere have undertaken the process of defining their goals, values, and mission statements. The process forces leaders and employees to analyze the very heart and soul of their existence. Today, increased competition in the global economy has placed values and ethics squarely on the table for everyone to evaluate and debate. The dialogue and debates inside of companies help us to answer important questions about who we are collectively and individually. What we stand for. How we will do business. How we will treat one another.

As Maslow foresaw, the more we immerse ourselves in the human side of the enterprise, the more spiritual we become.

seen as utopian thinking under conditions of accepting industry instead of rejecting it.

So far as the military is concerned, the case may be not quite as clear and simple as the ones above, but there's still a case. I should say it sums up mostly to the democratic army, the democratic society in 1962 going more and more toward the situation which demands that every man be a general. This is already true for the isolated jet fighter pilot, for instance, and there are many other situations in which single men or very small groups of men are on their own and have to take responsibility in their own hands. Of course, authoritarian people cannot do this as well as profoundly democratic people (I *think*).

I think I would stress also convincing the military of the necessity for making every soldier into an ambassador of the United States; that is, I would take the same tack about the military stalemate. The whole cold war could become a nonmilitary kind of competition for the friendship of the neutrals all over the world. The soldier then would have to win the love and respect of other people. I would also stress the dangers inherent in a military situation which requires a degree of authoritativeness and blind obedience greater than that required by any other institution in the whole society. This is a real danger politically and internationally because it has been the tendency of our military, with their authoritarian view of life, to be on the side of dictators rather than people's revolutionary movements throughout the world. That is, I would point out to them the dangers of the military becoming antidemocratic because of the demands of their own particular situation and their own particular professional obligations, just in the same way that policemen and detectives tend to become paranoid more easily than those in other occupations.

Finally, I think I would stress to the military the huge number of man-hours involved in general military service for a whole population, and the stupidity of wasting these millions and even billions of hours. They could be used for education, for social service, for psychotherapeutic and growth-fostering activities of all sorts in order to make better citizens. Perhaps it would be a desirable side research to make a careful study of the military groups which form themselves into brotherhoods, like Merrill's Marauders and other special service groups, where the authoritarian hierarchy was pushed aside in favor of participative management. Perhaps this would be the way to do the research, simply to make the hypothesis that for certain kinds of close-knit military units, the principles of enlightened management are better than the classical authoritarian military principles.

With respect to communication with educationalists and educational administrators, I think I would take the tack to start with, that education can be seen from the point of view of either bad management or good management principles, from the point of view of growth-fostering management or authoritarian management. In one blow, then, we can apply all the huge mass of research that has demonstrated that foremen and supervisors who are compassionate, helpful, friendly, altruistic, democratic, etc., produce better results of all kinds. The same would be true in the educational situation. It is an ironic fact that so much research has been done with the industrial situation (because of the money available and the money involved probably) and so little of the same kind of research has been done in the educational system. We have almost no data on the comparative results with good teachers and bad teachers. This, of course, should be remedied. The whole question of progressive education, which has got lost in such a tangle of semantic misunderstanding and of the political cold wars, had better be revived and resuscitated because from the point of view of management philosophy, progressive education was much like the participative management policy.

Also, I would stress to the educators the sharp difference between general education and professional training, i.e., the acquisition of skills. The main goal of the former is to make better citizens, happier people, better and more mature and more highly developed individuals. The goal of the latter is simply to make good technologists, and this is an amoral enterprise, carried on in just about the same way, perhaps, in a fascist or a nazi or a communist authoritarian society as in a democratic society. It is the former enterprise which shows how clearly different the goals of the two kinds of societies are, i.e., the authoritarian and the democratic. In the authoritarian society freedom, autonomy, self-sufficiency, curiosity, free probing, free questioning, are all very dangerous; in the democratic society, of course, they are exactly the opposite, i.e., they are extremely desirable and even necessary.

The trouble with education today, as with so many other American institutions, is that nobody is quite sure of what the goals and the ultimate ends of education are. Once the goals of democratic education are clearly set forth, then all the means questions will settle themselves overnight. Here we must be very bold; the goals of democratic education, once we leave aside the question of technological training, can be nothing else but development toward psychological health. That is, education must be eupsychian or else it is not democratic.

I think a very effective way of communicating the point and ultimate goals of enlightened management can be seen in this way: If a group of a hundred men all became partners and invested their pooled savings in an enterprise and they each had one vote, so that they would consider themselves both workers and bosses all of them, then the relationship of each to the enterprise and to each other would be very different from the classical model of a boss hiring a hand, an impersonal worker. The example is similar also to the situation of a group of patriotic people at war against a common outside enemy. In both of these cases anybody will do anything which has to be done.

For instance, in the Battle of the Bulge, when there was a great emergency, all the categories of the American Army broke down entirely. Physicians, bakers, chauffeurs, truck drivers, dentists, all of them in the stress of emergency were given a gun and told to fight—all the specializations broke down. Each individual suddenly became a whole American army all by himself. In the same way any partner would take upon his own shoulders in emergencies *any* of the functions of an enterprise if he happened to be the one closest to the emergency. Any one of them, for instance, if he saw a fire breaking out would without taking votes about it or anything of the sort immediately go to put out the fire; he would immediately respond to the objective requirements of the situation, to the demand character of the facts, without thinking of mutual exclusiveness of interests, and whether his contract said that he should do this, etc.

Now the point is this: All the experiments on enlightened management and humanistic supervision can be seen from this point of view, that in a brotherhood situation of this sort, every person is transformed into a partner rather than into an employee. He tends to think like a partner and to act like a partner. He tends to take upon his own shoulders all the responsibilities of the whole enterprise. He tends voluntarily and automatically to assume responsibility for *any* of the various functions of an enterprise which an emergency might call for. Partnership is the same as synergy, which is the same as recognizing that the interests of the other and one's own interests merge and pool and unite instead of remaining separate or opposed or mutually exclusive.

If it can be shown that partnership is really true or factual or scientifically accurate, then people are more apt to behave like partners, and this is exactly what is desired by everyone, and also what is factually, financially, politically more desirable, both for the individuals and the enterprise and the whole society. That is, it is to my advantage to be brothers with someone rather than to be mutually exclusive. One might use here the example of the Common Market in Europe to show what is meant by this shift over from mutual exclusiveness and the assumption of opposing interests, to the different attitude of brotherhood, of common interests, of synergy.

The same thing is true for the contrast between the whites and the Indians on this continent in the sixteenth, seventeenth, and eighteenth centuries. The Indians lost out partly because they could never get together, could never make real alliances, because they regarded themselves as enemies or rivals rather than as brothers against a common enemy; whereas the whites tended to pool together and to be loyal to each other, for instance, as in the thirteen colonies becoming a single United States of America. If one called this former process of mutual exclusiveness atomization or Balkanization, and if one asked a question about what would be the situation if we had fifty separate countries instead of fifty states in one country, then one can talk about the current situation in industry as parallel, that is as a kind of economic Balkanization. Against this kind of discussion as a background, perhaps even an authoritarian character might begin to see the advantages of taking an attitude of synergy rather than of Balkanizing.

Relationship between Psychological Health and the Characteristics of Superior Managers, Supervisors, Foremen, etc. (Notes from Likert)

This is a kind of holistic thinking, or organismic thinking in which everything is related to everything else and in which what we have is not like a chain of links or like a chain of cause and effects but rather resembles a spider web or geodesic dome in which every part is related to every other part. The best way to see everything is to consider the whole darn thing one big unit.

The trouble with the first few chapters of Likert's *New Patterns of Management*[1] and then, it occurs to me, with the half-dozen other books I've read on the subject of management, is that they all seem to be overlooking what is to me the clear relationship between what they're talking about and the general conception of psychological health. For instance, I played a little game of checking off in Likert's first few chapters all the empirically discovered characteristics of superior managers, that is managers of more productive groups or of groups of workers who were better in other things like turnover, or sick leave, or whatever. Listing all these characteristics and then putting in another column the characteristics of the supervisors found to be poor and inferior makes a clear pattern of psychological health and psychological illness, both in a rather general way. I think I'll try to do this more carefully a little later on. It becomes very clear and very obvious.

[1] R. Likert, *New Patterns in Management* (New York: McGraw-Hill Book Co., Inc., 1961).

This relationship makes Likert's findings relate to a lot of other larger considerations as well. For instance, I want to think some more about the possibility of considering politics and government as a kind of management problem; then science as a huge enterprise which is managed in a particular way; and then finally the colleges and universities which, it is already clear to me, are very, very poorly "managed."

Furthermore, these discussions of management can be enlarged by tying them to the whole literature of psychological health, of personal growth, of psychotherapy, of synergy, of theoretical social psychology, and God knows what else as well.

As I tried thinking about these matters it quickly became very clear that pure theory of theories must at once be involved. For instance, what we have here necessarily is a kind of holistic thinking, or organismic thinking, in which everything is related to everything else and in which what we have is not like a chain of links or like a chain of causes and effects, but rather resembles a spider web or geodesic dome in which every part is related to every other part and in which the best way to see everything is to consider the whole darn thing one big unit. Perhaps I'll try this later, but now I think what I'll do is try free association for one point after another.

First of all, are not good politicians and good statesmen good managers also? This raises a serious question about levels. Because it might be said that the good politician is a good manager only when conditions are good, that is when honesty is possible, when people are decent, etc., and that he cannot be a good politician or a good statesman when people are bad or immature or psychopathic. But even this is not altogether so, since a good politician or a good manager or a good supervisor for that matter can be called good in terms of doing the job with the human material he has and under the circumstances which prevail. The good politician will be "good" in the sense of doing the best that he can with the material he has and perhaps being one or two steps ahead of the crowd moving in the direction which is good for the crowd, even though they don't yet know it themselves.

One reason that it's necessary to bring up this question about good politicians and bad politicians in relationship to the level of goodness of the environment is that I detect a certain doctrinaire quality in much of the writing about growth or enlightened management policy. So many of the writers talk as if this new management policy were "good" in some platonic sense, in an absolute way. That is, the implication is that it's always good. And therefore there is a neglect of the circumstances in which these policies are to be applied. Or to put it in another way, the point tends to be lost that good management policies are pragmatically good, good in a functional sense, that they produce better results than the older style of management. That is, for the moment, they are not to be considered good in themselves, intrinsically, because God said so, but rather because they work better, they justify their existence in terms of increased productivity, or better quality of product, or greater growth of democratic citizens, etc. If we keep this in mind, then we will certainly not get pious about these management absolutes; we will not treat them as if they were good in themselves, independently of their consequences.

To be more specific, what I am feeling is that these new Theory Y enlightened management policies are in fact very fine in today's United States, with citizens who are fairly healthy, sophisticated, and autonomous, under cultural circumstances of a particular kind, in a democracy, etc. But suppose there were some kind of atomic catastrophe or great bubonic plague or something of the sort and the circumstances then changed to living under jungle law. What then would be good management policy? Obviously, it would be very different. What we now call good management policy would then be absolutely stupid and ruinous. You can trust people according to Theory Y in a wealthy society in which there is plenty of money, plenty of goods, plenty of food, but obviously you cannot trust people with a key to the pantry when most people are starving, or when there is not enough food to go around. What would I then do under such circumstances? Well, I'm very clear about it in my own mind. If there were one hundred people and there was food for ten, and ninety of these hundred had to die, then I would make mighty goddamned sure that I would not be one of those ninety, and I'm quite sure that my morals and ethics and so on would change very radically to fit the jungle situation rather than the previous situation of wealth in which these principles once had worked well.

This is what I get vaguely uneasy about in the reading on management, namely a certain piety, certain semireligious attitudes, an unthinking, unreasoning, a priori kind of "liberalism" which frequently takes over as a determinant, thereby to some extent destroying the possibility of maintaining the necessary sensitivity to the objective requirements of the actual, realistic situation. That management policy

or any other kind of policy is best which best fits the objective requirements of the objective situation. There is a strongly pragmatic
tinge in this approach. But it is also good Gestalt psychology of the
Wertheimer[2] and the Katona style, in which the best kind of thinking,
the best kind of problem solution, clearly depends on a good viewing
of the problem situation itself, of being able to see it objectively, without expectations, without presuppositions, without a priori thinking of
any kind but simply in the purest sense of the word, objectively, the
way a god presumably would be able to see it without being determined
by prejudices or fears or hopes or wishes or personal advantage or anything of the sort. This is the best way to see any situation. This is the
best way certainly to see any problem which is calling for a solution.
The problem to be solved is the problem out there in front of our noses,
not the problem tucked away in the back of our brains someplace on the
basis of past experiences. *That* is not today's problem, that was yester-
day's problem, and they don't necessarily coincide.

By the way, I might just as well make a general principle out of
that. I've got dozens of notes on dozens of statements in the management and organization and leadership literature that seem to me to go
off the beam somewhat for the above reason of piety and of loyalty to
a particular theory (like a vote for the straight party ticket, no matter
what). I think a formulation that will cover practically all the criticisms I had in mind would be in terms of "fitting to the objective requirements of the objective situation." This implies both the objective
perceiving (better write some notes on B-cognition) and also on the
suitable behavior in fitting to the objective requirements of the situation (write some notes on spontaneity, on creativeness, etc.).

To get back to the previous point, I think it could be illustrated
and empirically supported in several different realms. For instance, we
have a pretty fair amount of data on educational policies (management
of education) with various kinds of students. I think it's fair to say
that we *know* that handling authoritarian students, of the type found
in Germany right after the war, requires a very different kind of management from teaching or managing ordinary American students in
that same year. The authoritarian students preferred and required and
functioned best under an authoritarian teacher. Any other kind of

[2] M. Henle (Ed.), *Documents of Gestalt Psychology* (Berkeley: University of California
Press, 1961).

teacher was regarded as not quite a real teacher, and was taken advantage of, couldn't keep control, etc.

The correct thing to do with authoritarians is to take them realistically for the bastards they are and then behave toward them as if they were bastards. That is the only realistic way to treat bastards. If one smiles at them and assumes that trusting them and giving them the key to the pantry is going to reform them suddenly, then all that will happen is that the silver will get stolen, and also they will become contemptuous of the "weak" Americans whom they will see as spineless, stupid, unmasculine sheep to be taken advantage of. I have found whenever I ran across authoritarian students that the best thing for me to do was to break their backs immediately, that is to affirm my authority immediately, to make them jump, even to clout them on the head in some way that would show very clearly who is boss in the situation. Once this was accepted, *then* and only then could I become slowly an American and teach them that it is possible for a boss, a strong man, a man with a fist, to be kind, gentle, permissive, trusting and so on. And there's no question about it, that if the authoritarian disease has not gone too far, this kind of management will actually change the world outlook and the character of these people and reform them, at least some of them, over toward becoming democratic rather than authoritarian.

About the same thing would apply to a business situation. We are furnished American workers brought up under political democracy and in circumstances of wealth where they can tell a boss to go jump in the lake and can go off and get another job if they didn't like the one they have. But suppose we had Persians, or Peruvians, or Saudi Arabians or other people who had lived only under someone's heel, whose experience of the world had been only that there were wolves and there were sheep, and they knew damn well that they were sheep and not wolves, then it is quite clear that Theory X kind of management is realistically called for, at least for the time being, with a slow and delicate change-over to Theory Y management as the workers give signs of reforming their character and of being able to live well under conditions of being trusted, being considered honest, being considered autonomous, etc.

Something similar is true in democratic political theory as well. It is foolish for Americans to transport their political techniques wholesale and without any change-over to the Belgian Congo, let's say, where the conditions are absolutely different, the history is different, the individual people are different, the political structure has been different, etc. The political forms demand all sorts of prerequisites of sophistication, levels of education, levels of expectations, kinds of philosophy, etc. Democracy in our sense will simply not work in many situations of the world today, as any quick glance at the newspapers will prove; it is necessary to use another kind of management policy, even though our goal would be to transform the situation into a democratic situation ultimately. This is a matter of transitional management, a shifting over from Theory X to Theory Y kind of management.

In a fuller treatment, something of the same sort can be said for running a family, relations with wives and husbands, friends, etc. The kind of management policy which is best in each of these situations is that policy which will *work* best. In order to find out what this is, a full objectivity is required without a priori presuppositions or pious expectations. Realistic perceiving is prerequisite to realistic behaving, and realistic behaving is prerequisite to good results.

Further Notes on the Relationship between Psychological Health and the Characteristics of Superior Managers (Notes from Likert)

The best managers increase the health of the workers whom they manage.

I n general, what Likert is saying and proving is that under the circumstances of the researches he reports, that is, in the United States, enlightened management works best, in a pragmatic way. I suppose one could generalize this and say that American management seems to be better than management in other countries, again for the same reasons, simply that it works. Now here again, a realistic statement quite clearly would point out that there is a range of goodness of U.S. management. Most of the experiments that Likert reports compare good American managers with poor American managers, with the terms good and poor being defined pragmatically in terms of productivity, worker satisfaction, low turnover, low sickness, low absence, low labor trouble, etc.

Now a simple technique of handling this scientifically is the old process of iteration, which is a process of progressive refinement and purification by selecting out again and again, the best of the good ones. For instance, this is the way in which I constructed my personality tests of self-esteem and of emotional security (25, 53). What I did was first by the best criteria available at the time (and these were certainly not very good), do the best I could by way of picking out extremely secure individuals and extremely insecure individuals. I then studied these two groups as intensively as possible, comparing them with each other, and then on the basis of this study made up lists of characteristics and an improved definition of emotional security and insecurity.

Then I used this new and improved definition to go over my population again and to purify it. That is, it turned out by my new definition that some of my insecure group were not so insecure after all and some of my secure group were not so secure after all and that some others that I had overlooked might very well belong to the extreme groups. Once this was done and the new groups formed, they could be studied again in exactly the same way, and again this process of study led me finally to an improved and a finer definition and description of characteristics of the group. Then on the basis of this new and improved knowledge I could again constitute extreme groups and then study them, and so on and so on, moving all the time toward a purer and purer product. This is a little like the technique that Madame Curie used for refining pitchblende in order to finally get radium.

Well, to take the propositions one by one and so to build up the spider web of intercorrelations:

1. The best managers under the American research conditions seem to be psychologically healthier people than the poorer managers in the same researches. This is easily enough supported by the data from Likert.

2. The best managers increase the health of the workers whom they manage. They do this in two ways: one is via the gratification of basic needs for safety, for belongingness, for affectionate relationships and friendly relationships with their informal groups, prestige needs, needs for self-respect, etc.; the other is via the gratification of the metamotivations or the metaneeds for truth and beauty and goodness and justice and perfection and law, etc. That is, once granted a sufficiently high level of worker health to begin with, enlightened management increases worker health in these two ways of gratification of the basic needs and of the metaneeds (89).

3. The healthier the workers are to start with, the more they profit psychologically from enlightened management and the healthier they become. This follows exactly the parallel of insight therapy in which the healthiest people are the ones who profit most from insight therapy because they are the strongest ones, the least sensitive ones, the least paranoid and suspicious ones, etc. That is, the healthier people

have broader shoulders and can take a heavier burden of anxiety, stress, responsibility, depression, and threat to self-esteem, and actually use all of these for good purposes, i.e., for strengthening themselves. Sicker or more neurotic people under these very same stresses tend to crack up rather than get stronger. At this point it would be useful to describe my "continental divide" principle. I use this principle to describe the fact that stress will either break people altogether if they are in the beginning too weak to stand distress, or else, if they are already strong enough to take the stress in the first place, that same stress, if they come through it, will strengthen them, temper them, and make them stronger. In general this same principle is roughly the same for battlefield surgery. The physician who has too many patients to treat will pass by the sickest ones, the ones who will probably die, in order to give the little time that he has to those people who are most likely to recover and get healthy. Of course, this looks like a heartless and cruel thing to do, but that's what battlefield surgery is like. It would be absolutely stupid for a man who has only five hours to spend to devote all of those five hours trying to keep alive a man who has very little chance of living instead of using those same five hours to give treatment to fifty people who could recover.

4. As we move toward enlightened management policies, enlightened managers, enlightened workers, and an enlightened organization, so also do we move toward synergy. (The explanation of synergy needs a separate and full treatment [103].)

5. Any move toward social synergy is also thereby a move toward enlightened management policy, enlightened managers, enlightened workers, and enlightened organizations. (Describe here in some detail the isomorphism between the perceiver and the world [104], or between the person and the environment, pointing out that each has a feedback to the other, each affects the other.) The more integrated the person becomes, the more he is capable of perceiving integration in the world. But also, the more integrated the world becomes, the more integrated is it possible for individuals to become.

6. Any increase in intrapsychic synergy in any one person is simultaneously thereby a move in the direction of increased synergy in other persons and also in the direction of increased synergy in the society, the organization, the team, etc. (This says about the same thing as in the previous paragraph, only in a different way which possibly is more testable, experimentally.)

7. The better man and the better group are the causes and effects of each other and the better group and the better society are the causes and effects of each other. That is, a better individual person tends to make a better group out of the group in which he is. But also the better a group is, the more it tends to improve the person within the group. The same is true for the group in the larger society. They influence each other. A simple way of saying this is to quote Goethe: "If everybody in the world cleaned his front yard, then the whole world would be clean." Or another way of saying it is that every person is a psychotherapeutic influence or a psychopathogenic influence on everybody he has any contact with at all (32).

8. In general there is a reciprocal relationship between psychological health and McGregor's Theory Y kind of management. And also there is the same kind of reciprocal relationship between psychological sickness and McGregor's Theory X. This is to say that people who are healthier are more apt to hold to Theory Y in their spontaneous and instinctive management policies. And those who are sicker are more apt to express Theory X in their management policies. Contrariwise, those persons who are found to function by Theory Y will be found upon examination to be psychologically healthier than those persons who function by Theory X.

9. Those people who are psychologically healthier *and* who live by Theory Y, and who are the best managers under the good circumstances, are the very same people who will spontaneously themselves be synergic, and who will frame a synergic situation for the people that they manage. (Look up the fuller treatment of synergy [103] but stress for this purpose the contrast between the doctrine of a limited amount of goods versus an unlimited amount of goods; and also stress the contrast between synergy as a theory and mutual exclusiveness and antagonism of interest as a theory.)

10. Here, also, we have a network of interrelations. The better the society, the better the productivity; the better the managers, the more psychologically healthy the individual men; the better the leaders, the better the managers; the better the individual men, and so on and so on, the better the enterprise. And then, of course, by participation, the better are all the determinants of each of these variables. The better are *any* determinants of the better society for instance, like a good educational system, then the better everything else is, and anything that increases the psychological health of any one individual helps

to improve the society, the managers, the leaders, the enterprise, productivity, and so on and so on. This means, for instance, that an increase in the number of good psychiatrists is a determinant of all of these improvements.

Placing all of the foregoing discussions of management policy and organizational theory, leadership policy, etc. in a larger context, within the nation, within the community, and I would say, even within the United Nations, throws things into a somewhat different light. In general, we may say that management theory can stress roughly two products, two consequences: one is the economic productivity, the quality of products, profit making, etc.; the other is the human products, that is, the psychological health of the workers, their movement toward self-actualization, their increase in safety, belongingness, loyalty, ability to love, self-respect, etc.

On the international scene, especially as it is today with the cold war going on, the latter takes on a huge importance. I think this is so because on the whole my expectations are that there will not be a "hot war," that there will not be bombs dropped. The chances are that the present military stalemate will continue, because both sides are too afraid for it not to. If this is so, then an immediate consequence is that the whole of the military becomes of secondary importance. All they are doing is maintaining a holding operation, keeping up with the Jones's, so to speak, actually preventing their materials from being used. The main function of the military as a matter of fact, to say it very bluntly, is to prevent a war, not to wage a war.

Then again, if *this* is so, huge changes in public thinking are necessary, especially with relationship to the rivalry between Russia and the United States. It is impossible that in this race they will remain evenly balanced. Sooner or later, one will forge ahead. But how will a nation forge ahead? How is this possible if we exclude war as a probability? Well, obviously, it will be in terms of just these two sets of consequences of management policy. On the one hand are better fountain pens and better automobiles and better radios. In this respect the United States is far ahead of Russia because our fountain pens, automobiles, and radios are respected all over the world and the Russian ones are not. But on the other hand is the human consequence, which is just as important, and I think in the long run, more important. The question is who will be loved and respected more by the neutral nations, Russia or the United States? And how shall this

MASLOW PREDICTS PEOPLE WILL BECOME *THE* COMPETITIVE ADVANTAGE

Management theory can stress roughly two products, two consequences: one is the economic productivity, the quality of the products, profit making, etc., the other is the human products, that is the psychological health of workers, their movement toward self-actualization, their increase in safety, belongingness, loyalty, etc. On the international scene, the latter takes on huge importance. But how will a nation forge ahead? How is this possible if we exclude war as a probability? Well, obviously it will be in terms of just these two sets of consequences of management policy.

—Abraham Maslow, 1962

Maslow was predicting the end of the Cold War when he made this statement, yet his words are more applicable today than in 1962.

Almost every leader we interviewed for this book made mention of the competitive advantage that lies within the people of an organization. Most mentioned to us an increasing responsibility for business in a global marketplace. Many predicted that governments would increasingly take a backseat as businesses begin to play a much larger role in the new world order.

Thus business, through its products and workforce, would be in the most powerful position for leading world change. As one chief executive officer told us "business will be called upon to solve the problems normally delegated to governments. Increasingly, as our products are sold in a global market and our people work and live in the global community, we represent the future. Let's just hope we get our values straight before we undertake this task."

be judged except in terms of the individuals that people will see as tourists all over the world and from what they read in the newspapers about what goes on inside the United States? And, in effect, what else does this mean but that the cold war will be won by the nation that turns out the better type of human being.

Now Theory Y management (or eupsychian management) definitely turns out a better kind of human being, a healthier person, a more lovable, more admirable, more respectworthy, more attractive, friendlier, kinder, more altruistic, more admirable kind of person than does the Theory X or authoritarian management. My (unfounded) impression is that Americans are liked throughout the world, and, for example, the Germans are not, especially the Germans who were brought up under the older authoritarian regimes. The Nazis were about the most unpopular people there were. I have no information whatsoever about the popularity of Russian tourists and visitors and diplomats and so on in the neutral countries. (By the way, it's insane that we don't have such information in view of the foregoing. Such information is terribly important in letting us know how things are going on—just as important, let's say, as knowing how many submarines Russia has available.) Therefore, I would say that the theoretical discussions of management and organization and industry, the discussions from the professors, the researchers, the philosophers, certainly should include in the calculations this consequence of management style.

In the Morse experiment reported in Likert (p. 62) on authoritarian management and participative management, the rise of productivity was shown to be slightly higher in the authoritarian regime, but then, as Likert points out, all sorts of human variables improved under the participative management but were not included in the accounting system. In this kind of discussion the international scene and the cold war and the type of human being turned out by management should be taken into account. I'm going to dictate some time soon my thoughts on how stupid our present accounting systems are because they leave out practically all the important personal, psychological, political, educational intangibles, so I'd better not do it at this point. Anyway, in this "moral economics" and the "moral accounting" that I'm going to talk about (that I learned mostly from Walter Weisskopf and Bob Hartman), these considerations would have made a different result appear in the Morse experiment. It's true that they got a little more productivity, but this was at such a huge human cost in the long run and at such a cost even to productivity in the long run, and at such a cost to all the political factors that I'm talking about here, that the right accounting system would have shown the authoritarian system to be absolutely insane, absolutely inferior.

11. I'm trying to put all of this network of interrelationships into the form of single relationships which are testable, confirmable, or discomfirmable, and have therefore phrased them in a scientific rather than in a philosophical way. I think it can be said in still another way

that any of the characteristics reported to be found in self-actualizing people, or in the successful product of psychotherapy, or in psychologically healthy people measured in any other way, that if such a list of characteristics is made, each of these characteristics is predicted to be found in a higher degree in the better managers than in the poorer managers. (Here better and poorer are in terms of pragmatic results in productivity and so on.) It could also be, of course, that better and poorer should be defined in terms of the human consequences, i.e., the growth of self-actualization in the workers under the manager as well.

This can be put in classical experimental design because these are controllable variables. For instance, by psychotherapy or sensitivity training or group therapy or any other form of therapy, it should be possible to change deliberately the variable of, let us say, ability to listen well (this is certainly one characteristic of psychological health). Then this cause or stimulus or controlled change can be examined for its effects on any one characteristic or any one part of the whole syndrome of better productivity or better human consequence. For instance, to take a single example, one might speak then about sick leave or poor quality of the product. Then the hypothesis would take the form—any increase in the ability to listen well is predicted to lower the amount of sick leave, to lower the amount of unnecessary waste, and to increase the quality of the product. At this level of specificity hundreds of hypotheses can be made.

It is necessary in order to understand everything above to be aware of the distinction between holistic or organismic thinking and atomistic or discrete thinking. In other words there should be an explanation here of syndrome dynamics as I have presented it in Chapter 3 of my *Motivation and Personality*. There should also be an explanation of the nest-of-boxes relationship among facts explained in the same chapter; there should also be a discussion of hierarchical integration (in contrast with mutual exclusiveness). I'm going to dictate something about these things, so let this note serve as a reference to those other memoranda. That is the memorandum on syndrome dynamics and holism, and then the memorandum on hierarchical integration, and while I'm at it, a memorandum on synergy.

Memorandum on
Enlightened Management

*The most tough-minded person in the world would have to
draw the same conclusion as the most tender-minded person in
the world from these data: that a certain kind of democratic
manager makes more profit for the firm as well as making
everybody happier and healthier.*

P oint out the parallel between Dove's experiments on superior
chickens (p. 121 in Maslow 70) and the new literature on superior supervisors. In the case of the chickens, the superiors
were found to be superior in every way, i.e., they had healthier feathers and healthier combs, they laid better eggs and more of them, they
were heavier and stronger, they were higher in the pecking order, and
they chose spontaneously by free choice a better diet for physical health
when put in the cafeteria situation. When this dietary which was chosen by the superior chickens was forced upon the inferior chickens,
these inferior chickens improved in all the mentioned qualities to some
extent. That is, they got heavier and they laid better eggs; they rose
in the pecking hierarchy and they had more sexual contacts, etc., etc.
But they never rose as high in these qualities as the innately superior
chickens. They went about 50 percent of the way up.

The first researches on supervision were like this kind of naturalistic observation. It was found, for instance, in Jim Clark's[1] studies or
in many of the studies quoted in the Likert book that one department
was doing better economically than another department, that is, it had
a higher production rate or it had less turnover or it had better morale
or something of this sort, and the experiment was made in order to

[1] In P. Lawrence et al., *Organizational Behavior and Administration* (Homewood, IL:
Irwin-Dorsey, 1961, Section II).

find out what factors were responsible for this economic superiority. What was found in practically all of these cases was that a particular kind of foreman or supervisor-manager was responsible for the economic superiority of the working group. And the qualities of the superior managers have been worked out, i.e., they are more democratic, more compassionate, more friendly, more helpful, more loyal, etc., etc. That is, the whole thing has been done *pragmatically,* rather than on a priori, moral, or ethical or political grounds. The most tough-minded person in the world would have to draw the same conclusion as the most tender-minded person in the world from these data, that a certain kind of democratic manager makes more profit for the firm as well as making everybody happier and healthier.

Implied, but never clearly stated so far as I know, is the belief that what is true of the behavior and attitudes of these pragmatically superior supervisors should be copied or forced upon the pragmatically inferior supervisors, even if this is not their spontaneous self-choice. The unspoken implications can be read between the lines that the expectation would be that the pragmatically inferior supervisor would then get the same kind of results as the pragmatically superior supervisor who did all of these things intuitively and unconsciously and without having thought about it beforehand, i.e., just simply as an expression of his personality.

But this remains to be proven or disproven. It may or may not be true. A first and most obvious possibility is that the results would parallel those of the chickens, i.e., it may be that forcing the superior manager behavior on an inferior manager may improve the whole situation but not all the way up. Or it may turn out to have no effects whatsoever because maybe the spontaneous personality of the supervisor is all-important. Or it may turn out that the inferior supervisor behaving like a superior supervisor may get the same results as the superior supervisor. We just don't know—this is a matter for research.

It also raises all kinds of fascinating, theoretical problems about the relationship between the personality, behavior, expressiveness, and the like. We may say that the qualities which mark the inferior supervisor, e.g., authoritarianism, hostility, sadism, etc., etc., may all turn out to be psychopathological and therefore curable, rather than intrinsic, inborn, temperamental qualities of any human being. This we still do not know.

As I read the evidence, all the traits which make an inferior supervisor inferior are acquired in the course of a neurotogenic life, and therefore can be cured away by psychotherapy or by education or by good work experience. This remains to be proven or disproven. Another point is that all the good human qualities, perhaps, are inherent in all human beings, at least at birth, and are gradually twisted or lost. This is to say that human evil is an acquired or reactive kind of response to bad treatment of the individual. At least this is what the Third Force psychologists generally agree upon. This has, however, not yet been absolutely and finally proven to such an extent that anyone *has to* believe in it whether he likes this characterologically or not. If this is so, then teaching the inferior supervisors about the causes for their inferiority, setting before them the example of the superior supervisors and telling about all the relevant research data, might appeal to something deeply human in each of them so that they would spontaneously reorganize themselves into better human beings. This in turn would automatically mean becoming pragmatically better supervisors, i.e., in terms of better economic results, as well as in terms of greater happiness and self-actualization for everybody concerned. Again I must say that the only way to learn how to choose among all these various alternatives is through more research as well as more careful, theoretical phrasing of all these situations.

By-Products of
Enlightened Management

The man (or woman) who truly is influenced by enlight-
ened management should become a better husband (or wife)
and a better father (or mother), as well as a better citizen in
general.

There are plenty of data to indicate that a mother who truly and deeply loves her child can behave in practically any way toward that child, beating it or slapping it or whatever, and yet the child will turn out well. It is as if the basic attitude of love is important and not so much the particular behavior. There are all sorts of data to make this point quite clearly in this relationship at least. Behavior is not a very good index of character or of underlying personality or of attitudes. Anybody who puts on behavior like a cloak, as an actor would, finds that this doesn't work very well. People somehow are able to detect at some conscious or unconscious level that a person is acting and not really feeling deeply the attitude which he is trying to convey through his behavior. So in the same way we have the possible complication that the supervisor who takes all sorts of courses and reads all sorts of books and is trained in various ways and who agrees with the data and who honestly tries to behave like a superior supervisor, may not be able to get the same results if he does not deeply feel democratic, parental, affectionate, etc.

This brings up the profound existential question of the difference between *being* something, and *trying to be* something. We are involved here in the paradox that there must be a transition between being something bad and being something good. If a thief becomes conscious of the fact that he is a thief and wants to become an honest man instead, there is no way in which he can do this except by consciously trying not to be a thief and consciously trying to be an honest man. Trying to be an honest man is self-conscious, artificial, not spontaneous, not natural, and may look phony. This is very different from spontaneous honesty which is an expression of deep-lying character attitudes. And yet what else is possible? There is no other way to jump from being a crook to being an honest man except by trying.

This is just as true for the organizational situation. There is no way for an authoritarian supervisor to become a democratic supervisor except by passing through the transitional stage of consciously, artificially, voluntarily *trying* to be a democratic supervisor. This man who is trying to be a democratic supervisor is obviously quite different from the person who is spontaneously a democratic supervisor. We get involved in all sorts of philosophical arguments here which we had better be careful about. It is so easy to despise the "trying" state just because it is not absolutely spontaneous, and therefore it may be rejected, with the person doing the rejecting failing to realize that there is no other possibility than this as a pre-stage to becoming spontaneously and deeply what one is trying to become.

Another way of expressing the above is to say it so: We must try to make a particular kind of people, of personality, of character, of soul one might say, rather than try to create directly particular kinds of behavior. If we talk about creating a particular kind of personality, we at once move over into the explicitly psychological realm of the theory of growth, of personality theory, of the theory of psychotherapy, and take upon ourselves the huge mass of Freudian theory as well, because then we must talk about the unconscious and of various determinants of behavior which are not consciously known to the person. These unconscious determinants of behavior cannot be influenced directly, in general; we must overhaul the personality, create in effect a different kind of human being. (For such a reason as this the term "behavioral science" is not suitable to describe this realm of science.)

This emphasis on the person, and the consequent emphasis on behavior as a by-product of deep-lying personality, is one of the reasons that leads me to feel that the validation of enlightened management and enlightened supervision must come not alone from the behavior in the factory, not alone from the quality and the quantity of the product, but rather must be a test of these aforementioned by-products. Thus I would think that one quite practical test would be what the workers in an enlightened enterprise do when they go back home to their communities. For instance, I would expect that if the management policy were truly growth fostering and truly better-personality producing, that these individuals would, for instance, become more philanthropic in their communities, more ready to help, more unselfish and altruistic, more indignant at injustice, more ready to fight for what they thought to be true and good, etc. This can easily enough be measured, at least in principle.

Also, it should be possible to gather data on the change of behavior in the home itself. The man who truly is influenced by enlightened management should become a better husband and a better father, as well as a better citizen in general. Therefore, interviews not only with him but also with his wife and with his children would be a direct technique of validation. I am reminded here of Dick Jones's study[1] in which he tried psychotherapeutic teaching in a high school for a year and then tested for validity of his enterprise by checking the decrease in race prejudice in the girls he had been teaching. He found that there was a decrease in race prejudice, even though he had not even mentioned this topic through the entire year. This is what I mean by measuring the by-product rather than the behavior itself directly. After all it is too easy for passive people or for shrewd people to mimic any behavior or to put on any act which might be necessary for them to keep their job or to get ahead in any particular situation. They might *act* the way management wants them to, but their souls might be totally unchanged.

---

[1] R. Jones, *An Application of Psychoanalysis to Education* (Springfield, IL: Charles C. Thomas, 1960).

Notes on Synergy

*The more influence and power you give to someone else in the
team situation, the more you have for yourself.*

Social synergy as used first by Ruth Benedict to apply to the degree of health of the primitive culture she was studying meant essentially that a synergic institution was one that arranged it so that a person pursuing his selfish ends was automatically helping other people thereby; and that a person trying to be altruistic and helping other people and being unselfish, was also automatically and willy-nilly helping along his own selfish advantages. That is to say, it was a resolution of the dichotomy between selfishness and unselfishness, showing very clearly that the opposition of selfishness and unselfishness or their mutual exclusiveness was a function of a poorly developed culture (103). I have shown this to be true within the individual in about the same way, winding up with the statement that where selfishness and unselfishness are mutually exclusive, this is a sign of mild psychopathology within the individual.

Self-actualizing people rise above the dichotomy between selfishness and unselfishness, and this can be shown in various ways. One is that they get pleasure from the pleasures of other people. That is, they get selfish pleasures from the pleasures of other people, which is a way of saying unselfish. The example that I used a long time ago can serve here—if I get more pleasure out of feeding my strawberries into the mouth of my little beloved child, who loves strawberries, and who smacks her lips over them, and if I thereby have a wonderful time and enjoy myself watching her eat the strawberries, which would certainly give me pleasure if I myself ate them, then what shall I say about the selfishness or the unselfishness of this act? Am I sacrificing something? Am I being altruistic? Am I being selfish, because after all I'm enjoying myself? Obviously, the best way to say this is that the words selfish and unselfish as opposites, as mutually exclusive, have become meaningless. The two words have fused together. My action is neither selfish exclusively nor unselfish exclusively, or it can be said to be both selfish and unselfish simultaneously. Or, as I prefer the more sophisticated way of saying it, the action is synergic. That is, what is good for my child is good for me, what is good for me is good for the child, what gives the child pleasure gives me pleasure, what gives me pleasure gives the child pleasure, and all the lines of difference fall and we can say now that these two persons are identified and in certain functional theoretical ways have become a single unit. Very often this is so. We learn to treat a loving wife and husband as a single unit; an insult to the one is an insult to the other, shoes on the feet of one make the other's feet feel good, etc., etc.

This happens to be also a pretty decent definition of love, namely, that the two separate sets of needs become fused into a single set of needs for the new unit. Or love exists when the happiness of the other makes me happy, or when I enjoy the self-actualization of the other as much as I do my own, or when the differentiation between the word "other" and the words "my own" has disappeared. Where there is mutual property, where the words change into "we," "us," "ours." Another definition of love is that happiness of the other is the condition of my own happiness. Synergy is the same kind of thing, and it involves a kind of love-identification. One might say it means in certain respects different people can be treated as if they were not different, as if they were one, as if they were pooled, or lumped, or fused into a new kind of unit which was superordinate and included them both, fusing their separateness.

In her last manuscript, Benedict gave various ethnological examples. In my studies with my Blackfoot Indians I got examples aplenty also. Teddy Yellowfly was my interpreter, and was the one educated man in the whole tribe, that is, he had gone to college for a year or two, and when Teddy became prosperous this was good for the whole tribe. For instance, he became prosperous enough to buy a car, the only car in the whole reserve. But the old Blackfoot way was that anybody could ask any other member of the tribe for the loan of anything that he needed. In effect, the car belonged to the whole tribe. Anybody who needed it could have it. Teddy himself used it no more than other people did. About the only consequence of "owning" (the word no longer had any meaning) was that he paid the bills for gas and so on and so on. On the other hand, however, everybody was very proud of Teddy and in an identification way, in the same way that we might be proud of an American who won the 100-yard dash in the Olympics or proud that we have a great philosopher or scientist in our city or in our college. In this same way they were all very proud of Teddy and loved him very much and looked up to him and elected him chief and made him the informal spokesman and leader of practically all the tribe. There was no question about it, Teddy liked this, just as I suppose anybody else would. The respect and the love that he got from everybody was deeply satisfying, and I certainly never heard him complain about his car being used, except in a rather humorous way.

Another example of selfishness fusing with unselfishness was the custom of the "giveaway" at the annual Sun Dance. Through the whole year, or even for several years before, people would have saved money and worked hard and so on in order to make a big display of generosity at the Sun Dance, which was done very publicly. I saw White-headed Chief, for instance, stand up within the circle of the whole tribe, within the circle of the teepees of the Sun Dance in the very holiest moment of the year and make a very long speech that we would call boasting, about how smart he was and how capable he was and so on and so on, and then with a very lordly gesture give away the piles of blankets and food and even soft drinks for children and so on that he had stacked up beside him in a very impressive heap. He gave these away to widows, to old blind people, to children, to teenagers, etc.

The more money he made, the better worker he was, the more successful his farm, the more horses he bred, the better it was for everybody. This contrasts with the tendency in our society for a similar situation to breed envy, jealousy, resentment, and loss of self-esteem. When my uncle suddenly became rich by accident, in effect what happened was that he immediately lost the friendship of all his relatives, for reasons that any American would understand. His wealth did not redound to the advantage of any one of his relatives, and I remember for myself that I was pretty sore about it. He had a huge amount of money and I was an impoverished graduate student and he didn't help me in any way. I thought this was very selfish and I was never friendly with him again. If we had been Blackfoot Indians his wealth would have helped me. As Americans his wealth did not help me. And therefore it made us enemies rather than friends.

Perhaps in our own society, a kind of impersonal example that can be used is the one of the graded income tax. The more somebody makes, the more taxes he pays and presumably the better this is for me. Of course, it's very abstract and impersonal and I don't see the money and so on, but the fact remains that this is true and the fact is also therefore true that the graded income tax is a synergic principle and guarantees that it is to the benefit of everybody if some people produce wealth. This contrasts very heavily with the situation in Mexico and the rest of Latin America in which the more wealth comes into the society, the smaller the amount of food that poor people get, i.e., the higher prices for food go. This is because there is no income tax there and because rich people keep everything that they make, and the fact that they have more money to spend lifts the prices of everything and the poor people suffer rather than benefit. That is an anti-synergic principle by contrast with the graded income tax.

The Synergic Doctrine of Unlimited Amount of Good versus the Antisynergic Doctrine of Unlimited Amount of Good

All one can steal is a product, a by-product of creativeness or of good management policy. One cannot steal the creativeness or the good management policy.

The one psychological example that I can use for a certain audience is the Freudian doctrine of limited and fixed amount of libido in the individual. Freud assumed that one had only a certain amount of love and that the more of this love was spent on one person, the less was available for others. For instance, in his doctrine of narcissistic love, the person who loved himself was thereby less able to love others. The person who loved one person was thereby less able to love other people. It was as if one had a fixed amount of money and when part of it was spent, that was that and there was just that much less left over. This contrasts with the doctrine of love of Fromm, Horney and others, who understood that at least in the good situation, love breeds more love, that the spending of love creates more wealth of love. It is only when the young lover falls in love for the first time in a reciprocative way that he is truly able to love the whole world. The more he loves his sweetheart or his wife, the more he is able to love his children and friends and humanity in general.

Another example is in the economic realm of the use of money. It used to be that you had a certain amount of money and you watched over and spent as little of it as possible and buried it in the ground and kept it guarded. It was only in recent times that we have learned that spending money, using it, taking a chance with it, investing it instead of diminishing it, augments it, actually increases the amount of money. Generosity can increase wealth rather than decreasing it. This is also, I think, true of the differences between the attitude of the American businessman and the South American or European businessman. The latter is apt in his little grocery store to hoard his goods and to sell each item at the highest possible profit. The enlightened American has long since learned that it is better to have a big turnover even with a small profit and that this is the only way to make large amounts of money. The pinching, stingy, niggling Latin American storekeeper may make a huge amount on any one transaction but is not apt to get stinking rich in the American style, let's say like Henry Ford. (Maybe Henry Ford was one of the people who invented or discovered this doctrine of spending in order to make money, giving things away in order to pile up wealth, lowering prices in order to get richer, and the like.)

Likert's book[1] has one research example which leads him to speak finally about the "influence pie" and to try to say the same kind of thing. I quote from page 57:

> Another widely held view is that there is a fixed quantity of influence in a company or plant. Consequently if subordinates are permitted to exercise more influence as to what goes on in the organization, the superiors have correspondingly less. The pie, so to speak, is thought to be just so big, and if some people are given more, others must have less.

Then, on page 58:

> This better management system, while giving the men more influence, also gives the high-producing managers more influence. The high-producing managers have actually increased the size of the influence pie by means of the leadership processes which they use.

That is, the more influence and power you give to someone else in the team situation, the more you have yourself. This might be likened to the military situation which we must eventually develop; that is, our effort must be to make every man a general instead of hanging onto the old doctrine of just one single general. Under the circumstances in which a general is in charge of a whole group of generals to whom he has given high power, he will find to his amazement that he

[1] R. Likert, *New Patterns of Management* (New York: McGraw-Hill Book Co., 1961).

ROARING OFF THE FACE OF THE EARTH . . .

Abraham Maslow often asked his students the following questions: *Which of you believe that you will achieve greatness? Whom among you will change the world?* As the myriad of faces stared back at him, perplexed and confused, he continued his dialogue by asking: *If not you, who then?*

As is evident in these journals, Dr. Maslow believed that people sought meaning in their work, wanted to commit to causes larger than themselves, and were capable of "roaring off the face of the earth" when engaged with a task, role, or responsibility that was worth doing.

Our organizations are fertile grounds to allow people to roar. Yet, too many of them extinguish human potential rather than unleash it. In looking for an example of a company that provided the opportunity for employees to roar, we looked at the early days of Apple Computer.

In the early 1980s, Apple attracted hundreds of intelligent, idealistic, risk takers who were drawn to the founders' visions of developing computers for the masses. The cause was breathtaking—change the world through cutting edge technology. The commitment of employees during this time period became a legend in Silicon Valley.

Ask anyone who worked there during the early days (and we did) you'll get an earful: *It was an incredible group of visionary thinkers, a group of people who pushed themselves past self-imposed limits. Apple was my family during those days—we loved each other and knew we were doing something very special.* Its founder, Steve Jobs, stated, *"It was small teams of great people doing wonderful things."*

The company and its employees managed to garner more than half the personal computer market while singlehandedly claiming responsibility for pioneering the desktop computer market. Apple developed not only loyal employees but an almost fanatical and, at times, cultlike following among its customers. One might easily dismiss these achievements as being the fruits of those first to market. We think the success can be attributed to more than being first and to more than having great technology. We believe a great part of the success equation was the environment which allowed people to reach their potential, commit to a cause, and find great meaning in their work.

Although Apple's recent corporate performance card casts doubts on its future and far too many question its strategic choices, we think there is another chapter in Apple's history that hasn't been written: The firm's ability to develop high-technology leaders who "think differently" and who believe that they can "change the world." In our unofficial count, at least 34 former Apple employees are now chief executive officers and 11 more hold high-level leadership positions in other major firms.

Is Apple still roaring off the face of the earth? Perhaps not in financial terms, where stock prices measure value, but in human terms it continues to be a rich story.

has far more power and influence than he had before passing out power. The more he gives, the more he retains, so to speak.

We can use also the example of generosity and openness in science. The general lesson, at least so far as the scientists are concerned, is that the keeping of security, the keeping of scientific secrets, was actually more harmful to the American scientists than it was to the presumably spying Russian scientists. It was a way of hurting ourselves rather than hurting them. Why? Because science depends on generosity, because knowledge breeds knowledge. There isn't just a fixed amount of knowledge which you can pass out and share and divide and hoard and save and so on. Knowledge itself breeds knowledge. This is related also to the business situation, as for instance in the matter of business secrets. When I asked Andy Kay (of Non-Linear Systems) about what he did about business secrets, he said he didn't have any. The only things that were kept secret were plans for the future, and so far as the actual processes of producing voltmeters were concerned, all the knowledge was publicly available. He pointed out that if someone came in to copy the processes, this wouldn't do them very much good because part of the good management and of the good plant was that there was a continual improvement. By the time a copier had turned out the copied instrument, the good plant would have forged ahead and produced something far better. All one can steal is a product, a by-product of creativeness or of good management policy. One cannot steal the creativeness or the good management policy.

Or to say it in still another roundabout way, anybody who tries to learn the secret of making good voltmeters would eventually become a noncopier and would discover that the best way to make them would be to become a creative person, functioning with human beings in a particular way. I suppose it would actually help the economic structure of our society if we kept all the factories running at full blast and simply gave things away. Why? Because the continual process of running the factories themselves would make good factories, good managers, good workers, etc., far more than would closing down the factories or running them at a reduced rate. The same thing has been true in my experience. I learned long ago as a graduate student, through various incidents, not to worry about having my ideas copied or stolen. In short, what I discovered was that whenever they were stolen, it was by a person of such bad taste that he overlooked the good ideas and stole the poor ones. I finally turned from being angry and

INTERVIEW WITH ANDREW KAY

All human beings prefer meaningful work to meaningless work. This is much like stressing the high human need for a system of values, a system of understanding the world and of making sense out of it. . . . If work is meaningless then life comes close to being meaningless.

—*Abraham Maslow*

Andrew (Andy) Kay could well be one of the fathers of the digital revolution. His company, Non-Linear Systems (NLS), produced the first commercial digital voltmeter. In 1980, while attempting to move some computer equipment, he combined a number of components. He and his son thought that the complete "box" might make a productive product so they set about developing one package that would include a CPU, printer, monitor, and keyboard. Thus, Kay launched Kaypro Computer and was among the first American-based companies to offer desktop computers to the masses. Kaypro Computers grew quickly, soaring to $120 million in sales. As was the course of other pioneers in the digital revolution, Kaypro also took a beating in the evolving marketplace, ultimately declaring bankruptcy in 1984. Undaunted Kay continues today, always innovating and breaking new ground.

In addition to the technology revolution, Kay played a starring role in enlightened management practices. During the late 1950s, Kay experimented with ways to unleash the potential of the several hundred employees on the assembly lines in his Southern California-based manufacturing company. During those days, factories were not known as environments where people were appreciated, let alone valued. Yet, Kay wanted employees to "think like owners" and to participate in the overall decision making of the company. In his search, he embarked upon one of the most innovative managerial experiments in the country.

Relying heavily on Dr. Maslow's book, *Motivation and Personality,* Kay decided to make sweeping changes in the way work was organized. He dismantled his assembly lines and replaced them with small teams of six to eight people. Each team learned every aspect of production. The teams were also self-managed. They decided the hours of work, break times, even scheduling of work. Kay did away with time cards and he also paid his employees 25 percent more than the prevailing wage. He was among the first to offer stock options in the company to employees. Kay even created the post of vice president of innovation.

Today, such practices would seem unremarkable. Yet, three decades ago they were unheard of. Kay invited Maslow to spend a summer observing his company which inspired the writing of these journals. Currently president and CEO of Kay Computers, Kay invited us to spend a day in his San Diego office to discuss Dr. Maslow's summer at NLS.

How did you decide to bring Dr. Maslow to your company for the summer?

In 1958, several people in the San Diego area had started a seminar program for heads of various companies. One of the people was Richard Farson. Farson approached me with the idea. This group of people had introduced me to Maslow's book called *Motivation and Personality*. I read that book and also one that Peter Drucker had written. I was taking some of their ideas and putting them into work in the plant. During a trip to Europe, we stopped in Boston to visit with Maslow. I thought I should at least meet him before I offered him a summer at my company.

Maslow was very gracious. I remember knocking on the door, seeing this man with a head which reminded me of Stalin's—kind of rugged. Maslow was a very strong individual. His wife Bertha served us tea and we had a marvelous conversation. When I returned to San Diego, I told Dick Farson I would sponsor Maslow.

The Maslows arrived in San Diego that summer and Abe started writing a book. We thought we shouldn't be bothering him so we didn't interact with him much. Later on, it turns out, he was wondering why we weren't interacting with him!

After spending that summer with us, I was standing in line for a meeting that the National Training Laboratories put together for chief executive officers. Ahead of me in line was Bill Laughlin, the CEO of Saga Foods. He asked me about Abe. He said he had met him at a meeting and was interested in bringing him to his company. I said to Bill, "Hold my place in line." I went to the nearest pay phone and phoned Dr. Maslow. I told Dr. Maslow about Bill's interest. Later, he and Bill agreed to talk. Bill and Abe got together and the rest is history. Abe spent a year of his life in Northern California under a generous grant Bill and Saga Foods extended to him. Abe described that year as "heaven."

When you brought Dr. Maslow into your company, did you have any expectations? It sounds like you just opened up the company to him.

Yes, I thought maybe he'd want to spend the summer out here in a company that was supposed to be profit-oriented. He thought his time with us was a luxury because there was a secretary available to transcribe the tapes

(continued)

he dictated. The next day she would have a draft ready for him. He also spent time with other business leaders and thinkers in the Southern California area. Faculty from UCLA came down to visit with him.

He said in his journals that in your factory you were experimenting with all types of what would have been called "enlightened management." What gave you the idea to try those things? The business environment during those times certainly was not so enlightened.

Well, Drucker's book helped some. There's a funny story about that. I ran into Drucker in Palm Springs in 1962. He was speaking at the meeting there. I got him off to the side, away from people, and said, "I'm using some of the ideas in your book." You know what his response was? "Don't blame me! Don't blame me!" I guess it wasn't working for other people.

In your discussions with Maslow about proprietary or trade secrets, you told him it was the people that could not be duplicated. You said that if someone came in to copy the processes, it wouldn't work because part of the good management was that there was continual improvement.

That's right. In our business, the assembly line was crucial to our product. One person did this, another one did the next operation, and so on. Almost always, the people in the beginning of the line were unhappy. The happiest ones were at the end of the line that finished the job. We set out to manage so that all people on the assembly line felt like the people at the end of the line. Everyone was encouraged to learn as much as they could about all of the operations and to do them. At the same time, the product got more and more complicated. We also had a piece of test equipment we built to see if all of the wires were put in the right place. The goal was to keep it down to one or two errors per voltmeter. People would make up their own notes. We didn't have a staff to make up these things. The employees made up their own guides. Whatever they wanted to jog their memories on how to do things, we encouraged them to do. Throughout all of the procedures and changes, they did not decrease the rate of production. Essentially, each person on the assembly knew what role they played in the entire production and how their work affected the end product.

They turned out so many voltmeters a month. They kept on doing the same thing and finally it got to the point where each person in the group was able to do the entire assembly from beginning to end. Men tended to be the technician types and do final testing on the units. We had some women doing that for themselves. I remember a supervisor told me he had a person who was not willingly participating. I asked to meet this person. She was a young Mexican woman and among the first few employees we had hired. I watched her on the assembly line and she seemed to have her eyes focused a million miles away while she was doing a simple operation. It's all she wanted to do—so they told me. About 9 months later, I saw her checking out a digital voltmeter. I said, "I thought you told me she didn't want to do anything except the simple operation." The supervisor told me that they had discovered that she was afraid she wouldn't be able to do the other parts of the assembly, that she lacked confidence. She was afraid she would look bad in front of her peers so she was afraid to try. She had very low self-esteem. However, after she saw all of her colleagues performing the various functions, she decided that if they could do it, she could do it! So she got involved to the extent that she got beyond them to learn the technical aspects.

I used to get a number of Christmas cards from women who thanked me for letting them do so many different things in the factory because they never thought much of themselves. The complicated unit they put together made them proud of themselves and their work. Their self-esteem went right up from doing these jobs.

Maslow said that he learned a great deal from you in the summer he spent at NLS. Did you have any conversations with him that were memorable?

Yes, I talked to him about vocabulary, general English vocabulary. This researcher I met in 1954 had convinced me through his research that if one increased his vocabulary, he would also dramatically increase his learning by 10 to 100 percent. He said yes, you raise a person's vocabulary and you raise his awareness of the world. One other thing I discovered over a long period of years—and I tell this everywhere I go, every talk I do— the lower the vocabulary, the higher the paranoia. Think about it. If increasing the vocabulary raises a man's awareness of the world, decreasing it means it lowers the awareness. He's blind effectively.

Did you set out to raise the vocabulary of the people in your factory?

We tried. I spent $800,000 in the 1960s building some equipment to help our employees increase their vocabulary. We had this one supervisor who was using the vocabulary tapes we developed. Soon the women who were doing the inspection of silk screens were listening to the tapes all day long. Later on my son got involved in this venture. He started vocabulary improvement centers.

There was a fellow from the Navy, very talented but very frustrated because he couldn't explain things to people in the plant. He was a very

(continued)

talented designer. I kept after him and he went through vocabulary builders class twice. He successfully went from the 5th percentile to the 20th percentile—almost a college average. He talked to people about this vocabulary program and how it changed his life.

Did you keep in touch with Maslow after he spent the summer here?

All the time. Whenever we traveled to Europe we would stop in Boston first to see the Maslows. During one of our trips, I realized while talking to Abe that he had never met Douglas McGregor. Here they were living in the same town (McGregor at MIT and Maslow at Brandeis) and they had never met. So I said "Abe, grab your coat" and we drove over to MIT to see McGregor.

I keep going back to one thought that I think is important. It's about what I call enlarging the workplace. People grow through learning and I guess that is what I tried to do in my factory. Offer a place where people could grow.

---

making resolutions about keeping my mouth shut to finding the whole matter humorous and funny and thereafter never bothered to keep my mouth shut and never bothered to keep any of my ideas secret or to withhold them until I had worked them out myself. The very process of talking about ideas helps the creativeness, and thereby makes it more likely that there will be hundreds of ideas where there were only dozens before. Copying or stealing is a little like stealing the egg, instead of the hen that lays the eggs. In a word, money must be used; the mind must be used; creativeness must be used and one must spend it and be prodigal with it rather than to hoard it and be stingy with it and think that it can be used up or spent or decreased in quantity.

Point out that this is an immature way of thinking in the very literal sense because this is what one finds in young children and this is what they grow out of if luck is with them. For instance, the whole phenomenon of sibling rivalry rests upon the theory of a limited amount of good, i.e., the child who has had the exclusive love of his mother resents the newborn baby who is also loved by his mother because he thinks that when his mother loves the baby she can't love him any more. It takes him a long time to learn that it's possible to love two children, or four children, or eighteen children for that matter, and that the more one loves one of the children, the more is left over for the others, rather than less.

One thing about synergy is that you enjoy making other people happy or, to say it in the true synergic fashion, that you can selfishly enjoy other people's happiness. I suppose also it means that you can love other people more operationally. The point is that with such an attitude there would be somewhat greater tendency toward an economic system of unlimited production at lower prices rather than the antisynergic principle of limited production with high profit for each unit. This is because the more generous, the more loving, the more synergic person would actually enjoy passing out one thousand radios rather than one hundred radios on the grounds that this would simply produce more happiness and that he could enjoy his generosity more, since he exercised it one thousand times instead of one hundred times. That is, the unlimited production is a sign of greater care for others by contrast with the opposite attitude, which is one of greater care for myself in contradiction to others.

I suppose I'll have to make clear the matter here of the resolution of dichotomy, or at least try to make it clear, because it's not too clear to me. For one thing, point out that this is different from the Jungian and the Darwinian stress on the benefits of conflict, on the dynamic influences or consequences of conflict in strengthening people, and so on. Now, this may well be. There certainly are some good consequences of conflict along with the bad consequences. But this is not what I mean here. Actually what we have is a transcendance of the polarity between selfish and unselfish. That is to say, one rises above the conflict rather than benefits from it. It ceases to be a conflict, it ceases to be an opposition. One realizes or perceives or discovers that my good and your good, selfishness and unselfishness which we have always been taught to perceive as different from each other and mutually exclusive and even opposites, are really not so under the right circumstances. That is when we are healthy enough to perceive the higher unity, when the world is good enough and wealthy enough so that there is no scarcity, then we can see that our interests as human beings are pooled and that what benefits one person benefits me, or benefits anybody else for that matter.

Use the various examples from the self-actualizing people of this superordinate unity which has been constructed out of the selfishness and unselfishness which are now structured with each other, fused with each other, in some new way where we can talk about healthy selfishness, for instance, and also where we can talk about pathological unselfishness as a masochism. And where the particular syndrome in the self-actualizing person is a very peculiar mixture and fusion of selfishness and unselfishness in such a fashion that it finally becomes impossible to label a particular act either selfish or unselfish. One finds that they are both or that they are neither. This is also related to the great criticism of Aristotelian logic, especially the law of the excluded middle, the mutual exclusiveness of Class A and Class not-A. Look up Korzybski's non-Aristotelian stuff for his critique of the two-valued orientation of the polarizing and see also the general critiques of the black-and-white thinking, of either/or thinking and the like. They are all related here to the fact that synergy represents a transcendence of the dichotomy, not a profiting from the conflict.

It's going to be very difficult to think through and to describe some of the subtleties of the situation here in regard to what is truth and what is reality. I believe that synergy is an actual perception of a higher truth, of a higher reality, which actually exists and that the development over into synergy is like the development from becoming blind to becoming seeing. Of course, this is difficult to demonstrate, but I think it can be done so long as there is sufficient stress on the operational definitions and also on the pragmatic superiority of synergy in the operational, factual good situation. The truth is that human interests, especially when people know each other and love each other, are pooled rather than being mutually exclusive. Any analysis of good marriage can easily show this. Any analysis of a good partnership in business can easily show this. Any analysis of the scientific ethic, that is of the code of ethics among scientists can show this. What is good for any scientist is good for me as a scientist. What is good for my wife is certainly good for me. What is good for me is good for my children. What is good for the teacher can be demonstrated to be good for the students, most of the time, etc.

Part of the job here will be to show how either/or thinking or mutually exclusive, nonsynergic thinking is a sign of mild psychopathology. Maybe one way of approaching this is via my old analysis of the authoritarian character structure (33). I showed there that if the jungle world view was in fact correct, then the only realistic thing to be was authoritarian. I was trying to show how it was not crazy but that it was really all sensible and logical and rational and even necessary *if* one granted the original premise that life was a jungle and the people in it were jungle animals with mutually exclusive interests. Look this up again for the exact phrasings. I think I did use there the terms "mutually exclusive interests," and this could be a good pedagogical device for making the whole thing clearer, and more plausible, to make it communicate better. (Maybe this whole communication is not as difficult a thing as I think. I guess I'd better try it out and see if this notion of synergy is as subtle as I've been assuming it to be. Maybe it's quite obvious.)

Synergy is more holistic, and the more holistic is more synergic. (By contrast with atomistic, which is nonsynergic and which must be.) The more holistic a structure is operationally, that is, the more mutual interdependence there is, the better the communication, etc., etc., the more the team has to rely on each other—for instance as in a basketball team—the more synergic everything will be. Maybe I can take the example of a basketball team which is composed of five prima donnas who are each out for their own benefit and regard their own benefit as contradictory to the benefit of the others, that is in terms of points and scores, and then contrast this with a real "teamy" team in which the good of the team is above the good of any particular person. Observe that you can't even say it this way, because once that's true, then there is no contrast between the good of the team and the good of the person. The good of the team has become the same as the good of the person, and he can't tell the difference. Therefore, it doesn't matter too much who makes the score. All the five members of the team will be equally proud of the team and of each other and of themselves. And furthermore, anyone with any basketball sense will also perceive this, the person who is a good "feeder" to the man who is the good "basket shooter" deserves exactly as much credit as the one who actually puts the ball into the basket. When this kind of synergy breaks down, then you really have ultimately a lousy team. And the same would be true in the economic situation. If a group of five people are supposed to turn out a single product, the same principles would hold. The more teamwork there is, the more they rely on each other, the more they trust each other, and so on; this is the same as saying, the more synergy there is. And, of course, this all can be put in researchable form. Dozens of testable hypotheses can be generated here.

Something very similar is true of the doctrine of hierarchical integration, which also correlates very highly with synergy. Work this out.

Since synergy is true and realistic (under good conditions) and since also synergy correlates with psychological health—that is, healthy people are more synergic—*and* since healthy people have better perception of the truth and are more realistic, then a whole network of testable hypotheses can be affirmed here. For instance, the whole experimental design that I set up for showing that healthier college students have more efficient cognition, more efficient sense organs, more efficient thinking and perceiving processes—all of this set of tests can be turned to tests of synergy. This is true at the sensory level itself probably. And if I were setting up an experiment here I would certainly suggest testing the efficiency of color discrimination, of auditory thresholds, of two-point thresholds on the skin, of the taste buds, of the sensitivity of smell, etc., in *(a)* psychologically healthy people, in *(b)* synergic people, and in *(c)* better managers and supervisors. Presumably what is true for one is going to be true for the others, just as of better people in general. Now, to turn it over to making affirmations about the better managers and predictions for research, let's do it this way.

Better managers are better perceivers. That is to say, they would be predicted to have more acute visual discrimination, auditory discrimination, etc. And, of course, all of these can be tested by standard tests. Moreover, at the perceptual levels, good managers may be expected to be more logical, to detach perception from wishes more clearly, to be able to make better predictions about the future on the basis of what evidence is available today. I would predict specifically that good managers are less apt to follow the *Einstellung* in the Luchins[2] experiment. I would predict that they would be less likely to be yielders or conformers in the Asch[3] experiment. I would predict that the better managers would be less likely to be field-dependent (à la Witkin[4]) than the poor managers. I would predict that in the Sherif[5] experiment, the better managers would be less suggestible and less influenced by the stooges than the poor managers would.

[2] A. Luchins, "On Recent Use of the Einstellung Effect as a Test of Rigidity," *Journal Consult. Psychol.*, 1951, *15*, 89–94.
[3] S. Asch, "Studies of Independence and Conformity" (Part I) *Psychol. Monogr.*, 1956, *70* (Whole No. 416).
[4] H. Witkin, H. Lewis, M. Hertzman, K. Machover, P. Meissner, S. Wapner, *Personality Through Perception* (New York: Harper & Bros., 1954).
[5] M. Sherif, *Psychology of Social Norms* (New York: Harper & Bros., 1936).

As a matter of fact, any of the tests of general psychological health can be affirmed of better managers because if I am correct then what is now being turned up experimentally as good management policy is on the whole almost synonymous with what I've been calling psychological health and this in turn is almost synonymous with the ability to be synergic. And so on and so on. It would be possible very easily to make a hundred testable statements here. As a matter of fact I may suggest this, or at least the theoretical possibility that very soon it might be possible to set up a series of laboratory tests totally non-fakable, like electrocardiograms, like electroencephalograms, for making pretty decent predictions about the kind of people who would make better managers and supervisors and bosses and leaders later on in life. This would be a wonderful thing, of course, if it were possible, and the more I think of it, the more possible it seems. In any case, it's possible enough to be worth a try.

I guess I can go on with this; there are still other possibilities. If all this network of relationships is true, then anything that makes better managers also makes better human beings in general and improves the whole society. That is to say that all the techniques of sensitivity training, or of management training, or of writing books and doing researches, etc.—anything that does this benefits everybody in the long run. The same thing is true for psychological health. If a better school system is better for psychological health in general, and if we think in terms of the long run—that is, if we are preparing, as we should, for future executive material, or to say it in another way, if our executive training program looks fifty years ahead—then we should think about the kindergartens being of the right sort in order to create the future generals and bosses and managers and leaders that we will need for the next century. The same thing is true of any self-therapeutic technique of any kind whatsoever, or of psychotherapy in general. All of these interrelate; making a particular person healthier makes him more, shall I say, promotable, that it makes him a potentially better manager or better anything else, as a matter of fact, and the converse is true. Whatever improves the society at any point tends to improve the rest of the society. Whatever improves one human being at any point tends to improve the whole human being. Whatever tends to improve the whole human being tends to improve all other human beings, especially those in close contact with him. Whatever makes a man a better husband, for instance, tends to make

TRAINING KINDER-LEADERS

If our executive training programs look fifty years ahead then we should think about the kindergartens being of the right sort in order to create the future bosses and generals and managers and leaders that we will need in the next century.

—Abraham Maslow, 1961

We were delighted to learn that a group of volunteers from Oracle Corporation, a local company, was participating in the local Junior Achievement project. The volunteers were going to visit the classroom of our kindergarten. Through a series of classroom activities, exercises, and discussion, the business executives hoped to impart good citizenship and leadership skills to this group of 5-year-old learners. We decided to learn more about Junior Achievement as it seemed to fit Maslow's vision for the future. We learned:

- Junior Achievement is the world's largest and fastest growing nonprofit economic education organization. The programs are taught by class-room volunteers from the business community in both the United States and nearly 100 countries worldwide. The purpose is to educate young people to value free enterprise, understand business and economics, and be workforce ready. The predominately volunteer effort reaches more than 2.6 million U.S. students each year.

- Junior Achievement's Elementary School Program, for levels kinder-garten through sixth grade, demonstrates how economics impacts people's lives as individuals, workers, and consumers. As they progress in school, students will grasp important economic concepts that enhance their understanding of the world and positively affect their future. The program's focus is as follows:

  —Ourselves: Economic roles of the individual.

  —Our Families: Role of families in the local economy.

  —Our Community: Responsibilities of and opportunities available to citizens in their economic community.

  —Our City: Economic development, local businesses, and career opportunities.

  —Our Region: State and regional economies, businesses, and economic resources.

  —Our Nation: Business operations and economic issues in the United States.

—Our World: World resources, economic systems, monetary exchange, and global trade.

Volunteers share their life experiences through stimulating, age-appropriate activities. These programs promote important life concepts that foster individual success.

Today's elementary school children are part of a rapidly changing and challenging world. Through interactive, hands-on activities, students can better understand the relationship between what they learn in school and success later in life. Students learn to value and respect:

- The relationship of basic economic concepts to the life experiences of the students
- The role of the individual as a consumer and producer in the market economy
- Practical applications of classroom theory to real life
- The ability to effectively work with others and as a member of a team
- The importance of staying in school

As we observed the business volunteers working with this group of kindergartners, we understood the importance of training our youth to take their place as leaders in society. Maslow's words echoed in our heads as we watched the 5-year-olds: *"Whom among them will change the world?"* We truly understood Maslow's words that day.

him a better worker and a better citizen and a better basketball player and everything else.

A few more notes on copying secrets. If the American conception of human nature is true, that is to say the enlightened management, Theory Y, best American conception is true, then no real copying is possible. The only way to copy the American style or the American product is to *become* American. That is, to become the kind of person who spontaneously emits creativeness and so on. Also there is the point here that I'd better think about some more, about "know-how" and what "know-how" consists of. The style of organization, the style of management, and everything that goes with Theory Y management, when it's realistic and under good environmental conditions with the self-confidence and the self-respect that goes with it, and with its tendency to create steadily a better kind of human being (more self-respecting, less fearful, less timid, less masochistic, less sadistic, less hostile, more affectionate, more friendly, more trusting, more honest, and the like), all of this is part of the "know-how."

It may ultimately be that American know-how will really be, so to speak, the American character. This is an important point, especially these days when so many other societies can beat us in so many different ways. For instance, labor is cheaper in many places. Most places in the world are much easier for authoritarian bosses, people under the spell of fear, of starvation, of losing jobs will certainly do what they're told quicker than the American workman will. There are places in the world where the raw materials are available in greater quantity than we have, where just simple quantity of labor is available in endless amounts, where police systems will prevent any strikes of any kind, and so on and so on. That is, there is no question that other cultures have certain "advantages."

Addition to the Notes on Synergy

Poor social or environmental conditions are those which set us against each other by making our personal interests antagonistic to the group, to those of others.

There is a possible empirical relationship between the concept of synergy and the concept of good conditions which might be exploited for research purposes. Ruth Benedict has defined synergy as the social-institutional arrangements which fuse selfishness and unselfishness, by transcending their oppositeness and polarity so that the dichotomy between selfishness and altruism is resolved and transcended and formed into a new higher unity: This is to be done by institutional arrangements so that when I pursue my selfish gratifications I automatically help others, and when I try to be altruistic I automatically reward and gratify myself. Various testable hypotheses can be deduced from these statements which might put the definition to the test:

1. A good society is one in which virtue pays.
2. A good society is one in which selfishness pays and in which other people approve of one's selfishness because they understand that they will ultimately benefit thereby. (The point here is that virtue or altruism or unselfishness are no longer different from selfishness and no longer have different directions or different goals or different consequences.)
3. The more the synergy in a society (or in a pair, or within a self), the closer we come to the B-values.
4. Poor social or environmental conditions are those which set us against each other by making our personal interests antagonistic to those of others, or mutually exclusive, or are

those in which the personal gratifications (D-needs), are in short supply so that not all can satisfy their needs except at the expense of others.

5. Under good conditions we have to pay little or nothing for being virtuous, or for pursuing the B-values, etc.

6. Under good conditions virtue (or selfishness) in a person is approved by others (that is, the person is loved and respected, sought for, etc.).

7. Under good conditions the virtuous or altruistic (or the healthily selfish) businessperson is more successful financially.

8. Under good conditions the successful person is loved rather than hated or feared or resented. (This statement can stand plenty of expansion, which I think I'll do below.)

9. Under good conditions admiration is more possible (unmixed with contaminating factors like erotizing or dominatizing or Nietzschian resentment, etc.).

10. We can be selfish as we please at these highest levels and yet feel virtuous.

11. We can feel as virtuous as we should like and yet permit ourselves to be selfish.

12. Re-examine Adam Smith's philosophy which implies something of this same sort. Perhaps he could be rephrased to read: "Under what conditions does enlightened selfishness work for the good of the whole society?" In the same way we can ask, "Under what conditions is it true that what is good for General Motors is good for the United States?" Or, "What is good for me is necessarily good for you?"

At these highest levels of B-psychology it will soon be necessary to redefine not only altruism and selfishness and unselfishness so as to transcend the dichotomies between them, but also such a concept as humanitarianism badly needs redefining or at least it needs to be purged of its exclusively good connotation. Or I might ask the question this way: "Under what conditions is humanitarianism bad?" Another question of the same sort, "Under what conditions can we drop all our guilt over our good luck or good fortune or our talent or our capabilities or our superiorities?" Clearly, at the level of synergy when altruism and selfishness work toward the same ends and are fused, then our stress on being kind to others and being good to others and going out of our way to help others and not being able to eat heartily while somebody else doesn't have enough food, and not being able to enjoy our wealth if somebody else is poor, and not being able to enjoy our good health if somebody else is sick and not being able to enjoy our own brains if somebody else doesn't have any, and the like, at the level of synergy—all of these considerations for others become either unnecessary, that is to say neurotic, or else they may become positive hindrances on the free and spontaneous expressions and behaviors and pleasures of the superior or of the fortunate person at that level.

This is very difficult to say because it involves rising above a distinction that we now take for granted, but it must be worked out. For instance, another way of looking at it is that this implies a fusing into one of the two different Hindu conceptions of Buddha. The one who seeks his self-actualization alone, privately and selfishly, and seeks Nirvana for himself by concentrating on himself; and the other exemplifies the legend about Buddha that he came to the gates of Nirvana and was so unselfish that he couldn't possibly go in so long as other people were not in, and turned back from Nirvana to go teach and help other people, with the implication that nobody can ever reach Nirvana or that nobody can ever reach full self-actualization unless everybody else in the world simultaneously does too. Under good conditions the superior person is totally freed, or anyway more freed, to enjoy himself completely, to express himself as he pleases, to pursue his own selfish ends without worrying about anybody else or feeling any guilt or obligation to anybody else in the full confidence that everybody else will benefit by his fully being himself and expressing himself and pursuing his own selfish ends. Everybody else benefits as a by-product of this.

Still another way of saying this is that under conditions of synergy, that is to say under the best or ideal conditions, there is no need to fear the evil eye or any of its modern parallels. There is no need to fear counter-resentments or the counter-values, i.e., the hatred for excellence, the hatred for truth, for beauty, for justice, for goodness, for virtue in general, which is now so often the case and which we must expect to some extent.

Under these ideal conditions the superior one would not have to fear resentment, envy, jealousy, hostility simply because of his excellence or superiority. (As is now the case, especially with less evolved and less mature human beings.) That is to say, he can unleash himself, he can show his genius or talent or skill or superiority freely without building up defenses or guards, and without protecting himself against expected counterattack. (One thought here: Probably at this level, boasting and modesty would also disappear as a dichotomy, because presumably at this level knowledge would be objective enough so that one could talk about one's own superiorities or inferiorities just about as efficiently and calmly as about other people's superiorities or inferiorities.)

(I suspect also that we will have to redefine our continuum of political liberal and political conservative, if all the above is true or even if it is only *partially* true. For instance, political liberalism simply assumes that humanitarianism is good—period, under any circumstances whatsoever and without any amendments or compromises. The weak are to be helped. But we can see that at these high levels of development, which is to say what might be expected in a eupsychian social setup, this is no longer true. Helping other people may now be seen as an intrusion, as an insult, as unwanted, unnecessary, as implying feebleness, etc. Also we know now and have enough clinical information to know that in truth there are many situations in which indiscriminate helping of someone else does in fact tend to enfeeble him, e.g., serving as a crutch for a person with weak legs will make his legs atrophy altogether eventually. We should talk here also of our information about the compensation neuroses. Certainly, many of our social security customs in this country are all mixed up from this point of view. For instance, the limitation on income for sick people or old people can do this kind of harmful thing. I know of one disabled man who is able to make his own living in a heroic way, but who is penalized for this by not being given any of the help that he is entitled to otherwise. The only way under which he can get help is to give up his self-reliance altogether and become totally the baby of the county hospital. Certainly this is no encouragement of self-reliance.)

(It occurs to me also that if I were to try to apply in a systematic way the principles of scientific management to our political situation—for instance, the stress on federal decentralization which has proven so wise in the industrial situation—then this would be in opposition to many of the shibboleths of contemporary political liberals. For instance, this would imply the town-meeting kind of democracy, it would imply decisions from below as often as possible, it would imply steadily cutting down of federal responsibilities in favor of more and more local responsibilities. The fact that the political reactionaries have used states' rights and local rights for evil ends should not confuse us about the generalities and the principles here. I wonder how applicable our new information about the efficient supervisor and the efficient manager is applicable to the efficient political leader at the various levels right on up to the senator and the President. This could be tried out systematically too, I think. In any case, I think there is little question about the usefulness of re-examining all these political and economic and social concepts under the terms of B-analysis, that is to say to see what they would be under eupsychian conditions. Clearly they would be different in various ways.)

Memorandum on Syndrome Dynamics and Holistic, Organismic Thinking

Good management and good workers and good enterprises and good products and good communities and good states are all conditions of one another and of good, mutual relations. If an improvement in the community does not have an ultimate effect on the goodness of the product, then something is wrong someplace.

The data that I've been reading about in the books on management can either be organized in an atomistic, cause-effect, beads-on-the-string manner, and treated like a pile of bits of facts, or they can be perceived in organismic terms, that is, as if they were all related to one another. Now, the latter way is actually more true, more real, more pragmatically successful. For instance, the reason I bring this up at all and would want to include it in any ultimate discussion of the theory of management of an enterprise is that it is necessary to point out that much of the writing on management, and especially the older stuff of the 1930s and 1920s, was based on the atomistic conception of the enterprise, that is, viewing it as if it were a world in itself and had no relationship to anything else, as if it were selfishly conceived. This is on the paradigm of a boss owning a little grocery store and feeling absolutely independent about it and beholden to nobody in the world; he runs it, he's the boss, and it's as much his property as the keys in his own pocket. Now, the fact is that this was untrue in the first place and that as our society, like any industrialized society, gets more and more interdependent, this conception gets to be less and less true until finally it just becomes stupid and unreal altogether.

The fact is that the enterprise, let's say Non-Linear Systems, is embedded in its immediate community; in all sorts of specifiable ways this immediate community is embedded in the larger community, let's say the Southern California area, which in turn has very definite and functional relationships with the state of California, which in turn is embedded in the United States, which in turn is embedded in the Western world, which in turn is embedded in the whole darn human species and the whole darn world. These are all functional relationships in the sense that demonstrable causes and effects can be listed, and they can be listed by the thousands. The fact that these are normally overlooked and taken for granted has nothing to do with the case. For instance, the fact that Non-Linear Systems has just one night watchman instead of a private army of three thousand people equipped with machine guns and cannon is taken for granted, but this can be taken for granted only when the relationships work so well. Or the fact that the enterprise is dependent upon the town for the supplies of water, electricity, and gas, for the maintenance of roads, for fire and police departments, not to mention dozens of other services like restaurants and shopping centers and markets and the like, which make it possible for people to live in the area, which makes it possible in turn for them to work in the plant. If anybody who worked at Non-Linear Systems took a risk of being assassinated on the main street, then the enterprise would, of course, disappear. This should be spelled out; it should be consciously understood that Non-Linear Systems rests on a whole network of assumed relationships, services, etc. It is, in a word, "contained within" as in a syndrome, or even more accurately it is "contained-and-structured within." The same is true of the various levels, and we can talk about taxation and about the services rendered in return for it. The United States maintains an Army and an F.B.I. and a Library of Congress and does all sorts of federal things without which Non-Linear Systems would collapse and be impossible. The same is true for NATO, the U.N. perhaps, and so it goes.

If this plant is taken as a syndrome itself, that is as a kind of organism within which all sorts of analysis of interrelationships could be made, then this syndrome is embedded in a larger syndrome, which is embedded in a larger syndrome, which is embedded in a still larger syndrome, and so on. This is what I meant in (57) Chapter 3 by a nest of boxes, that is, of one syndrome being contained within the next larger, more inclusive syndrome. Another figure of speech that I used there was the "level of magnification." One can see a histological slide under different magnifications of the microscope, and so one can see in closer detail, closer up but with a narrower field.

Now, the intracorrelations within syndrome 1, that is, the inter-relations *within* Non-Linear Systems as a syndrome, the friendliness, the ties, the mutual dependencies, the mutual necessities, the mutual leaning upon each other, let's say, can be measured as correlations of the order of .6. Now the correlations between the details within syndrome 1 and the details within syndrome 2, the more inclusive, larger syndrome *within* which syndrome 1 is embedded, these correlations are somewhat less and might average out to .4 instead. One would get a lower and lower correlation between syndrome 1 and syndrome 3 and syndrome 4 and larger and more inclusive syndromes. This means among other things that any change within syndrome 1 will affect everything else within syndrome 1 a lot more immediately and strongly than it will affect syndrome 3. *But* any change in syndrome 1 will in theory have *some* effect on syndromes 2, 3, 4, and so on.

What this means in other words is that any change for the better or for the worse in Non-Linear Systems is going to have an effect on Del Mar, on Southern California, on the state of California, on the United States, on the Western world, and on the whole world, and these effects will be steadily weaker as the syndrome gets larger and more inclusive. Unemployment, or let's say an explosion in Non-Linear Systems that would wipe out the whole plant, would be a real catastrophe for Del Mar and would certainly have a measurable effect on the state of California and would be almost unnoticed in China, but would even so have some very slight but real effect.

The intrasyndrome effects are greater than the intersyndrome effects. The same is true the other way about—changes in China or Bulgaria or Iran or anyplace else in the world ultimately will have ef-fects upon Non-Linear Systems and upon each single person within it. The fact that they may not be aware of it for a century doesn't matter. The effects are measurable, discernible, and pragmatically there. A shift in regimes, an assassination of, let's say, the Shah of Iran would have a definite effect upon Non-Linear Systems. The same is true at all the levels up and down the nest of boxes.

Now what does this mean in testable theoretical and experimental terms? It means that all sorts of hypotheses or affirmations can be stated and put to the test, and these hypotheses are just about the same as the ones that I have already generated from relating management policy to psychological health. For instance, I can say that the better the world, the better the country, the better the local government, the better the enterprise, the better the managers, the better the workers, the better the product. This is an overall statement which could be split apart into ten thousand specific hypotheses, each of which would be testable. And, of course, the whole thing can be stated the other way about. The better the product, the better the workers, the better the managers, the better the enterprise, the better the community, the better the state, the better the country, the better the world. And this also can be put to the test.

Another way of saying it is (this is a little more startling and a little more debatable), what's good for the world is good for the country, which is good for the state, which is good for the community, which is good for the enterprise, which is good for the managers, which is good for the workers, which is good for the product. (This borders very closely on a statement of synergy.) This comes close to the statement that roused so much fuss that "what's good for General Motors is good for the country," and yet the fact is that in an ideally holistic or organismic or integrated world situation exactly this would be true and should be true. What's good for me is good for the whole world. What's good for the whole world is good for me. What's good for the locality is good for the state, and so on, and so on, and so on. And ultimately, if one asks the question about what is necessary to turn out a good voltmeter, we would find ourselves in a series of concentric circles, larger and larger circles of explanation, until finally we would be talking about conditions on the sun and geographical conditions, and what is happening in ocean currents, in the stratosphere, and so on, and so on. For instance, an increase in temperature on the surface of the sun due to some huge explosion might very well wipe out the whole earth. And then, of course, no voltmeters would be possible. So good conditions on the sun are one of the prerequisites for good voltmeters, to take the most extreme instance that I can think of, and yet an instance which is clearly true and real.

Now, another way of twisting the whole thing about for the sake of understanding it better but also for the sake of testing it better and

INTERVIEW WITH BRIAN LEHNEN

It's not so much foreign capital that is needed in most poor countries, it's entrepreneurs of this self-confident type.

—*Abraham Maslow*

Brian Lehnen, cofounder of The Village Enterprise Fund, brings Dr. Maslow's words to life in some of the poorest countries in the world. The Village Enterprise fund was started nearly 10 years ago by Lehnen and his wife Joan. Through $100 mini grants and a worldwide network of field coordinators, The Village Enterprise Fund helps people rescue themselves from poverty through the tools of capitalism. The dreams of thousands of would-be entrepreneurs in the world's poorest nations are becoming a reality through the Village Enterprise Fund.

Why did you decide to leave a steady career path to launch the Fund?

A church trip to the Dominican Republic sparked our interest in developing countries. As with anyone else, we had this desire to have an effect. I equate it to the quintessential search for meaning in life, I suppose. I remember in college one of my professors told me that "you can't find happiness searching for happiness. You can only find happiness in service to somebody else." Our actions truly came about from our religious beliefs, those beliefs form the motivation for our work. Primarily, our mission is showing a holistic message—that entrepreneurship and capitalism can help the very poor create businesses and experience the dignity of long-lasting jobs. I'm just a piece of this—a tool. We can't take the successes too personally or the failures too personally.

How do you accomplish your mission which is "helping the poor help themselves with entrepreneurial grants"?

I think one of the keys to our success has been something we learned early on and which, for me, has had a lasting effect. In every person we work with, we see a spark of humanity. In America, we tend to think of the poor or of being poor as a very dehumanizing experience. Yet, when one is face to face with the poorest people in the world, the similarities—the spark of humanity—are striking. We are all so similar.

Maslow speaks of something like this in his journals regarding his experience with the Blackfoot and Plains Indians. First and foremost, he said he found them to be humans and then secondarily to be Indians. Is that the spark of humanity you refer to?

Yes, and I think we are so far removed from the international scene in this country that we expect human nature to somehow be grandly different. For example, I recently took one of our major contributors with me through Haiti. We had been there a few days, meeting some of the people we had sponsored in start-up businesses. One of the Haitian women we had funded explained her business to my guest and then excused herself to feed her twins. My guest, who had started and sold several successful U.S. companies, said to me, "If they had had half the opportunity I've had, I would be working for them." I think his reaction was one I hope to help people understand. We are not out to "save" the poor; we are really out to lend them a hand, one person at a time.

You have stirred quite an interest from the venture capital community—those hard-charging numbers guys who make and break companies every day. How did you manage to get their attention and their dollars?

The venture capital (VC) community are really of two types in my mind. The first type is the Donald Trump *Art of the Deal* type. Even if it's returning a pair of socks to Kmart they want a deal! That type of VC is attracted to our ability to help someone start a business for a hundred bucks! Once they see the results, they want to be a part of starting businesses all over the world. Although they take no profit or ownership in those businesses, they love to be in the start-up phase—helping the very poor develop simple business plans, scoping out the competition—if it exists. So for them, it's the art of the deal and the innovation behind the thought process. However, every one of them is thrilled to see the "human results."

The second type of VC are older, in their 50s and 60s, who grew up with a sense of philanthropy. Since they are going to give money anyway, they feel much better about giving money to a fund that helps people start businesses. They know how powerful and empowering ownership can be. Therefore, they tend to relate to what we are attempting to do more so than giving dollars to some of the other nonprofit foundations.

So you are really a social entrepreneur?

Yes. I use the same language, the same tools and techniques as for profit entrepreneurs. We coach poor, hard-working people through the process of starting a small business. They learn to create a simple business plan and if we think the plan has a chance of working, we fund the plan. Money is dispersed in three parts: the first part upon approval of the plan, the second part after the business is launched and operational, and the third part when specific goals have been achieved.

The social entrepreneur enjoys the sense of accomplishment, the excitement of knowing the effect, and witnessing firsthand the results from sometimes less than a hundred dollar investment. It's really not much different in approach from for-profit launches. We just have a different end result—our income is intrinsic income.

(continued)

Please explain to me how someone can launch a business on $100?

I think it's difficult for Americans to realize that what they pay for dinner for two in a nice restaurant is sometimes the equivalent of one year's income in a developing country. It is a very large amount of money in the backroads of Haiti, Bangladesh, Ethiopia, Burma, and a whole host of other countries. Thus, we are able to make a difference with a $100.

The types of businesses your group has helped launch are decidedly low-tech yet you have a number of high-tech investors. I would guess you would be encouraged to be pursuing technology or launching technology-oriented companies?

Although technology has an important role to play in the world, in the countries we work in, many of the people have yet to even make a telephone call. The world of television is still foreign to them. We help people launch businesses that have a chance of success in the world they live in today. For example, farming, furniture making, grocery shops, tailoring, bicycle repair, carpentry, auto repair. We have access to some of the best and brightest business minds and we bring their brains to these "low tech–high success ventures."

In his journals, Maslow speaks of people as being meaning seeking in their work. I can't think of a better example of meaning seeking than the work that you do. What do your three children think of this work?

I think our three children are proud of the work we do. However, they are still children and many times the effect rings rather hollow with them. It's hard getting around the fact in a child's world that you can't have a better house, drive a better car, have the newest tennis shoes, or gadget because your parents work in a field that doesn't lead to a lot of money. However, I can only hope that as they grow older and are able to look back, they see value in the way we've chosen to spend our lives.

In terms of people seeking meaning in their work, there was a time several years ago that I felt for financial reasons I really needed to return to corporate life to better support our family. We listed an advertisement in a local paper for someone to take my place. The ad said something like "low pay but high rewards!" It listed the work of The Village Enterprise Fund. We received over 200 resumes and letters from potential applicants!

Most carried the theme you speak to—a real search for meaning in their lives and work. I hope my children, as adults, see that I was one of the lucky ones!

making it more scientific is that all of these holistic interrelationships, this whole next of boxes, is in effect a theory of unity, of integration, of coordination, of harmony, and of good working together. That is, all of these signs of integration and mutual effect that I have mentioned are themselves symptoms of the degree of goodness of the integration. What I mean is this: the better the integration, the more will these effects that I have mentioned prevail; the worse the integration—the more the atomizing, the more the mutual exclusiveness, the more the splits between communities and states and countries and individuals and enterprises and classes and castes and so on—then the less will these effects exist.

I can say it in still another way. Good management and good workers and good enterprises and good products and good communities and good states are all conditions of one another and of good mutual relations. If an improvement in the community does *not* have an ultimate effect on the goodness of the product, then something is wrong someplace. The system is not integrated enough, the communications are bad, or groups are set against each other instead of being synergic or something of the sort. This is in effect a pathological situation. Perhaps the parallel with the human body would be useful here. The less the coordination and integration within my body, the more dangerous it is for me. For instance, if my nervous system has one mechanism of coordination thrown out of whack, then my left hand doesn't know what the right hand does, and they simply can't work together, which in turn is bad for me rather than good for me.

Thus, I think a pretty interesting theoretical and research study could be made of those factors which split the society, disintegrate it rather than integrate it—for instance, like the treatment of the Negroes in industry, the fact that they are split off, could ultimately be shown to have bad effects upon the products, the workers, the managers, the plants, the communities, and so on and so on, if we think in this syndrome way and especially if we think in a long-term way. To give one single example, the counterhostility that is now developing among the Negro population in the United States may ultimately take the form of burning factories, or of assassination and Civil War. Certainly it already has taken the form of aggression, criminality, delinquency, and so on—it is dangerous for a white man to walk in Harlem in New York City, for instance, because all the pent-up bitterness of past bad treatment is taken out on any particular white person who happens to walk by. The person who gets slugged and then viciously beaten for no purpose at all, after being robbed, is paying the price for a lot of other bad treatment he had nothing to do with. It is conceivable that in the management situation in Non-Linear Systems this kind of thing could happen—sabotage, criminality, or whatever. Therefore, what some vicious person does in Mobile, Alabama, will ultimately have an effect on the quality of the voltmeter in Non-Linear in Del Mar, California, perhaps thirty years later.

Said in another way, the best conditions for making good volt-meters are to have a perfect world. Or contrariwise, any falling short of goodness in the world will ultimately have its effects on our volt-meters and fountain pens and automobiles and so on.

It is very necessary to make the long-run–short-run distinction in this context. Be sure to include this is the discussion of synergy, of moral accounting practices, etc. It is perfectly true that swindling, let's say, a particular Negro today, or exploiting the Italian workers and making them feel unwelcome, or being nasty to redheaded people, or not giving women a fair chance in industry, or whatever, can have short-run advantages. It is obvious that if I run a grocery store and shortchange a particular customer, this is to my monetary advantage at this particular moment; long-run considerations and one-world considerations, however, added into the balance sheet will make the whole transaction look different. For instance, the more I am a crook, the more I affect other people and the more I affect the world at this moment. I may not see that bad effect of this immediately, but my children or my grandchildren will. If I am contemptuous of Mexicans and treat them badly in my grocery store by swindling them or what-ever, it's perfectly true that my checking account at the end of the month may be bigger and there may be no discernible harm to me immediately; but my children or my grandchildren would certainly be affected sometime in the future if, for instance (which is quite con-ceivable even though not probable), some great military catastrophe in the United States would destroy the whole society and we Americans would then go streaming into Mexico to beg for food. I wonder what would happen if whites went into Harlem to beg for food today.

The same thing may be true in a more diluted form with the vio-lent hatred that some Chinese have for the Americans. The war in Korea was certainly partly determined by the fact that the American Congress and the American people had been so stupidly insulting to the Chinese in their immigration policies. We are paying for these past sins. And this is all to make the point that whatever sins we commit today we and our children will eventually pay for.

All of this kind of thing is made much stronger, much more obvious, more to be taken for granted, more commonsensical by organismic thinking, by holistic thinking. The truth is that everything in the world is related to everything else and everybody in the world is related to everybody else and everybody now living is related to everybody who is going to live in the future, and in this way we all influence one another, and we might as well know this scientifically.

Of course, this kind of understanding of mutual interrelations in time and space takes a pretty large and sophisticated and educated mind to understand. However, if it can't be achieved in a total way, at least the management theorists and philosophers can press steadily in this direction of demonstrating larger and larger interrelationships, larger and larger "cause-effect" syndromes, in any particular local situation. Thus, for instance, the experiment in 1956 of Morse and Reimer[1] is terribly important not only for its own sake, but also as a paradigm, as a model, as a kind of an example of what could be the case: What Morse and Reimer demonstrated was that long-run human consequences are different from short-run productivity consequences, that it's easy enough to increase profits and production and to make a good balance sheet by putting on pressure in the short run, using up reserves and strength and throwing away long-term investments, and so on. I'd say that this insight of the management people would be part of their citizen's responsibility, their eupsychian responsibility, part of the thing that they must teach the world. This citizen's responsibility is in full accord with scientific responsibility to the absolute truth. What is necessary here is to teach the larger truth. There's no implication here of telling an untruth, of telling a lie.

Now another point that I want to deal with at length, I've already dealt with a little bit is the fact that synergy, mutual interdependence, mutual advantage, the "what's-good-for-me-is-good-for-you" kind of philosophy, is all very true in the long run *under good conditions*. It is definitely not true in the short run, in emergencies, under bad conditions, especially under conditions of scarcity. When there's a need

---

[1] N. Morse and E. Reimer, "The Experimental Change of a Major Organizational Variable," *Journal of Abnormal Social Psychology*, 1956, 52, 120–129.

for ten lamb chops and only one lamb chop exists, then in fact my interest is antagonistic to your interests. Whoever gets the lamb chop is hurting the other people. What is good for me is bad for you under such circumstances. We must be very aware of this. All of the qualities that we call moral and humanistic and good—the kindness, altruism, unselfishness, kindliness, helping each other, etc.—all depend upon a rich, good world which furthermore is holistically integrated with good communication from every part to every other part, so that the full benefits of interdependence can flow rapidly.

If I ever do any more writing on this holistic point in relationship to social psychology in general, I think I would start with Kurt Goldstein's[2] stuff, and perhaps the work on the integrative functions of the central nervous system and go on up from there to more and more complex, wider and wider implications, finally winding up in the social psychology of one world. I would use also the basic tenets of the Gestalt psychology.[3] Chapter 3 in my *Motivation and Personality* is a theoretical foundation for this kind of thinking. Maybe this is simply an application to social psychology of what I have there.

To go back to the very beginning of this memorandum, I forgot to expand: When syndrome 1 is "contained within" syndrome 2, this is different from the statement, syndrome 1 is "contained-and structured-within" syndrome 2. Simply to be contained within does not necessarily mean having real functional relationships with, just in the same way that my body can have something contained within it if somebody simply implants a pebble below my skin by a surgical operation. This is different from the way in which my liver is contained and structured within my body because there are definite functional and necessary interdependences and interrelationships. The same thing can apply to the relationship of an industry to the community in which it is imbedded. It can either be structured within it, or it can be contained within it like a lump which is indigestible and has no relationship with it.

It will soon be necessary to make the explicit tie between syndrome dynamics–holism, and hierarchical integration and synergy. They overlap, but they are not quite the same. Each needs a special treatment and a special explanation.

[2] K. Goldstein, *The Organism* (Boston: Beacon Press Paperback, 1963).
[3] M. Henle (Ed.), *Documents of Gestalt Psychology* (Berkeley: University of California Press, 1961).

Another point important for this general context of holism is that the truth in general tends to become more and more holistic, more and more homogeneous, more unitary, more integrated, more whole, more single. At every point within the body of knowledge there are definite strains toward consistency. Of course, the most perfect examples are mathematics and logic, but this is also true for science in general and as a matter of fact for all knowledge in general. Human beings just don't like inconsistencies, and the only way they can manage them is by repression, by overlooking them, by paying no attention to them, and so on; but once the inconsistency or the contradiction is called to the attention of the human being, the wheels are set in motion, and he must whether he wants to or not, keep on thinking about it and trying to make it consistent. One could talk here about the cognitive dissonance experiments. To some extent this is related to my discussion of metamotivation and metaneeds in my *Notes on the Psychology of Being* monograph (89, 97). One of the B-values is integration, unifying, tendency toward oneness. Everything that is said there can be integrated with everything that I have said so far in this memorandum. For instance, it can be treated as a human metaneed, i.e., as a particular kind of higher motivation. Also it generates its countermotivation, countervalue, i.e., it generates fear, distaste, threat, and resistance just as every need and metaneed does. The consequence is a kind of dialectic, as for instance between the need to know and the fear of knowing.

All of this theoretical stuff can be applied to the specific management books and theories. I think also that I may want to fold into this whole theoretical structure eventually the doctrine of isomorphism between the person and the world (104), that is, the tendency for the person to perceive the world as if it were like himself and to make it into something like himself, on the one hand and, on the other hand, the tendency for the world to model and mold the person into a consistency with itself. That is, the person and the world tend to become more and more like each other. They have a mutual cause-effect, feedback, mutual-influence relationship. The more integrated I become, the more able I am to see integration in the world and the more annoying disintegration becomes to me, so that I will try when I see it to change it into integration. And contrariwise, the more integrated the world becomes, the more pressure it will exert upon my disintegrations to change into integrations, the more one the world becomes,

Aspen Skiing Company: A Story of Connectivity

The fact is that the enterprise is embedded in its immediate community; in all sorts of specifiable ways this immediate community is embedded in the larger community. . . . It can either be structured within it with form and harmony or it can be contained within it like a lump which is indigestible and has no relationship with it. More should be said on the relationship between the enterprise and the society, especially if we take into account the ways to keep the organization healthy over a period of a hundred years.

—Abraham Maslow

Aspen, Colorado, has always been a different kind of place. Unmatched physical beauty, a world-renowned institute for educating leaders, great music, and more world-class restaurants per square block than any other place on the planet. It is also a company town where the Aspen Skiing Company not only employs a large number of residents of the Roaring Fork Valley but affects the lives of nearly everyone who lives, works, or visits the community.

As is often the case in company towns, Aspen Skiing Company has not always been popular with residents. Cooperation was not a word that would have described the company or the residents just a few short years ago. Aspen Skiing Company was viewed with suspicion in the past because many residents felt that the company did not share the values of the community.

When the leadership team of the Aspen Skiing Company met in 1995 they sought to discover ways to build cooperation with residents while improving the value received by the hundreds of guests and tourists who visited Aspen each year. They knew they had to find a cause that both the company and the community would be willing to work together to achieve.

Aspen Skiing Company was faced with the daunting task of discovering ways to attract more skiers to Aspen (even though the number of people participating in the sport was declining). The company also knew that the visitor's experience while in Aspen was affected by the airline, hotel, taxi, restaurant, and shopping experiences. In fact, those experiences left an impression on the guest more so than how they were treated during the short time they spent on the mountain with Aspen Skiing Company personnel.

The goal was clear that the leadership team of the skiing company was determined to lead the town in improving the guest experience throughout their stay in Aspen, Colorado.

As the group struggled to articulate their purpose, they began to see how their values and the values of local residents could help provide a unique experience for guests. They deemed their goal as the providers of opportunity for every guest to "renew the human spirit" and for more residents to be able to participate in the process.

When CEO Pat O'Donnell offered Aspen residents the opportunity to work one day per week without pay (a ski pass and uniform were the only compensation) to give tours of Aspen to guests, many of us thought he was crazy! However, O'Donnell believed that given the opportunity to participate in a meaningful way, the residents of Aspen would jump at the chance. Early volunteers were attracted to the newly articulated values of the Aspen Skiing Company. They took pride in the company's commitment to service and the high standards of service they hoped to achieve. In fact, the volunteer meetings with townspeople soon became opportunities for people to tell outrageous service stories. The meetings were so entertaining that a local television station started broadcasting the "events" on local TV! Aspen residents began to see that serving visitors could be fulfilling and fun.

The second year into the all-volunteer brigade posed a problem for Pat O'Donnell. There were twice as many resident volunteers as positions. Imagine officers of some of America's largest corporations (many of whom happen to be Aspen residents) complaining to the CEO of the skiing company that they were being discriminated against because they couldn't ski well enough to be a part of the all-volunteer brigade! Pat and his crew quickly looked for other ways to use the all-volunteer brigade. A group of volunteers now works at the Denver International Airport, greeting passengers on their way to connecting flights to Aspen with the vision that they can somehow make up for the poor service the arriving visitors may have encountered by the airlines!

The excitement, the sense of belonging, the feeling of accomplishment is what the volunteer brigade say they get from the venture. As a "guest" one senses all of that and more even during a short visit to the town.

Although we have always believed in Dr. Maslow's theory that people long for a shared sense of purpose, to be a part of something larger than themselves and their search for meaning is often found in work, we were amazed to see firsthand his words come to life in an entire community. Great music, world class skiing, gourmet restaurants—and a community proud to welcome, no, absolutely delight a guest. Aspen has changed. It's not only better for guests, but in the process has become a better place to live and to work.

the more it will tend to make me one. The more one I become, the more I will tend to make the world one. This is what I mean by isomorphism. This itself, by the way, is an example of the pressure toward homogeneity and unity of knowledge, toward the oneness of knowledge. Differences and discrepancies between knower and known tend to obliterate themselves, i.e., to transform themselves into a unity.

Notes on the B-Values (the Far Goals; the Ultimate Goals)

We fear our highest possibilities (as well as our lowest ones).
We are generally afraid to become that which we can glimpse
in our most perfect moments. We enjoy and even thrill to the
godlike possibilities we see in ourselves. And yet we simulta-
neously shiver with weakness, awe, and fear before these very
same possibilities . . . .

In the discussion of enlightened management as a direction, and
also in the discussion of any other social institution which takes
this same direction toward eupsyschia, it is best to give up the
"one-big-value" kind of theory (e.g., "All is love"; or as one enlightened industrialist said, "All my efforts are in the interests of service to
other people") in favor of a pluralism of ultimate values—at least for
the present. This is true, or at least it is expedient practically, even
though we can already today extrapolate to the future this notion of
the one-big-value which is over-arching. This is because *each* B-value,
if it is fully defined to its limits, turns out to be defined in terms of
each and all of the other B-values. That is to say, when I tried to define truth and honesty totally and ultimately and went on as far as I
possibly could with it, I found that truth was defined in terms of each
and all of the other B-values on my list. For instance, truth was beautiful, it turned out; truth was good, truth was just, truth was final,
truth was perfect, truth was complete, truth was unitary, truth was
rich, and so on for the whole list of B-values. This was an exercise that
I actually did; I haven't yet done the same for the other B-values, but
even with the little effort I made in this direction, it already becomes
clear that beauty—if it is examined totally and ultimately—will finally

wind up having as part characteristics of its own nature each and all of the other B-values, and so on down the line (102).

What this means is that one day in the future we may find some kind of way of phrasing this unitary nature, this oneness of all the B-values. I suspect that the technique of factor analysis will be useful for moving in this direction.

But this gives us a criterion for judging whether something is really a B-value or not. Thus if the Christian Scientist talks as he does about love as the one supreme value, or a particular scholar talks only of truth, or Keats talks only of beauty as the supreme virtue, and the lawyer talks of justice as the ultimate one value, then we can use our principle of criticism to judge whether this is phony or OK. For instance, what the Christian Scientist defines as love is in contradiction to medical and biological truths, and at once we realize that it has been dichotomized away from the other B-values, it has been isolated or encapsulated or cut off from them. This, of course, ruins it at once. This indicates that it is not fully defined—or that the Christian Scientists have a cut-off notion of love, i.e., that it's not inclusive enough or big enough. The same is true for the truth as the ultimate goal of certain pure scientists who look for truth without regard to the other B-values. For instance, there's a question about whether a blind, atomic physicist or rocket expert, or the Nazi concentration camp physicians who did all those horrible experiments, might not have all of them thought that they were pursuing the pure truth. Perhaps they were, so far as they were concerned introspectively. Perhaps they felt virtuous enough. And yet the fact remains that this truth of theirs was in clear contradiction to other values of love and goodness and beauty and so on, and therefore must be presumed to be an imperfect or partial or false or cut-off definition of the truth. That is, no B-value may be defined in such a fashion so as to contradict or exclude any other B-value. There must be no isolation or dichotomizing or cutting off one B-value from any other B-value.

Also this implies that it is OK to stress any of these far goals or B-values just so long as this continues to be defined by all the other B-values. It is possible for a scientist, for instance, to pursue the truth wholeheartedly and still to be correct and OK in all respects because the truth that he is looking for is compatible with or includes all the other far goals or B-values. This is certainly true for the principles of enlightened management. One could speak of limited goals or of single values like service, and yet not include all the implications of a fully defined service. Perhaps I should say it this way: B-love or B-truth, etc., is equal ultimately to any of the other B-values. Or it can be said: B-love is defined by all the other B-values, or B-love is the sum total of all the other B-values.

Or still another way to say it, if we keep in mind simultaneously the present pluralism of B-values and their future extrapolated oneness: One may approach the oneness of being via *any* of the B-values. One may foster truth *and* beauty *and* justice *and* perfection, etc., by devoting one's whole life to the B-truth, *or* to B-justice, etc.

Notes on Leadership

. . . the person who seeks power for power, is the one who is just exactly likely to be the one who shouldn't have it. Such people are apt to use power very badly; to overcome, over-power, use it for their own selfish gratifications.

I am dissatisfied with the material on leadership in the management literature; I think again there's some tendency, as in McGregor, to be pious about the democratic dogma, rather than using the objective requirements of the situation as the centering point or organizing point for leadership. I think the way that I'll approach it will be from the point of view of the perfect (paradigmatic) situation, or the enlightened situation, in which the objective requirements of the situation, or of the task, or of the problem, or of the group reign absolutely and in which there are practically no other determinants. This would then provide an answer to the question, Who is the best leader for this particular situation? In this paradigmatic situation, I would have to assume very good cognition of the skills, talents, and abilities of every single person in the group, of one's self as well as others. I would also assume a totally innocent B-cognition (89) of all the relevant details of the problem situation. I would also assume healthy characters in all the people involved (so that there would not be too much sensitivity, or feeling insulted or hurt, or of anybody having such weak self-esteem or weak ego that he has to be handled delicately or diplomatically and with lies, politeness, etc.). I would also then have to assume in this perfect situation that the task, problem, or purpose was totally introjected by everybody in the situation; that is to say, that the task or duty was not any longer something separate from the self, something out there, outside the person and different from him, but rather that he identified with this task so strongly that you couldn't define his real self without including that task.

A good example to use here is the man who loves his work and is absorbed in it and who enjoys it so much that he can hardly think of himself apart from it. If I am a psychologist and I love psychology and I was born to be a psychologist and I get total satisfaction out of it, etc., etc., then it becomes totally meaningless to try to imagine me not being a psychologist—I would simply not be the same person. I might not even be a person in the fullest sense of the word if this were amputated from me. Well, this kind of total identification with the task or the duty is an aspect of B-psychology (86) that people probably aren't ready for yet, so I'd better figure out easier ways of communicating it. It's difficult because it jumps the dichotomy between work and play, between a person and his labor, between the self and nonpsychological reality, etc. The concept of the task or the vocation or the duty becoming part of the self, a defining and necessary part, a *sine qua non* part, this I think is difficult to understand in the culture which cuts these things apart and makes dichotomies out of them.

Well, granted all these ideal conditions, then the kind of B-leadership which would emerge would be the same kind of functional leadership that I saw in the Blackfoot Indians, or that I see in a group of youngsters who form a basketball team, perhaps, and who have good team spirit and who are not selfish prima donnas. The Blackfoot Indians tended not to have general leaders with general power, for instance, like our President of the United States, but rather to have different leaders for different functions. For instance, the leader in a war party was the one whom everybody thought to be the best person to lead a war party, and the one most respected or the leader in raising stock was the man best suited for that. So one person might be elected leader in one group and be the very last one in the second group. Of course, this is all very sensible, logical, and rational, because in truth we do have different capacities and powers and certainly in any group of hundreds of people, we should not expect that the person who is best suited to arrange the Sun Dance must be exactly the same person who is best suited to be the political representative to the Canadian government, let us say. The Blackfoot were very realistic about themselves and about each other and about their talents and always chose for a particular job just exactly that person who was the best one for that particular job without getting sentimental about his being good or not good in some other job. This can be called functional leadership, or as I would prefer, B-leadership. It corresponds to the objective requirements of the objective situation, of reality in general, both natural and psychological reality.

Now, another aspect of this B-leadership in the Blackfoot was that the leader has absolutely no power whatsoever that wasn't deliberately and voluntarily given to him *ad hoc* by the particular people in the particular situation. That is to say, he didn't really influence anyone or order anyone about. There was a kind of a mutual give and take between the group and the chosen leader because generally the chosen leader considered himself quite objectively to be the best one for the job and the group considered him to be the best one for the job. It was assumed that they all had the same purposes and that the leader then was a kind of quarterback who called the signals and coordinated the group toward common ends rather than one who gave orders, who used power, who tried to influence them or control them in any way. In fact, he was really asked by the group to be an arm of the group or servant of the group in order to pattern it and organize it, to give the right cues and signals at the right time just as in a football team, because otherwise there would be confusion. And by the way, the Blackfoot Indians didn't bother with leaders when there was no necessity for any leader, and in some situations there were simply amorphous, unorganized groups, quite unstructured, and this worked well too.

In such a situation the relationship between the group and the leaders is quite different from the kinds of things I've been reading about in these books on management. For instance, in the Blackfoot groups and in other B-groups that I have seen, the group tends to be grateful to the leader rather than resentful of him. That is, it is as if they recognized that they have placed a burden of responsibility upon his shoulders because he happens to be the one best fitted to do the job. Since he also recognizes in the perfect situation that he is the one best suited to do the particular job, he may take the job whether he enjoys it or not, whether he likes it or not, simply out of a sense of responsibility.

This is very different from our American political situation, for instance, in which leaders tend to choose themselves. Some guy gets ambitious to be governor or something of the sort. Then he throws his hat in the ring and says, "I want to be governor." Then he goes out in a campaign to fight against all the other people who want to be governor, and this is what we call campaigning and making a hard fight, and so on. From the point of view of B-psychology, this is a very unsuitable and even dangerous way to do it. And in any case, is a very poor way of getting the right functional leaders for the right jobs.

It's dangerous because it tends to leave the selection of candidates to just exactly those self-seekers, those people who neurotically need power in the sense of power over other people (D-power), rather than getting into office the person who is best suited to the job and who may be modest and humble about the matter and would not like to push himself forward. Or, as I put this in my old article on leadership (24), the person who seeks for power is the one who is just exactly likely to be the one who shouldn't have it, because he neurotically and compulsively needs power. Such people are apt to use power very badly; that is, use it for overcoming, overpowering, hurting people, or to say it in other words, they use it for their own selfish gratifications, conscious and unconscious, neurotic as well as healthy. The task, the job, the objective requirements of the situation tend to be forgotten or lost in the shuffle when such a person is the leader. He is essentially looking out for himself, for a kind of self-cure of neurosis, for a self-gratification.

Then if we look at the person who would be best suited to be the leader—that is, the one who is best suited actually to solve the problem or to pursue the task successfully, i.e., the one who is most perceptive about the objective requirements of the situation, and who is therefore most selfless in the situation—just that person, because by definition he is psychologically healthier, gets absolutely no kick out of being able to order people around or to boss them. It simply doesn't give him kicks or gratification. Therefore, he generally has to be sought out by the others, and he definitely feels he is taking on a responsibility or he is doing the group a favor rather than the other way about, as is the situation with most of our politicians who are self-chosen and who seek for power instead of waiting humbly to be asked to take it. The pushy people are exactly the ones who shouldn't have power. The safest person to give power to is the one who doesn't enjoy power. He is the least likely to use it for selfish, neurotic, or sadistic purposes, or for showing-off purposes, all of which can be motivations for the D-leader and all of which mean obscuring or neglecting or overlooking the objective, realistic requirements of the group or of the situation or of the job. As I recall it, in that old article on leadership I pointed out that these are pretty decent criteria for judging whom you should want as a leader or not want. If a man doesn't have any hankering for leadership, this is one point in his favor. If a person struggles for leadership and for bosshood, then this is one dangerous point against him that should make us question his suitability.

Another way of saying this is to make the distinction between B-leadership and D-leadership, and a parallel one between seeking for power over other people and for power to do the job well. And this latter leads me up to the point of trying to explain what B-power is.

B-Power

B-power is the power to do what needs doing, to do the job that ought to be done, to solve the objective problem, to get the job done that needs to be done or to say it in a more flossy way, B-power is the power to foster and protect and enhance all the B-values, of truth and goodness, beauty, justice, perfection, order, etc., etc. B-power is the power to make a better world, or to bring the world closer to perfection. In its simplest conceivable form, it is like the Gestalt motivations in which crooked things are set straight or unfinished things are finished. For instance, I take as a paradigmatic example straightening the crooked picture on the wall. For practically all people such a situation is slightly irritating and "calls for" the person who sees the crooked picture to get up and straighten it. This straightening is a satisfaction. The crooked picture is a stimulating trigger. This is a matter of setting things right, of cleaning up a dirty room, of bringing order where there was disorder, of doing things right, of completing an incompleted job and the like, of producing closure, and of producing a good Gestalt. We all have such tendencies more or less, although some of us are far more irked, far more motivated by one B-value than by another. For instance, the aesthetically sensitive or the musically sensitive may really squirm if a particular chord is played badly on the piano. There is an anecdote about Brahms that illustrates the point. Somebody had been fiddling around at the piano and was idly playing notes and chords and in the middle of playing, left the piano. Brahms had to get up and finish the progression and said, "We cannot let that chord go unresolved forever."

This is a little like the business of waiting to hear the other shoe drop in the apartment above before one is able to go to sleep. Or the impulse that the good housekeeper gets to straighten things out and to clean up things, not to leave a dirty kitchen after a meal. These are all small examples of situations which have demand-character à la Kurt Lewin in which the environment, or reality, or nature, or the situation call for something to be done. Well, we can very easily step up from these trivial examples to the larger examples which make huge motivations for large segments of life. For instance, the straightening out of injustice, or unfairness, or of untruth. We all have some sensitive spot with relationship to the B-values where we will get indignant and are impelled to set things straight. For instance, there's a little anecdote which illustrates this is the *Saturday Review* of a man in an airport restaurant who just got stubborn about the lousy steak that he was offered which he couldn't eat and which was very high-priced. He sent it back to the kitchen and then they sent him another bad one, and he sent that back to the kitchen and then they sent him another bad one, and he sent that back to the kitchen and then they sent him another bad one, and he sent that back to the kitchen, but the point was that he got stubborn about this injustice, I guess it could be called. This is what I would call righteous indignation—a very desirable kind of indignation. Or this is the kind of impulse that will sometimes impel us to trace down some crook or swindler, even if it has not been us who has been swindled. Or especially for the scientist and the intellectual, this is the sort of situation in which a lie has to be straightened out and the truth has to be told and, of course, there are situations in history in which people risk their lives for truth or would rather go to execution than tell a lie.

Well, for people who are pretty good, or pretty healthy, or pretty decent, i.e., for fairly well-evolved human beings, the world is full of situations of this sort which call for straightening out and which cause irritation until they are straightened out. It is for the power to straighten out such situations, to make things more perfect or more true or more beautiful or more correct or right or suitable or whatever, that B-power is such a wonderful thing, and one which should be sought by all decent people, rather than avoided. If we think in this way, then, B-power is the most wonderful thing in the world rather than the bad thing that we in the United States have gotten used to thinking it. This confusion is a confusion between bad power, unhealthy power, neurotic power, D-power, power over other people and not differentiating this from the power to do a good job, and to do right, and do good. It is as if we assumed that the only kind of power was this sadistic or selfish power. But this is simply psychologically untrue.

If then we understand B-power, the B-leader is the one who seeks for B-power and who uses it well for the purposes of the B-values. This is a very different conception of leadership and of power from the ones that I've seen in these management books. It is almost synonymous with responding to duty.

The B-leader in the work situation, if we follow the above objective type of analysis, can be defined as the one who can get the job done best or who at least can help to organize things in such a fashion that the job gets done best. I cannot see any other definition of leadership of the ordinary sort, e.g., one who can influence people, one who can control people, one who can twist people around his finger, or anything of that sort. For one thing, that's too general and not pluralistic enough, i.e., I may be perfectly willing to take orders from a good functional leader who can do better than I can, let's say on a hunting expedition, but I wouldn't dream of taking his orders in a publishing situation, for instance. If any man has the power to twist me around his finger whenever he pleases and regardless of the situation, then I would have to be an extremely sick man and so also would he have to be an extremely sick man if he wanted to twist me around his finger.

The B-leader doesn't want to twist anybody around anybody's finger, and while I'm at it, I might as well talk about the B-follower here who can really be defined in about the same way as the B-leader, as one who has introjected the goals or directives or objectives in the problematical situation and who is so identified with them that he wants them done in the best possible way; this might mean that the other guy is the right man for the job rather than the follower himself, so that the B-follower is presumably exactly as eager to have the B-leader become the leader as the B-leader is himself.

The requirements of different kinds of situations in which there are different kinds of leaders range very widely. For instance, in a perfectly democratic way we may elect a leader and give him a huge amount of power, even power over life and death, just because that particular type of situation requires that particular kind of leadership,

Interview with Linda Alepin and David Wright

The old style management is steadily becoming obsolete. The higher people get on the hierarchy (of needs) the more psychologically healthy, the more enlightened management policy will be necessary to survive in competition and the more handicapped will be an enterprise with an authoritarian policy.

That is why I am so optimistic about enlightened management. . . . why I consider it to be the wave of the future.

—Abraham Maslow

David Wright is the CEO of Amdahl Corporation and a leader in the high technology region of California, referred to as Silicon Valley. At the helm of one of high technology's industry leaders, he works in an environment that sometimes changes overnight. Visionary, pragmatic, and values-based, he fits the role of the leader in the new economy that is highly competitive, driven by risk, fueled by knowledge, and fast on its feet.

Linda Alepin is CEO of Pebblesoft Learning Inc., a start-up Internet company, typical of the hundreds of fast-paced ventures that change the landscape of American enterprise daily. A veteran corporate strategist and Silicon Valley leader, she embodies the leader of the future.

Linda and David were colleagues before their ascent to the top echelons of corporate America—colleagues who did not get along, embodied brash leadership styles, and generally viewed one another as enemies. Yet, today they are very different leaders. The lessons they learned fit well with Dr. Maslow's journals. Through the process of transforming their own working relationships, they found they were also improving the work environment for their colleagues. We met with them in the corporate headquarters of Amdahl in Sunnyvale, California. What we discovered were two examples of the leaders we think Maslow would have called "enlightened."

Linda: I had just completed this management development course where one of the first exercises or the first thing I was supposed to do was list a coworker with whom I had difficulty working or relating. I was supposed to list the way in which I viewed this person. The person was David and I remember I described him as:

- Mr. Action
- Running for CEO
- Doesn't like me

(continued)

- Out to get me
- Not strategic
- Jealous
- Only the bottom line

Now this particular management course didn't allow you to just write things down. So the next thing I was instructed to do was write down what I was going to do about our relationship. In fact, the instructions were to identify specific actions you can take or avoid taking. The goal was not to attempt to change him but to change my interactions with him so the relationship would change. I wrote down:

- Avoid strategic topics
- Review conversation and change it to a more "what's in it for him" type of conversation
- Start with practical
- Be impersonal

These are the first things I had written down. I see now I had completely misjudged you. I think this type of misjudgment goes on all of the time within organizations.

David: I agree. I sensed that Linda did not care for me. I've always been pretty good at trying to figure out what the landscape looked like. Coming from a sales background, you learn pretty quickly to size up the relationship. You know quickly if customers relate to you or not. You just intuitively know. I never really got into what the issues were with Linda. I never really had time to get into the issues. It's not that I didn't care, I was just extremely busy. What changed me was to realize that everything looks different depending on where you sit. I was running on a path. I was very focused. I didn't know if I was running for CEO at the time or not.

It's interesting. When you have smaller organizations, some leaders take the *"my way or the highway"* type of attitude. Either you do it my way or you're gone and you are out the door. As you move more and more into the business world, you have to realize that there's a lot more balance than that. You have to have a much larger perception of the world and people. You have to really start to understand everybody else's perspective on things. Linda brought so much more to the table than the cronies that I had around me—the ones who would say yes all the time. They were like me and I realized that if I was going to exist in this business world very long in this Valley, that I couldn't have people around me just like me. Now the problem with that is "like me" is real simple. In fact, there is a company stereotype that exists right now in this organization called "friends of Dave." I had no idea it even existed until I had to go through the process of becoming CEO of Amdahl.

Linda: Yes. It's perceived that if you are a friend of Dave's you are going to succeed in this company and if you are not you won't go far.

David: However, I was oblivious to the whole perception. I think what really opened up my eyes was when Linda started taking a different approach to me. It became very confusing. I remember thinking is this a blessing or should I look at it with a little apprehension? You have a feeling the person really isn't supportive of you and then all of a sudden she comes across a little differently.

When we started talking, I said to myself, this is a person who has something that I don't have. She fits a different perspective. When we really started talking, I realized she was a blessing. She is very strong financially, has better strategic thinking than I do (and still does today), can see things differently than I can see them.

Linda: Unless you are making a strategic effort to listen for different voices, to add diversity, to pick out people who are knowledgeable in certain areas, you really get sort of cushioned. Particularly when you get in a period when you're at the top in an organization as opposed to when you are in the middle. When you're in the middle, you pick up a wealth of conversations and knowledge from others. When you are at the top, you get very cushioned by whom you communicate with.

David: You really do. Besides the fact that I found out I really liked Linda, and, by the way, I think at the same time she started figuring out she liked me. Then all of a sudden that energy started working in a much more positive way.

Linda: As a leader, I am more a facilitator. My role is definitely getting everyone's views out on the table and to make sure they understand each other's views and from that exercise come the answers. For example, I'm in crisis right now as happens with many startup firms. I had this brain trust meeting a few days ago. We spent hours covering scenarios and strategy. Several days after the meeting, I questioned whether or not I should be more of an authoritarian leader because I am in a crisis. This is despite the fact I don't believe in authoritarian management. Yet, the one place I had left for that style of management was crisis. I realized I still believed that when a company gets into crisis that's when you, as leader, must revert to authoritarian leadership. Why? Because it's your job. However, I now no longer even believe there is a place for authoritarianism in crisis. I saw that after our meeting, I already had voice mails from every person who was in the room giving me an update on the steps they had taken since our meeting. I know that no amount of authoritarian

(continued)

leadership would have motivated the people outside of my company who had critical roles to play to take the action they took.

David: An authoritarian relationship is one of direction, not necessarily control and command.

Linda: Right, I agree. Yet, I still believed it took a dictator when things were in crisis. That would have been the best way to cut through the whole situation. It certainly would have been much simpler. Yet, I don't believe it would have led to the same results. I would now, from this one experience, dispute the need for authoritarian leadership in crisis. I have some extraordinary people with whom I am working. I would say my perception has really changed. I think management consists of getting good people, not just experts in their field. They are people who are willing to express their opinions, who leave their egos at the door. I had 3 or 4 former CEOs in this meeting and every one of them checked their ego at the door. A good team member is not necessarily what the old paradigm was either. It's more about the whole way you as a leader interact with the rest of the team. It is very important to be part of the team. And it isn't acquiescing either. It's a strange combination of strength and willingness, and vulnerability, and the willingness to listen and participate rather than always having to be right. It is *very* different from the way both of us operated 10 years ago.

David: It's a belief system I had 10 years ago. No question about it. However, it wasn't the way I was operating 10 years ago. I think you see these kind of people in the Valley today. It's an interesting study. John Chambers of Cisco was here the other day. He is an exercise in what we're talking about. He's a pretty balanced guy. Understands where he came from, what's going on. He allows people to be the leaders they need to be in the time they need.

It used to be knowledge was power. Now knowledge is everywhere. If you try to be the knowledge power broker today, you will die in the marketplace. You will completely lose where you are. Therefore, I think that the role of CEO today changes based on the circumstances. But the style shouldn't change, just the role you play. Sometimes you will be the head of the class, sometimes you will be in the class listening to somebody else. I think when one walks through the door, it doesn't matter if you are a man or woman, the scientist or the accountant or the CEO or the project manager. It is that you're part of this whole organization as long as you and the organization share common goals.

I think these issues became clearer to me when I started the practice of writing down the goals and commitments I had as well as those of others within the company. The process enabled the people I work with to realize that I had some of their same fundamental values and direction.

Linda: The profit-and-loss side of the business is easy. It's getting people to execute, to commit, to create that has always been the most difficult piece.

David: I think what's going to fix this world is the business community. It's not politics or governments. Business leaders who realize that the people issue is a lot bigger than just a company. As we continue to use technology to educate and to learn things, we have to be concerned and focused on our values and about the "have nots," especially in the Third World countries. Because there are no barriers in technology, we are really global and where you don't have the infrastructures and the values, it becomes a very large world problem. This "soft stuff," the issues of people, becomes increasingly more important in the world we live in today.

as in a lifeboat, for instance, or in an army group or in a surgical team. Then, in such situations there may be flat orders, without apology, without diplomacy, without delicacy. In such a situation, of course, the B-leader would have to have the ability to give orders without feeling guilty about it, feeling that he was taking advantage or getting into a tizzy about it in any way. Furthermore, if his job is to give out life sentences or death sentences, then he must be able to do this too without falling apart. That is one of the objective requirements of the objective leader in that objective situation. Of course, this might be extremely unsuitable in another situation. I think what I'm trying to say here is that there are many situations in which the boss ought to be very strong and authoritative boss, although in large-scale industrial situations my guess is that participative management and therefore participative managers are more often needed objectively than the strong boss who can bark out an order and have it executed immediately without any question.

But to some extent my vague feeling is that we can generalize about practically all leaders or bosses that they *should* be able to pay attention to the objective requirements of the situation without fussing too much about the delicate sensitivity of the followers or of the employees, of the people who have to take orders. For instance, I think most leaders have to be able to withstand hostility, that is, to be unpopular, without falling apart. The kind of person who must be loved by all probably will not make a good leader in most situations (although I can conceive of a few in which just this quality would be an asset rather than a liability). The leader must be able to say "no," to be decisive, to be strong enough to do battle, if that is objectively necessary, to be tough, to fire, to hurt people, to give pain, etc. Or to put it in another way, the boss in most situations cannot afford to be what we call weak, which is the obverse of what I've been saying. He must not be ruled by fear. He must be courageous enough for the situation.

(Therefore, I would say certain kinds of neurotic people are probably excluded from bosshoods of most kinds. For instance, a man stuck at the safety-need level could not be a good boss in most situations because he would be too afraid of retaliation, because he would seek safety rather than problem solution or productivity or creativeness or whatever; in short, he would be too vulnerable. So also the man who is stuck at the love-need level, whose main purpose is to be loved by all, to be popular, to be appreciated, and who, therefore, could not bear to give up the love of any particular person.)

Ideally here the strong boss would be, then, one who has all his basic needs gratified, that is, the needs for safety, for belongingness, for loving and for being loved, for prestige and respect, and finally for self-confidence and self-esteem. This is the same as saying that the closer a person approaches toward self-actualizing, the better leader or boss he is apt to be in the general sense of the largest number of situations.

Of course, the same thing is true for the B-follower as well, since the personality requirements for him are about the same as for the B-leader. This latter statement reminds me of a slogan which helps me in many such theoretical situations, i.e., "Every man a general." That is, every man in the ideal or perfect society or situation would be able to become a functional leader wherever he was the most suitable one for the job. He could take control, be boss, give orders, gauge the situation, etc. Every man in a democratic society ought to be a general, ought to be able to be a boss, or a leader in some situations at least. This is a little like saying that he ought to value the B-values, ought to be able to have righteous indignation, and ought to *want* to foster truth and beauty and justice, etc. Every man, then, ought to have broad enough shoulders so that he can enjoy taking on responsibilities, rather than feeling burdened and overloaded by responsibilities.

INTERVIEW WITH NANCY OLSEN OF IMPOSTERS

It is not that people are divided into leaders and followers. Everybody knows exactly what the goal is and is doing his best and making his own best contribution toward this goal. He is therefore as much a general as anybody else.

—*Abraham Maslow*

Nancy Olsen is an entrepreneur extraordinare. Having launched several successful businesses, she is most noted for her launch of the national retail jewelry store chain called Imposters. Under Nancy's leadership, the chain grew to 120 stores nationwide.

★ ★ ★

What do you believe the role of the leader is?

The process of becoming a leader is analogous to that of a musical conductor. At the start, you spend many years acquiring the knowledge and skill required to play an instrument. Perhaps you learn several instruments. You begin by playing a solo where you are the lone element. Before too long, you play with another person in a duet. The duet is still rather easy because you are close to the other player, can look into his or her eyes to keep the beat and create the harmony.

As your grasp of the music and your experience grows, you find yourself leading a quartet, then a chamber orchestra. You learn how important each and every player is. If the first violin is off key, or the French horn is off beat, the entire musical piece is affected. Instead of the audience focusing on the beauty of the music, they focus on the one weak player or the one fault in the whole. At this point, you might be able to fill in for one of the musicians, in a pinch.

Eventually you are in the position of conducting a full symphony orchestra. As you look out, you know all of the musicians *want* to be there. They want to perform. After all, nobody practices bass for years and doesn't want to play. You also know that as the conductor, they are looking to you to bring them together. To bring the passion and feeling of the music together. To make each musician a part of the whole. You realize that not only can't you dash about playing each instrument yourself, you don't even know how to play many of them! So, you begin. You begin by pulling together everything you know, everything you've learned, everything you are, and you lead.

As the music ends, the musicians take in a large breath and say "WOW! I am so glad I was a part of that magnificent piece." As you turn to the audience you see through their applause that they are also thinking "WOW, I'm so glad I was a part of this audience."

Another aspect of this is that the good boss or the good leader in most situations must have as a psychological prerequisite the ability to take pleasure in the growth and self-actualization of other people. That is to say, he ought to be parental or fatherly. If one had to define a father, very briefly it would be about the way in which I've defined the perfect boss. He must be strong in the above senses, he must enjoy responsibility, that is, of supporting a wife and children; he must be able to mete out discipline as necessary, to be stern as well as loving; he ought to be able to be a captain or a general; he ought to be able to get great gratification out of watching his children grow up well and out of watching his wife develop her personality well and grow on toward greater maturity and self-actualization. Each of these are requirements for the good manager as well. The only point is that the good manager must also be able to be a good B-follower, that is, he must be able to take the reins and be the boss in that situation where he has to and to do this well, but he must also not need to be the boss in every conceivable situation, i.e., he must be able to play second violin when there is a better first violinist and must be able to enjoy this situation exactly as much as when he himself plays first violin or is the soloist.

Oh, another thing about the good father and therefore also about the good leader is that if he is really and sufficiently sensitive to the requirements of reality, then he is able to be unpopular with his children for the time being. That is, he must be able to say "no," to discipline, to deny, and to be stern in situations where his superior knowledge or his superior ability to renounce or to delay gratification tells him that his children's impulsiveness and inability to delay is a bad thing. The father who says "no" under such circumstances is apt to become unpopular, but he must be able to withstand this in the faith that in the long run truth, honesty, justice, and objectivity will win everybody his just rewards. That is, one must be able to be unloved, unpopular, to be laughed at, to be attacked, and still to be able to see the objective requirements of the situation and to respond to them rather than to these interpersonal satisfactions for the moment.

(I think science, taken as a social institution exemplifies all of these points. It is "leaderless," or better said, each scientist is a leader.)

The Superior Person—
The "Aggridant"
(Biologically Superior and
Dominant) Person

The nice thing about this whole new management business (enlightened management) is that from which ever point you start, whether from the point of view of what is best for personal development of people or from what is best for making a profit and turning out good products, the results seem to be almost exactly the same—that which is good for personal development is also good for turning our products and so on, the results seem to be almost exactly the same.

I think it will be pertinent to use the Dove[1] experiment here on the aggridant chickens (bigger, stronger, dominant) who were the good choosers, and who were thereby distinguished from the poor choosers. None of the writers that I have been reading on management dares to confront the profound political implications of the fact which is so unpopular in any democracy that some people are superior to others in any given skill or capacity and also that there is some evidence to indicate that some people tend to be generally superior, that they are simply superior biological organisms born into the world. For the latter I can use the Terman[2] kind of data which indicates that all desirable traits tend to correlate positively, i.e., those people who are

---

[1] W. F. Dove, "A Study of Individuality in the Nutritive Instincts," *American Naturalist,* vol. 69 (1935), pp. 469–574.
[2] L. M. Terman and M. H. Oden, *The Gifted Group at Mid-Life* (Stanford: Stanford University Press, 1959).

superior in intelligence tend to be superior in everything else, or those people who are selected out because they are physically healthy tend to also be superior in everything else. (A thought here. Could this general superiority be part of the explanation for those who seem to be unlucky all the time, or lucky all the time? Or maybe this is the place to talk about the schlemiel personality.)

Dove's superior chickens were superior in everything. That is, they got the best of everything; they were higher in the dominance hierarchy; they were bigger, stronger, healthier, they had better feathers, they had more sex drive and more sex contacts, they got the best of the food, etc. But the important point was that when Dove analyzed their choice of diet in the cafeteria situation, it was from the human point of view a superior diet to that chosen by the inferior chickens—the smaller, weaker, less dominant, less healthy ones. Dove tied up the whole business neatly and avoided all sorts of difficult questions by then taking the diet which the superior chickens had chosen and feeding the inferior chickens with it. What turned out was that the inferior chickens improved, they got bigger and stronger and more dominant and had healthier feathers, etc., but they never got as superior as the superior chickens. That is, they went about 50 percent of the way up from their inferiority to the superior chickens. They gained weight and got stronger, but never quite as strong as the chickens that were superior by sheer constitution and heredity in the first place.

What this might imply for the management and the work situation is a little startling. If we seek for B-leaders, that is, the people who are by constitution and heredity and by biological endowment good functional leaders or bosses for a particular job—for instance, they might be the most intelligent ones—then there are several assumptions implied here, one is that they are born that way and, of course, this must be investigated in the long run as a possibility. (Just how hereditary and constitutional is the I.Q., the good body, the superior physical ability, superior energy and forcefulness, superior ego strength, etc.)

Another question is, what to do with these people and how to handle them. Such people would gravitate to the top of the society as cream rises to the top of the milk. And to some extent this may contradict the whole notion of functional leadership as I described it above, because maybe, after all, the superior person tends to be superior in everything, that is, maybe the one who is the best person in one leadership situation is a little more likely than chance to be superior, to be the best leader in a different situation. This is like saying that there are superior and inferior leaders and followers by nature and by biology and what is the society going to do about this? How does this fit in with democracy and so on. It also raises the question of the "countervalues," of Nietzschean resentment, of the resentment of the superior, of the jealousy of excellence, of the hatred or hostility to the person who is more beautiful than we are or more intelligent than we are or more lucky than we are or whatever. No society can function unless the inferiors have the ability to admire the superiors, or at least not to hate them nor attack them. Also, no society and no enterprise can be really efficient unless superior people are freely chosen and elected by the other people. This is part of the requirement of the ideal situation. A person should be able to detect objectively the particular level of I.Q., for example, or physical strength in the other person and then be able to say to him, "You are physically stronger than I am; therefore, you will make the better leader for this particular job," and then be able to do this without resentment, without feeling a loss of self-esteem, without destroying self-respect.

It's a funny thing how this whole delicate problem is ducked by everybody in the whole society. For instance, we talk about every man having a vote while the fact is that a good 10 or 20 percent of the population don't have votes and never will. For instance, the people who are locked up in jails and insane asylums, who are feeble-minded, who are physically so handicapped that they live in hospitals all their lives and can't move, the senile people who have to be taken care of, the helpless cripples, and god knows how many other kinds of people. This must be a good 10 percent of the population at least whom we simply tell what to do, whom we care for as if they were pet animals or something of the sort. They don't have a vote; nobody listens to the insane person or the feeble-minded person. And if we remember that 2 percent of the population is technically feeble-minded, this is already one person in fifty who is not a really functioning, autonomous member of the society. I haven't thought this through, but I'm sure it needs thinking through. I think the thing to do is to reread Nietzsche on the slave morality or the morality of the weak in contrast to the morality of the strong. It raises questions.

For instance, in our society there's some tendency for people who are superior at anything to feel sort of guilty about it and to be apologetic. There are many people who are "losers" in the sense that they simply can't win; they get too disturbed and too guilty and feel too selfish and too crass and too overbearing. This loser type or better say, the one-who-doesn't-dare-to-win type has really not been studied or analyzed sufficiently. Well, if we are to understand leadership and bosshood in a democracy, we had better study them and get to know more about them.

Another question that comes to my mind is this: While on the whole it's better to have one vote for each person no matter what the facts are about constitutional superiority, this is clearly not a good idea in the ordinary industrial situation where under competitive circumstances simple pragmatic success and productivity means industrial life or death. Whether in a socialist society or capitalist society or communist society or fascist society it really shouldn't make any difference in this regard. The particular factory is supposed to do a good job or it will fail just so long as there is a free and open market or competition. Therefore, factual superiority simply must be sought out. In this area people are definitely not interchangeable and definitely don't have one vote per person or at least shouldn't have. The only circumstance that I can think of that would permit this to happen would be a cutting out of competition or a kind of protected situation like the one that exists in Spain now, where a factory can be absolutely inefficient, and since there is no competition it doesn't matter. So long as there is the free-choice situation in the world, or open competition as in the common market now, just so long will there be the factual necessity for discovering the factually superior managers and workers, and also will there be the factual and objective necessity for doing things in the best possible way. The ones who do things in the best possible way are the ones who will corner the whole market for automobiles or radios or whatever and the others will simply die economically.

With respect to the aggridant person, then, the question is, how much self-respect or openly admitted superiority or arrogance or boastfulness or healthy selfishness shall we allow such a person to have? In our society, in the United States, certainly superiority is generally hidden. Nobody runs around saying in company how superior he is. This just isn't done, but the fact remains that as psychological science moves forward, we know more and more about ourselves and in a very objective way, I know what my I.Q. is and I know what my personality test scores are and what the Rorschach is and so on, and while it's permitted to me to say in public what my weaknesses are, it is certainly not permitted to me to say what my superiorities are. This is a real weakness in the society, I should say, so far as managers and bosses are concerned. We arrange things in such a fashion that the boss or leader or general or successful person tends to be put on the defensive. But should this be so in a perfectly mobile and ideal society in which cream does rise to the top, and contrariwise that which rises to the top is therefore cream?

I'm reminded of my Blackfoot Indians where the correlation between wealth and skill, intelligence, and so on was almost perfect. Wealth there was a very good indication of capability. In the ideal society this would certainly happen. Success and wealth of any kind and status would then be perfectly correlated with actual capacity and skill and talent. As a matter of fact that's the way we could define a good society if we wanted to, as one in which all those who are on the top deserve to be there; or those who were elected to high office were the very best persons in the society; and those who were the best people in the society were necessarily elected to the highest offices, etc. For instance, in the United States we are very careful not to be ostentatious. But this is certainly different from the Blackfoot Indians who were very boastful, not in our bad sense necessarily but in just about the same spirit in which we put degrees after our names, as a simple sign of achievement which we have a right to have.

The Plains Indians generally for each coup that they managed or each success were entitled to put an eagle feather in their war bonnets. We have all sorts of situations of the same sort, especially in the Army where medals are put on the chest to show how good we are or the little red ribbon in France means that you are a member of the Academy or Phi Beta Kappa key means what a good student you were, etc., etc. My guess is that this kind of innocent boastfulness, innocent showing off, has deep roots in human nature and had better be allowed or maybe even encouraged.

All of these considerations bring up the question that I've brought up in other contexts of the relationship of the leader or the boss to the people whom he might have to order around or fire or punish. Again I think that we might as well be realistic about this, the truth of the matter is that our attitude toward anyone who has power over us, even if it's the most benevolent power, is a little different from our attitude toward those who are our equals, i.e., who have no power over us. This has to do with participative management, with democratic management, with the interpersonal relations in the industrial situation. It might in some situations, perhaps in many situations, be better for the manager or the boss, as it is now for the general in the army, to remain in a certain isolation and to maintain a certain distance and objectivity and detachment from the people that he might have to discipline, just exactly in the same way as we now recognize that therapists should not stand in any other rewarding or punishing relationship to the patient; for instance, the psychotherapist cannot be a teacher and give grades to his patients, because this could destroy the therapeutic function.

Also I think I would affirm again that the leader in many situations ought *not* to be as expressive and open about himself as other people are permitted and encouraged to be. Again here I think of the example of the captain of the ship which is in danger, or the surgeon or the general in the army who may entertain all sorts of dark suspicions and fears and so on but who had better keep their mouths shut rather than open up freely about their anxieties. This is for the simple reason that such open expressiveness would be dysfunctional by tending to break up the morale of the organization, by destroying confidence, etc. Perhaps it had better be added as one of the requirements for general bosshood that he should have the power and the ability to keep his mouth shut and not express anything which is dysfunctional for the group, but that rather he must take upon his own shoulders the responsibility for the worry and the anxiety and the tension that may be necessary. (Make sure that there's no confusion here about the openness and the sense of listening. Certainly, one characteristic of any good manager or leader is that he be able to know what's going on. Therefore, he must have his ears wide open and be able to assimilate and to receive information. So also for his eyes; he ought to be able to see clearly. But this is different from openness in the sense of talking and of revealing yourself and your inner experiences.)

One of the advantages of being a leader is that one can have one's own way. This implies that the boss is one who particularly needs to have his own way or gets special pleasure from it. And then, with the assumption that the B-leader enjoys and fosters the B-values, having his own way means the ability, the power to set things right in the world that needs setting right, and of getting great personal pleasure from this. If I'm to be the B-boss, then I must get a special kick out of doing a good job or seeing a good job done, of forming a good and efficient, smooth-running organization, or of turning out an especially good product, or the like. This is a kind of instinct of workmanship at a higher level which has to be taken very seriously in the future.

Another thing that is implied by this ideal situation is that then it would be best for the B-boss to be what Fromm[3] calls healthily selfish. Presumably if he follows his own private impulses, does just what pleases him most and what he instinctively tends to do, gets rid of what irritates him most, and tries to please himself and have pleasure in gratifying himself, then this is exactly what is good for the world. (Because what pleases him most is to improve the world, and what irritates him most is to see the B-values destroyed.) Here again is a beautiful example of synergy. He can demonstrate by permitting himself to be perfectly selfish and by our perhaps wishing him or urging him to be perfectly selfish, and by following his own impulses about what to do, that this is exactly the best way to make a better world.

Another way of putting this concept of the B-leader into three dimensions is this: Suppose that there were an enterprise which was cooperatively owned, let's say by 300 people, then what management principles would these 300 people choose in the long run, i.e., what would be to their various interests. Let us assume that they were intelligent and fairly healthy. Then I think it could be shown that they would inevitably have to come out with enlightened management principles; that they would have to employ or elect a B-type leader (if they needed a leader); that they would have to become B-type followers; and that they would have to introject the directives and objectives of the plant, in pursuance of all their own perfectly selfish interests, both in terms of productivity—of the factory, of profit, of a good growing organization—on the one hand and on the other hand, in terms of all the questions of personal development, of growth, of self-actualization, of a happy place to work, etc. All of these things in the ideal situation must be theoretically synergic.

Certainly, this group of 300 people wouldn't want the factory to fail. Well, the best way of having the factory not fail is to have the best kind of management and social organization and personal growth

---

[3] E. Fromm, *Escape from Freedom* (New York: Farrar & Rinehart, 1941).

and so on and so on and so on. Everything follows in a logical and orderly fashion here. For one thing, it would obviously be very desirable, especially since each of these 300 people was a general, to vote, I am sure, for setting up conditions under which they could enjoy their work, that is to say, in which they could enjoy living, enjoy their lives. Point out that the nice thing about this whole new management business is that from whichever point you start, whether from the point of view of what is best for personal development of people or from the other point of what is best for making a profit and turning out good products and so on, the results seem to be almost exactly the same. That which is good for personal development is also good for turning out good automobiles, in the long run at least. And that which is good for turning out good automobiles in the long run, and for having a good functioning factory which is to last for a long time, then it turns out that this is good for personal development of the workers.

I quote from the Tannenbaum[4] book on leadership on page 74: "Managers differ greatly in the amount of trust they have in other people generally and this carries over to the particular employees they supervise at a given time." This emphasis on "trust" reminds me again of the contrast between the new piety and the new dogmas of democratic management which can be contrasted with realism and veridical diagnosis of the realities of the situation. In this passage Tannenbaum goes on to point out that the question of trust in people certainly varies as a character trait from manager to manager, but that there's also involved the realistic question of "who is best qualified to deal with this problem." Sometimes it is realistic to trust; sometimes it is unrealistic to trust. To trust psychopaths or paranoiacs is a very foolish thing. Any dogma that says we must trust everybody is apt to be unrealistic.

On the same page the question is raised also of the differences in the character trait of directiveness. "There are some managers who seem to function more comfortably and naturally as highly directive leaders. Resolving problems and issuing orders come easily to them. Other managers seem to operate more comfortably in a team role, where they are continually sharing many of their functions with their

[4] R. Tannenbaum, I. Weschler, and F. Massarik, *Leadership and Management* (New York: McGraw-Hill, 1961).

subordinates." Not only is this a variable in characterology; it is also a variable in situations. There are some situations which demand the highly directive leader as in a captain of a ship or the commander of an army group or of a submarine; there are other situations which demand realistically the team sharer. This is to say, we have to accept both of these variables as realities and then try to fit the right manager to the right situation. But *certainly* we must be very careful not to fall into the trap of regarding the highly directive leader as, e.g., un-democratic. Some people are built this way constitutionally and the thing to do is to understand this and to accept it as much as possible and put it to the most profitable use in the most profitable situation. The one danger here is again of dogma.

I think we should add one element that has not yet been discussed or pointed out sufficiently in the psychological makeup of the highly directive leader: that is, a stronger Gestalt motivation. He is more irked than other people are by lack of neatness, lack of order, lack of aesthetic rounding out, lack of completeness, etc. This is the kind of person who simply *has to* straighten the crooked picture on the wall. It just bothers him more than it bothers other people. This is the person who needs to perfect the environment more than other people and for him, having power to do this is a very wonderful thing. As a matter of fact, it may be the main reward for having power. Such a person may be willing to take on all the nuisances, responsibilities, irritations, and self-abnegations of power just so that he can retain in his own hands the power to get rid of irritating incompletions, lack of neatness, lack of closure, and the like.

This kind of thing should supplement the usual discussions which seem to focus more around the question of constitutional endowment, with urge to dominance. Even with respect to dominance the picture has not been drawn well enough by the students of leadership theory. They seem not to know about the great amount of work that's been done with animals and especially with the monkeys and apes. There seems (to me) little question from all of this material that dominance has, among other determinants, a constitutional determinant as well. That is to say, we can assume that people are born different with respect to the qualities of need to be in control, of need to defer, need to be passive or to be active, proneness to anger or to flight, etc. They should add also the new physiological information on the difference between adrenalin and noradrenalin. This factor alone, probably hereditary, is enough to account for a good deal of the personal variation in proneness to fight or to flee, to be active or to be passive (9, 12, 19, 28, 78).

And yet I don't want to lose among the complexity and multitude of variables which have influence in a discussion of leadership, the neglected variable or the frightening variable, perhaps, of general biological superiority, of general aggridance. The leader in all averaged-out situations tends to be superior in all the desirable characteristics. And this is just as it should be. In accordance with the objective demands of reality, the leader ought to be more efficient, more capable, more talented than the follower. It just makes more pragmatic sense, and is more likely to ensure successful outcome. Tannenbaum[5] on page 79 stresses very correctly the perceptiveness which is desirable in the successful leader. (Obviously, a leader who was blind or who was not open to information could not assess the situation well and therefore would be more likely to be unsuccessful.) But this superior perceptiveness, this greater ability at B-cognition, correlates with psychological health; which means again that psychological health co-varies with successful leadership.

[5] *Op. cit.*

The Very Superior Boss

*The objective requirements of the particular situation or prob-
lem should be the main determinant of leadership policy and
followership policy.*

There is a special realistic situation which sometimes occurs, and which makes all of us democratic people very uncomfortable: that is, great factual superiority of a particular person over his colleagues. This tends to confuse the whole point of the requiredness of the situation, and the kind of leadership which should prevail. For instance, discussion and participative management style is obviously less possible, or at least is more costly, in a situation where five people with I.Q.'s of 120 are teamed up with a leader of I.Q. 160. To talk things out, to let people discover things for themselves, to let people participate slowly in working their way toward a good solution to a problem—all of this is much more difficult in this situation than in the more average one. For one thing, the superior person is apt to get extremely restless and irritated in such a situation, and the strain upon his body is apt to be much greater because of the necessity for controlling himself and inhibiting his impulses. He may easily and quickly see the truth that all the others are struggling toward very slowly and keeping his mouth shut can be physical torture.

Another trouble is that at one level or another of consciousness, everybody perceives this discrepancy in I.Q. The tendency then will be for the less intelligent ones slowly to fall into the habit of waiting for the more intelligent one to give the solution. That is, they are less apt to work hard because the work is useless and senseless. Why should they sweat for three days to work toward the solution of a particular problem when they know all the time that the superior can see the solution in three minutes? The tendency, therefore, is for

177

all the others to become more passive. By contrast they may feel less capable than they actually are, more stupid than they actually are, etc.

In addition to these direct consequences, hostility and resentment are almost certain to develop at the unconscious level. The less conscious everybody is of the actual situation, the more likely there are to be the counterresentments. The person who is made at some deep level to feel stupid is apt to think himself the target of malevolence, i.e., he thinks the other person is *trying* to make him feel stupid, and then he gets hostile and angry in defense of his self-esteem. I would predict that the more conscious everybody is of this situation, the more insight they have into it, the less this counterresentment and counterhostility might be, at least in decent people. There would then be less need for repression and defense mechanisms to safeguard the self-esteem.

Another variable in this situation, then, would be time and the time span. Obviously, where quick decisions are needed, the superior must make these decisions quickly and directively, authoritatively, and without much discussion. Orders must be given, without explanation if necessary. On the other hand, if the situation has a long time span, as in building up a business which is to last for fifty or a hundred years, and especially if it is to be stable enough to last past the death of the superior, then greater patience is required and greater participative management, more explanations, more giving out of facts, more discussion of the facts, and common agreement upon the conclusions. This is the only way to train good managers and good leaders in the long run. I suppose there's apt to be some contrast here between the two main goals of good management. The simple goal of production and profit would press the admitted superior toward more authoritativeness; the goal of developing personality and thereby developing promotable possible managers and sucessors would press the admitted superior toward more discussion and participative management and away from directive and authoritative leadership. This is a little like saying again that the ideal management policies are best under good conditions in a good world for management of good people. If we had a peaceful, one-world society in which there were none of the present emergencies and in which we could patiently work toward the improvement of mankind, then the more participative management would be more desirable, even under this very special condition of admitted superiority.

The same thing roughly can be true of admitted superiority in certain personality traits, especially the one of ego strength, which for the moment I could define as the greater-than-average ability to tolerate anxiety, depression, and anger. If the boss is very much stronger in this trait than his managerial colleagues, then we are apt to work into a similar situation as with the admittedly high I.Q. Such a manager will take all sorts of things upon his own shoulders without explanation, without participation, simply because he recognizes that he is better able to handle the problem than any of the others.

(I think that I could use here my analysis of the paranoid leaders. The general point was to understand why it was that obviously borderline people like Hitler or Stalin or Senator McCarthy or some of the Birchers or people of this sort can gather so many followers. It seemed clear that one reason that they could was because they were so decisive, so sure of themselves, so unwavering, so definite about what they wanted and didn't want, so clear about right and wrong, etc. In a nation in which most people do not have an identity, or a real self, in which they are all confused about right and wrong, about good and evil, in which they are basically uncertain about what they want and what they don't want, then they are apt to admire and succumb to and look for leadership to any person who seems to know definitely what he wants. Since the democratic leader, the nonauthoritarian person in general, is apt to be marked by tolerance and by admission of ignorance, by willingness to admit that he doesn't know everything, sometimes for less educated people the decisive paranoid authoritarian then can look very attractive and relieve the follower of all anxiety. Quote here the Grand Inquisitor section in Dostoievsky's *The Brothers Karamazov*. Quote here also David Riesman's "other-directed" person. Also Fromm's robot personality. Well, this is obviously a relevant variable in any discussion of leadership of any kind in any situation.)

The person who is able to be decisive, who is able to make a decision and then stick to it, who is able to know definitely what he wants, to know that he likes this and dislikes that and no uncertainty about it, who is less apt to be changeable, who is more likely to be predictable, to be counted on, who is less suggestible, less influenced by contradiction—such a person is in general more apt to be selected out by others as leader. I think this may be one reason why so frequently obsessional persons are more apt to be chosen as the administrative type or the executive type or the leadership type. They are simply more predictable, more definite about what they like and dislike, less changeable, etc. The fact that this may be for pathological reasons need not be visible to the psychologically unsophisticated person.

I can quote here also from McGregor,[1] page 139, his section which is labeled "Confidence Downward" and which is much like the Tannenbaum passage: "Consider a manager who holds people in relatively low esteem. He sees himself as a member of a small elite, endowed with unusual capacities and the bulk of the human race as rather limited." But then I ask the counterquestion, suppose he *is* actually endowed with unusual capacities? Suppose he *is* actually a member of a small elite? Suppose he *is* unusually superior in some quality? McGregor is not taking this sufficiently into account as a real possibility. I must point out to McGregor that such a realistic perception of an unusual superiority can be absolutely compatible with holding to Theory Y. The greatly superior manager can in fact agree with McGregor in having a relatively high opinion of the intelligence and capacity of the average human being. Page 140:

> He sees most human beings as having real capacity for growth and development, for the acceptance of responsibility, for creative accomplishments. He regards his subordinates as genuine assets in helping him fulfill his own responsibilities, and he is concerned with creating the conditions which enable him to realize these assets. He does not feel that people in general are stupid, lazy, irresponsible, dishonest, or antagonistic. He is aware that there are such individuals, but he expects to encounter them only rarely. In short he holds to theory "Y."

But the admittedly superior manager can absolutely agree with all of this and still recognize the facts of an unusual situation. I think this whole discussion of Theory X and Theory Y can be clarified a little bit in this way. (By the way, I should also mention that this is no longer quite a theory, but is rather a fact. There is empirical evidence to support Theory Y for most American citizens, and there is empirical evidence to disconfirm Theory X for most American citizens. It can almost be called fact "X" and fact "Y.")

I am interested that McGregor on page 145 still uses the managerial and leadership terms which are very inappropriate to the Theory Y kind of approach. For instance, he talks about superior-subordinate

---

[1] D. McGregor, *The Human Side of Enterprise,* (New York: McGraw-Hill, 1960).

relationships. He talks about the principle of authority, the chain of command, and so on. Obviously, these words do not apply very well to B-leaders and B-followers, no more than they would apply to a really well-integrated basketball team, for instance. We had better find other words (which do not yet exist) to describe the B-psychology type of authority, leadership, etc., *not* using the words which are our heritage from an authoritarian situation which was thought to be the *only* kind of leadership situation. (Support for this conclusion comes from the lack of words to describe the B-psychology of leadership and followership.)

One conclusion I came to from trying to analyze this strong man, strong boss situation was that in view of the fact that openness of communication could hardly be expected in a perfect form in such a situation, in either direction—that is, upward or downward—then one technique by which the boss could handle this situation and avoid being the overpowering, overwhelming force which he ordinarily has to be, is simply to absent himself frequently from the group discussions. Undoubtedly, if he is highly superior, he will inhibit the whole group. If he wants them to develop personally, if he wants to cultivate them and their capacities, then he had best recognize that they will talk much more freely, be themselves more freely, actualize themselves more freely, when he is absent. This is one way that he can demonstrate his love for them, his respect, his trust, and his pleasure in their self-actualization.

It might be a loss for him to absent himself from all sorts of situations, but I think the objective facts require it rather frequently, just as the kindest thing that a very beautiful mother can do for her less attractive daughters is to get out of their way when the boys are around and not be a perpetual reminder to them of their own inferiority. Very intelligent or very creative or talented parents frequently will have to do the same thing in order not to overwhelm their children or to make them feel inferior, to make then feel helpless and passive and hopeless about ever rivaling their parents, whether in ability to paint or to be beautiful or to be intelligent or to be strong or whatever. Self-actualizing people pretty often have had rather unfortunate effects upon their children. This makes a very dramatic and very convincing demonstration of this point, because everybody a priori expects that wonderful people will make wonderful parents and that wonderful parents will make wonderful children. Point out that it's not so good for kids to have wonderful parents. Or at least say it this way, that bad parents create certain problems, but wonderful parents also create certain problems which may be *different* but which are still problems.

I think I would recommend also to the strong man to watch out for the trap of condescension, i.e., of phony discussions, of phony asking of opinions, of phony group dynamics. If the strong man knows the answer all the time and is simply trying to figure out some sly way of tricking the group into thinking that they have discovered it all by themselves, then most often this will not work and will simply breed resentments. This is, of course, an extremely difficult problem, a profoundly human and existential problem, which in truth has no good solution even in theory. The fact is that great superiority is unjust, undeserved, and that people can and do resent it and complain of injustice and unfairness of fate. There's no answer to this because the fact is that fate *is* unfair in giving one newborn baby a good body and in giving another one a bad heart or bad kidneys or whatever. I don't know of any good solution to this situation which demands honesty but in which honesty and truth must necessarily hurt.

In the ideal society, in eupsychia, it seems very clear that the ability to admire, the ability to follow, the ability to choose the most efficient leader, the ability to detect factual superiority, all these are needed in order for it or *any* culture to work, and they must all go together with a minimum of antagonism and hostility to the superiors. This antagonism and hostility varies in different ways in the leadership situation. What I'm trying to say is that it can be teased apart into different variables. For instance, one of the variables in our present cultural situation which the leadership people don't seem to talk about or to realize is the one of class antagonism. The armed forces used to be able to handle this very well because officers were upper and middle class and were therefore gentlemen, and the enlisted men were lower class and were therefore not gentlemen. The antagonism between them and the contempt and condescension and this, that, and the other were taken for granted. I think something of the same sort is probably still true in the Navy, the Army. My guess is that it is also true even in our upwardly mobile society. It must be conceded that in the Army and Navy or other huge organizations or in total societies, a "book of laws" is needed, perhaps all written down in great detail, much like our written constitutions and actual lawbooks and coded laws and so on. This is partly because such populations are so heterogeneous and so

THE LOOKY LOOS

We were surprised by the sheer number of inquiries from executives, literally from all over the world, regarding these journals. We asked colleagues, leaders, and management experts for their insights regarding the intense interest in a journal that was nearly 37 years old. One comment stuck with us.

Allan Webber, founding editor of *Fast Company* magazine summarized the interest best when he told us that *"it's true that management in the United States has a tendency to look for silver bullets and fads. It's also true that we've been down this path before with the sociotechnical movement. All that said, this is still the hardest thing to do and to do right. Maslow's ideas deserve to be raised and examined and promoted. All of the technology in the world only makes the human element more important."*

In the eye of this hurricane of interest, it appeared that two categories were emerging: the "looky loos" and the "participants." Looky loos, first coined by Professor Dave Hickey of the University of Nevada Las Vegas, in his book, *Essays on Art and Democracy,* are nonparticipants, people who do not live the life—people with no real passion or dedication to the ideas. They pay their dollar at the door, listen to the music, buy the art, play around with the ideas, but never really embrace the essence or participate. Participants venture into the unknown with a set of values and beliefs which guide them. They contribute to the cause, through good times and bad, through popularity and criticism, in times of prosperity and uncertainty. In art and democracy, all progress lies with the participants.

We've run across our fair share of looky loos and participants. Those leaders who take on the roles not so much because they are true believers but because "it" is the next fad, the next big thing, the next silver bullet. They try on the ideas without embracing the essence and without truly understanding the body of knowledge. When we hear corporate boardroom conversation reciting terms such as "human capital," "intellectual resources management," "unleashing the potential of employees," and other such terms, we are unequivocally convinced that revisiting the human side of enterprise will become the next big thing. We wonder how many of us will be looky loos or participants.

We have many role models for becoming "participants." People such as Warren Bennis, Peter Drucker, Douglas McGregor, Joseph Scanlon, Chris Argyris, W. Edwards Deming, Carl Frost, and Abraham Maslow have presented us with a body of knowledge and a way of life for nearly 50 years. Through good times and bad, they continued in their quest,

(continued)

often ridiculed, called naive, heroes in one decade and pious dreamers in another. Yet they participated.

Participation calls for courage and tenacity and an adherence to values which embrace the importance of people. It is not espousing values, a mission statement, and a corporate mantra while pushing motivational techniques which do little more than manipulate employees. Participation calls for fundamentally altering the system, revamping the organizational DNA in order for the human side to flourish.

The fundamental outcome, we believe, of this rush to unlock the intellectual assets of our companies and organizations will be in the form of looky loos and participants. Unfortunately, to be nothing more than a looky loo in the next decade will, we believe, lead to apathy, cynicism, and a discordant distrust of the very institutions and organizations we hope to reinvent.

unselected and include such a large proportion of very sick people, very incompetent people, very psychopathic people, insane people, vicious people, authoritarian people, immature people, etc., that it is necessary to make impersonal rules and not to rely on the good judgment of individual judges, captains, generals, and so on. Here again we must underscore the high selectivity of the T-groups, of the group "Y" managers, of the selected U.S. citizens that you'll find in a well-run industry, etc. Any reasonably intelligent set of managers will exclude in their personnel policy many of these bad and poor and diminished and inadequate people that one can find in a total society. *Therefore* Theory Y, enlightened management can work where there has been such selectiveness of personnel, while it might not work for the total heterogeneous unselected society.

I think that even in our upwardly mobile society class differences between the upper managers and the lower ones may partly account for differences in interests, hostilities, counterhostilities, and so on. So also for the strong/weak variable, superior/inferior variable, and the dominance/subordinate variable. For instance, I think here there would be illumination not only from the monkey material on dominance and the physiological stuff on constitutional strength and weakness and on the factual superiorities and inferiorities of intelligence and talent and so on, but also from such a situation as that of the prostitute. The terrible hostility, hatred, contempt, and so on that the prostitutes have for their customers, if fully explained, would, I am sure, throw a great deal of light on the situation in which there is exploitation of one person by another, or at least in which one person fancies he is being exploited by another.

Another constitutional factor to add to this discussion is the one of activity and passivity as discovered in the brain waves, as discovered by Fries[2] in newborn babies, as discovered by the psychosomatic people in the gastric ulcer character type, and as discovered by the endrocrinologists as effects of male hormones, for instance, in the Fröhlich syndrome. This kind of evidence certainly adds up to a pretty clear fact of inborn differences in activity and passivity, or dependency or receptivity. This, of course, would have to do with leadership and followship (the same for Funkenstein's data on adrenalin and noradrenalin).[3]

Partly, the whole enlightened development of management policy and leadership policy depends on bosses being able to give up power over other people, permitting them to be free, and actually enjoying the freedom of other people and the self-actualization of other people. This is exactly a characteristic of self-actualizing people, and of growing psychological health. Healthy people have no need for power over other people; they don't enjoy it, they don't want it, and they will use it only when there is some factual need in the situation for it. It is as if the growing out of pathology into health took away all the necessities for power over other people, and then simply changed automatically the whole philosophy of management and leadership of these people from a Theory X to a Theory Y kind of thing, even without any conscious effort to do so.

I think the way I'd sum up some of my uneasiness about the management and leadership literature, and my fear of a new kind of piety and dogma would be to shift the whole center of organization of the theory from the person of the leader to the objective requirements of the particular situation or problem. The latter should be the main determiner of leadership policy and followership policy. The stress should be on facts, knowledge, skill, rather than on communication,

[2] M. E. Fries, "Factors in Character Development, Neuroses, Psychoses, and Delinquency," in E. Drolette (Ed.), *Mastery of Stress* (Cambridge, MA: Harvard University Press, 1957).
[3] D. Funkenstein, S. H. King and M. E. Drolette, *Mastery of Stress* (Cambridge, MA: Harvard University Press, 1957).

democracy, human relations, good feeling, and the like. There ought to be more bowing to the authority of the facts. To stress a point here, this is not a dichotomy or a contradistinction. Bowing to the authority of the facts, being pragmatic, being realistic, and so on, all tend to support the participative management theory, the Theory Y type of management, etc., at least insofar as the culture is good enough, the people involved are pretty healthy, and conditions in general are good. All of this adds up to functional leadership in which all personality traits of a general sort are secondary to skill and capability and to the general requirements of the situation. So also should there be more stress on perception of the truth, the creative cognition of the truth, the creative cognition of new truths, of being correct, of being able to be tough, stubborn, and decisive in terms of the facts; that is, when the facts say "yes" and the public says "no," the good leader ought to be able to stick with the facts against the hostility of the public. There ought to be a little more stress on knowledge and experience, that is, on real objective superiority, than there now is.

I don't think there's any great problem here because I'm sure that all of these people would agree with me that this was desirable and that it's just simply a matter of a slight shift in emphasis and in theoretical organization and communication. It may be that I am stressing this a little more than the writers in the field because I am so aware of the fact that real, factual superiors tend to be strongly resented as well as admired, and that, therefore, they are less apt to be chosen on the democratic vote basis. This is a little like the Eisenhower-Stevenson kind of situation where the obvious intellectual inferior was chosen in preference to the obvious intellectual superior. Why is this so? I think my phrasing of leadership would lay a little more stress on this counter-hostility, secret resentment, secret jealousy, and accept more realistically the fact that excellence may be loved and admired, but it is also hated and feared.

Also I take into consideration here the new data on the creative child from Getzels and Jackson[4] on the one hand, and Torrance[5] on the other. There's just no question about it; creative kids are persecuted and disliked and resented not only by their agemates but also by

---

[4] J. W. Getzels and P. W. Jackson, *Creativity and Intelligence* (New York: John Wiley & Sons, 1962).
[5] E. Paul Torrance, *Guiding Creative Talent* (Englewood Cliffs, NJ: Prentice-Hall, 1962).

their teachers. We must work out some better criterion for selecting leaders than popularity, and it may be that if we shift our center of organization to what the facts demand, to factual superiority, to the authority of the truth, to the demands of reality and the like, that we are then somewhat more apt to get the best leader from the pragmatic point of view, even if he happens to be unlovable or unpopular or whatever.

I think I would quote here also the type of data that Drevdahl (unpublished) got when he picked out twenty highly creative psychologists. Every single one of them had had a somewhat unhappy childhood, or at least reported a feeling of being an outsider. Probably they were all somewhat rejected by the society, and I doubt that they would have won any popularity contests, any of them. And yet their factual superiority is in most situations highly desirable. We must learn to choose such people and to value them even if we don't love them or even if they make us uncomfortable and ambivalent or if they throw us into conflict or if they make us doubt our own worth a little bit. I guess this comes down to what I stress so much in my enlightened writings, a good society is impossible unless we develop the ability to admire superiority.

Notes on Unstructured Groups at Lake Arrowhead[1]

Maybe even the discovery of identity of self is helped along more by being given feedback from a whole group of other people of how I affect them, what influence I have on them, how they see me and so on.

I have many impressions, in fact a whole confusion of them, and it will take time for them all to settle down and structure themselves. However, I want to fix some of them before they disappear.

Some of them were made a little stronger by an article by Charles Ferguson in the *California Management Review*.[2] Ferguson's stress on the fact that the group was unstructured really helped to give form to many of my own vague thoughts. Once I started comparing these groups—their effect and phenomena—with the characteristics of the Rorschach tests and other projective and unstructured tests, I began to see the relationship between the lack of structuring in the psychoanalytic situation and in the groups. Also apparent was the relationship to the Taoistic philosophy of permissiveness and noninterference—letting things happen of their own accord and in their own style.

This also suggested a parallel with Carl Rogers' nondirectiveness, and here again, I could understand pretty well how this should bring the kind of results that it does.[3] All these parallels made the

---

[1] During this summer I was invited by Dr. Robert Tannenbaum to visit the Lake Arrowhead Conference Center of the University of California, Los Angeles. A series of training groups (T-groups) were being held there, and I would have a chance to observe and participate for two days. I had never been to such a group nor had I read anything about them. This was a first confrontation.

[2] Charles K. Ferguson, "Management Development in 'Unstructured' Groups," *California Management Review*, Vol. 1 (Spring, 1959), pp. 66–72.

[3] C. Rogers, *On Becoming a Person* (Boston: Houghton Mifflin Co., 1961).

T-groups much more understandable to me at once. I could integrate them with my theoretical knowledge of a half-dozen other phases of life. I'll suggest to the people in this field that they do the same thing. They all seem to overlook the fact that the dynamics of nonstructuring has already worked in a half-dozen other fields.

And now I have another thought: I go back to Max Wertheimer's talk about nonstructuring in thinking and remember how useful this concept was in the experiments of Sherif and in the experiments and writings of Asch, and this makes still another parallel.

All of these parallels add up to show how powerful the withholding of structure can be. My first thought follows the lines of what I put into the psychotherapy chapter in my Motivation and Personality, in which I compared psychoanalytic free association with the effects of using unstructured ink blots in the Rorschach tests. Mainly the idea is that where the world is structured and organized and lawful, we tend to adapt ourselves to it. We tend to be good boys, to play along with the gag, roll with the punch. We fit ourselves into the structure. I learned with my Taoistic and permissive Graduate Department of Psychology at Brandeis that lack of structuring and permissiveness provides the very best atmosphere to encourage the deepest psychic strengths, the self-actualizing tendencies, to emerge into the open; but I also learned that this same lack of structure in the department could bring to the surface all the weaknesses in the person—the lack of talent, the blocks and inhibitions, and so on. That is, the unstructured situation tended either to make or break them; many turned out either marvelously well or else failed altogether.

And then I realized that many of the people that were failures in our situation would have been, perhaps, successes in the more conventional graduate situation where they could take course after course, pile up credit after credit, take exam after exam, and live in a world that was structured and therefore authoritative. In such a situation life would be a step-by-step enterprise. They would always be told what to do, and it would not be necessary for them to have any initiative. Well, then I realized that the situation in our department was a good one—even for failures, because they learned at the age of twenty-five instead of at forty-five that they really had no profound interest in psychology or even that they were really not the dedicated intellectuals at all that they thought they were.

Well, it's just this sort of thing that seems to happen in the unstructured groups too. The people who have been living in a world
which always told them what to do—which made life easy for them
and told them what the next step was, and put them on an escalator
so to speak—this world never let them discover their weaknesses and
failures, not to mention their strengths. In my psychotherapy chapter,
the formulation I finally wound up with is, I think, a pretty good one
for this purpose, too: that if you take away the external determinants
which shape behavior, behavior gets to be shaped by the internal and
intrapsychic determinants. And that, therefore, the best way to find
out what these intrapsychic determinants are, is to take away the external determinants, i.e., the external structuring. This is precisely
what happens in the Rorschach tests and on the psychoanalytic couch.
And I think it is precisely what happens in the unstructured groups
which I saw at Lake Arrowhead. One way I've phrased it there follows:

> This is an introduction to the psychic world and the world of psychic
> knowledge. This is done via experiencing from within (rather than lec-
> turing or reading), (and by feedback from others which makes us more
> conscious of ourselves as psychic creatures and thereby helps us to ex-
> perience our inner happenings in a less chaotic form). These turnings
> inward and these becomings aware of inner experiences are best set forth
> in an unstructured situation (à la Freud, Rorschach, Rogers, Tao, per-
> missiveness, etc.).

Come to think about it, another very homely example, one which
I think I can use for communication, is what so frequently happens to
women who are married to authoritative husbands, especially in a
patriarchal situation. For forty years they may be "good wives," being
very dutiful, running from necessity to necessity, doing what *has to be*
done, nursing children, taking care of the household, etc. Then something happens, the husband suddenly dies, or the woman divorces him,
or she leaves him, and suddenly and unexpectedly, to everyone who
knows her and even to herself, there comes out a different kind of
human being altogether. Totally unexpected talents come out. For instance, I've known one who turned out to be a fine painter in her late
forties and hadn't the slightest suspicion that she had this talent or even
an impulse toward it ever before. It's as if a lid were lifted, and as if
this permitted the squashed, the hidden, inner person to emerge for the

first time. Many widows, let alone the divorcees, certainly heave a kind of sigh of relief, and after the initial shock and fear and so on, feel the delicious freedom, realize how they have been held down for decades, realize that they have been self-abnegating, self-sacrificing, that they always put first the interests of husband, children, and home, pushing their own interests into the background. Okay, this makes a very fine example, almost a visual image of how unstructured groups work. Structuring acts as a kind of lid, a suppressor, a concealer of what lies below. If you keep a person busy running from place to place and from duty to duty, then he'll never have time to sit down and let the deep, inner springs bubble up to the surface.

What I had started to say was that my very first impression in the very first group that I sat in on was one of real shock and amazement. These people behaved and talked in a spontaneous and free way that I have ordinarily associated with psychoanalyzed people, that is, with people who have been under psychoanalysis for a year or two at least. This threw me off balance at once, and I had to think my way through this. I had to rearrange my attitudes toward all group dynamics, toward what I had always thought of as being ineffective talk, talk, talk, more Pollyannish than realistic. Well, I'll just have to rearrange my thoughts on this point. I have always assumed, I think without quite realizing it, the psychoanalytic point of view that any change in the character is going to take two or three years to make. Well, apparently it can happen a lot faster, *very* much faster in this kind of social situation. I guess this is the most important change that I carry away with me from the experience.

Another difference from my previous way of thinking, I think comes from the stress on interpersonal and social and group relations as determinants of psychic, social, and interpersonal behavior. The change here comes via becoming aware, right now in this situation, here-now (rather than via genetic or historical or depth explorations within the depths of the single person), of his neurotic tendencies or of his primary process tendencies. That is to say, the psychoanalysts have assumed that the main determinant of behavior lay hidden deeply within the person, i.e., that it was intrapersonal rather than social or interpersonal. These group people are showing that we had better lay a great deal more stress on the current social interpersonal situation as a determinant of interpersonal behavior and even of self-awareness.

(What I'm trying to say here is something like this: Maybe even the discovery of identity of self is helped along more by being given the feedbacks from a whole group of other people of how I affect them, what influence I have on them, how they see me, and so on. This helps me to see myself as a passive person or a dominating person or a gentle person or a hostile person or whatever it might be.)

This is exactly what we mean by discovering one's self, who one is. This is all to say that the current social situation is more stressed as a determinant of behavior, and the deep psyche is less stressed, and the past history of the individual as it now exists unconsciously within the psyche is also less stressed as a determinant. Since these group people do get such results without probing into the history of the person, into the origins of his neurotic attitudes, this itself is a kind of a proof of their contention that you don't have to probe so much.

I suppose what we'll come out with eventually is some kind of much more complex statement or equation about the proper relationships between all these kinds of therapy, or self-improvement, or search for identity. It may turn out that the best kind of prescription is maybe to start with a T-group for a couple of weeks, then to go into individual therapy for a while, maybe then to come back to a T-group, and so on. In any case, the orthodox piety of the conventional Freudian psychoanalysts certainly must be shaken by these kinds of results. I even have the suspicion that there are some kinds of things that can happen in these T-groups that can *never* happen in the individual psychoanalysis, no matter how long it takes. There are certain kinds of feedback we can get from other people that we simply cannot get from just one person, even if he becomes active rather than passive or nondirective.

We'll have to stress, or anyway think through, some more of this whole business of self-knowledge that comes through feedback from other people who have learned to be sensitive enough to perceive in the first place, and spontaneous enough to express freely in the second place, and who can manage hostilities well enough so that they can say criticizing and damaging things without arousing defensiveness. I think all of the people who have talked about the search for identity—Wheelis, Fromm, Horney, etc., etc.—have not stressed sufficiently this very fact of a lot of other people mirroring back to us the impression we make upon them so that ultimately we get a pretty clear picture of ourselves, at least of our social-stimulus value.

Interview with Michael Murphy

Most know him as the cofounder of The Esalen Institute or through his best selling books, *Golf in the Kingdom, The Kingdom of Shivas, The Future of the Body,* and *The Life We Are Given,* Michael Murphy has spent his life in much of the same way Maslow did: exploring the self and examining how people can develop their capabilities. Studying meditation before it was fashionable, examining the connection between mind-body health practices, much of Murphy's work has become mainstream. Yet, our interview with this American icon were on issues very close to his heart. Maslow described Michael Murphy as *"the son I never had . . ."*

These two men were brought together in what could mirror a scene from Carl Jung's concept of synchronicity. Maslow and his wife, Bertha, were returning from a conference in Southern California. Driving up the coast in Northern California, the Maslows were looking for a place to lodge for the evening. Outside of the small city of Big Sur, they noticed a place that offered rooms and decided to stop. Upon check in, Dr. Maslow was asked to sign the register. The front-desk clerk, after reading the signature said, "THE Abraham Maslow?" Excitedly, the clerk yelled for Michael Murphy's partner, Richard Price, cofounder of The Esalen Institute.

In their search for overnight lodging, little did Abe and Bertha know that they had walked into a hotbed of writers, lecturers, philosophers, students, and therapists interested in humanistic psychology. During the 1960s, Esalen hosted conferences led by B. F. Skinner, Abraham Maslow, Carl Rogers, and others. Audience participation ranged from the common man to luminaries such as George Harrison, Joan Baez, Bob Dylan, and Allen Ginsberg. Gonzo journalist Hunter S. Thompson, age 22, was a caretaker on the grounds. The rest, as they say, is history!

Michael Murphy and Abraham Maslow shared a friendship that lasted until Maslow's death. We met Michael in his San Rafael, California home to talk about Dr. Maslow and his work. Although the topics in our discussion were far ranging, in a case of irony and paradox that Dr. Maslow would probably enjoy, we thought Michael Murphy had a valuable lesson to teach corporate America.

Ironic and paradoxical because Michael Murphy doesn't profess to understand the world of corporate America, yet is an astute and successful businessman. Like Maslow, Murphy has refused to play the guru role, yet has become a guru in the human potential movement. Maslow became a cultural icon in the turbulent sixties, yet was considered by those who knew him to be conservative. Murphy was at the helm of Esalen during that time—a hotbed for counterculture ideas. Yet, Murphy has always been the very straight guy in the middle of the "Summer of Love" movement which was anything but straight. As he says himself, "First off, very early I developed a powerful allergy to hallucinogens. Second, I was too fond of cashmere sweaters. And third, I didn't buy into the enthusiasm for a lot of these

(continued)

techniques. I was constantly skeptical about what was being tried. I was kind of an in-house critic . . ." Wise words for any corporate leader.

We have witnessed a resurgence of great interest in Dr. Maslow's journals. What do you make of it?

Every one is groping for something. We have the Enreagram, the Meyers Briggs test, different leadership models, and the ten steps to this and that. All of us need structure, guidance, and leadership.

There is intense interest because Abe had tremendous depth and substance. He was a researcher, psychologist, theorist, and philosopher. He hated panaceas. Part of Abe's theory about self-actualization was that such people abhor being rubricized.* He would have hated to see all of this. He didn't get into the issues of what type of leadership model or framework would sell. He truly studied and researched. He studied almost every aspect of human behavior and interaction. From his work in the 1940s on human sexuality and his studies with Harry Harlow to his work on self-actualization and human motivation, he had a body of knowledge from which to draw.

The problem is that human nature is so extremely human. We have such a capacity for self-transcendence that to peg someone as, for example, an INTP or ENTJ or whatever the latest tool du jour, is to limit them. To peg yourself or your colleague or team member is to sell our human creativity short, our capacity to begin again, to create, to be creative. It happens to us as kids, we get typed into family roles. We have such a potential for self-actualization that to typecast people is to sell them short.

Knowing Maslow as you did, what do you think he would have to say about organizational trends today?

He would have hated many of the panaceas, tools, movements, going on in business today. When a business guru comes into a company, it can almost be cultlike. Let's say you are an employee, you want to move ahead so you have to take this training or do this or that. You have to join up! The book *Cults of Everyday Life* demonstrates the destructive side of all of this.

However, there is a creative side. For example, sometimes to have a cultlike atmosphere within a company, as part of a strong corporate culture, can help people become more creative. It can serve as a shared sense of purpose. You have to keep an eye on the issues.

---

* Maslow defined rubricizing "as a cheap form of cognizing—a quick and easy cataloguing whose function is to make unnecessary the effort required by more careful, idiographic perceiving or thinking. To place a person in a system takes less energy than to know him in his own right. . . ." (*Toward a Psychology of Being*, p. 126)

This reminds me that I recommended to several of the people of Lake Arrowhead this old, old hobby thought of mine that for self-therapy, for quick therapy purposes, talking motion pictures of us as we go about our business, a totally candid picture from behind as well as in front would teach us a hell of a lot about what we are—not just what we *look* like, not just our *persona,* not just the mask, but in addition what we really, deeply are, what our identity is, what the real self is. Of course, there is danger in this. We can finally make the Harry Stack Sullivan kind of stupid mistake of defining self as nothing but our reflections in an awful lot of mirrors. But I think it's easy enough to avoid this mistake since the person who has strong enough identity anyway is powerful enough to reject false statements about himself, projections of the Freudian sort, etc., even if they are agreed upon by a lot of other people.

Maybe this would be a kind of test of strength and maybe we could even teach people, give them exercise of this sort, that is, like the Asch[4] situation or the Crutchfield[5] experiment, where five or six stooges will all agree in disagreeing with the experimental subject in telling him an untruth. We know that about two people out of three will finally disbelieve their own eyes in such a situation. Could we not use this kind of training in the group to teach the person when to believe his own eyes, when to trust the pooled judgment of a lot of other people, and so on.

One thought that kept going through my head while I was watching things, was that another approach to this whole business is to call it honesty training or spontaneity training, training in innocence of perception and innocence of behavior (89, 98). Or another phrase that maybe sums it all up that went through my head is intimacy training. The strong impression I got so often was of people struggling to drop their defenses, their guards, and their masks as they got less afraid of being hurt once this happened, in the hope that this would be a signal to others to do the same in turn; also, that this would be a signal for the others to reassure them that, well, "Your secret doesn't look so terrible after all," or "You think of yourself as such a dull and uninteresting person but you really give the impression of being deep and interesting to get to know."

[4] S. Asch, "Studies of Independence and Conformity" (Part 1), *Psychol. Monogr.,* 1956, *70* (Whole No. 416).
[5] R. Crutchfield, "Conformity and Character," *Amer. Psychologist,* 1955, *10,* 191–98.

I remember saying in one of the groups as I participated that the thought came to me again about Kurt Lewin's[6] and Walter Toman's[7] belief that Americans need so many more therapists than the rest of the world needs because they just don't know how to be intimate—that they have no intimate friendships, by comparison with the Europeans and that, therefore, they really have no deep friends to unburden themselves to. I agree with this in a general way. Much of what goes on in a therapist's office or in these T-groups or in group psycho-analysis really is a kind of artificial making up for the fact that you don't have a bosom friend to talk intimately with, to express your deepest wishes, fears, and hopes, to unburden yourself. Kurt Lewin said this a long time ago comparing the American character structure and the European character structure, and I suppose other people have said it too.

My own impression is that it's correct. For instance, in the two other cultures that I know, the Mexican and the Blackfoot Indian, I know that I envied them the closeness of their friendships. I know that I have to admit, whenever anybody thinks about it or asks about it, that I don't really have many friends in the world of the kind that I would love to have. There are certainly plenty of *approaches* to this friendship and I have good friends with whom I can discuss half my life, anyway, but there is nobody in the world with whom I can be as intimate as I was with my psychoanalyst. That's why we have to pay $20 or $25 an hour in order to have him simply listen to us and respond once in a while, and for us to have the blessed privilege of spilling our guts, of talking freely as one might to a totally trusted person, of whom we wouldn't be afraid, one who wouldn't hurt us, one who wouldn't take advantage of our weakness, etc., etc.

I suppose that I would extend this principle if I were thinking in terms of the whole culture, that is, this principle of self-disclosure, of trying to be honest, of trying to be intimate, of trying to learn to ex-pose ourselves, at least in the right company, in order to learn how nice this feels and how good the effects are. How many fears are dropped, how many phobias just automatically disappear, how much freer we can feel after we've given up some kind of guilty secret like having a wooden leg or expressing a fear of being crippled or the fear

---

[6] K. Lewin, *Resolving Social Conflicts* (New York: Harper & Bros., 1948, Chapter 1).
[7] Private conversation.

of remaining unmarried or whatever it might be. Certainly, I think I'm going to add to my map of eupsychia that all people feel it to be an expression of love and responsibility for their brothers and sisters to speak freely to them when there is approval and disapproval. That is, the enlightened is going to tell everybody, especially children, quite freely and without dishonesty that I am glad that you did that, or that was a nice thing to do, or that was not a nice thing to do, or what you did made me sad and disappointed, etc., etc.

As I remember it, this is the principle on which the Bruderhof works. They consider it one aspect of Christian love to be honest in this way with everybody else. They claim that they have no neuroses in their societies. This is also what I learned from Van Kaam, the priest. Apparently, in his order it is a priestly duty to be honest with each other in this way, even when it hurts. So if one person in his faculty is a bad teacher because he mumbles on and on, it is then considered to be a brotherly duty to tell him so. It is considered to be unloving to let him go on making the same mistake forever just because one doesn't have love enough and courage enough to take the chance of hurting him and of having him strike back.

Well, certainly in America we don't do this very much. The only time we ever criticize anybody is in anger. Our definitions of love don't ordinarily include the obligation to criticize or to feed back or to reflect back. But I think we'd better change our minds about this. The funny thing is that if this kind of feedback of unpleasant fact can take place, it breeds love in both directions. The person who is criticized honestly may be hurt for the moment, but ultimately he is helped and cannot help but become grateful. Anyway, it's a great sign of respect to me, for instance, if someone feels I'm strong enough, capable enough, and objective enough so that he can tell me where I've pulled a boner. It's only those people who regard me as delicate, sensitive, or weak, or fragile who will not dare to disagree with me. I remember how insulted I felt when it dawned on me that so many of my graduate students never disagreed with me. The conclusion I finally drew was, by God, what did they think of me? Was I so delicate a creature that I couldn't stand a debate? And then I went and told them so, and it helped in both directions. I felt much better about them, certainly.

What this adds up to, I guess, is a little exercise in interpreting all these group processes from the organizing center of "intimacy training" and then seeing some of the consequences of structuring the whole theory and the whole set of observations from this point of view. It's a real help. I think it brings up certain things that do not come up when we use the other centering point of honesty, or the centering point of openness to experience, or the centering point of becoming more spontaneous and expressive, or whatever it might be. Each centering point has its own advantages and throws into relief some things that the other centerings do not. A full exercise here would be taking every conceivable centering point and then trying to structure all the data from that point of view.

In any case, and to continue with this notion about the T-groups in enlightenment, I go back to my experiments in 1938 and 1939 with my Brooklyn College group therapies.[8] The general point is (and I think I'll try this on these group people and see what they think of it), from a social, philosophical, enlightened, world-improving point of view, that all of this self-disclosure and increase in intimacy makes better individuals, makes better groups, and makes for better inter-personal pairing relationships. I had so many examples of this, of the same sort that I've got from individual therapy, that it would be very easy to make a long list of them for the sake of convincing other people that this would be a good freedom, for instance, to add to the United Nations' basic freedoms. That is, the freedom or the obligation or the responsibility to our brothers (and all men are our brothers) to expose ourselves as much as possible and to feed back to them honestly and as gently as possible what impression they make upon us. Certainly this would be a way of tying the whole human species together, of making for greater individual psychological health, for making healthier groups, and large groups and organizations, and for making a better world in general.

Of course, there are questions which come up—questions that I can't really answer, questions that I guess nobody can answer yet. For instance, these T-groups are really hothouse affairs. The delegates are students who are self-selected and pay a lot of money and come up to a beautiful spot and work under the very best auspices. The trainers and leaders, my impression is, are very high-grade in general. They all seem to be capable, and certainly all seem to be exceptionally decent and nice people. Well, this is very fine for small pilot projects. I remember how it was at Brooklyn College when a small group of

---

[8] Unpublished.

enthusiasts created a new course in general social science, putting to-gether psychology, sociology, anthropology, and God knows what else, and we gave the most wonderful course the students had ever had there. Everyone was so admiring and so happy about it that what they did was to make it required for all freshmen, and immediately there was a shortage of teachers who were worth anything. The whole thing finally came to a pile of junk for the simple reason that the first group, which was taught by four or five selected instructors who were just right for the job, gave way to ten groups with fifty or sixty instruc-tors, and there just aren't that many people in the world who are right for that job. Certainly, there weren't that many people at Brooklyn College. So all sorts of incompetent unsuitable people became in-structors and ruined the whole thing.

We need for leaders in such groups, trained people, and also people of a certain character structure. They must be a little motherly, a little parental, a little of the eager-to-help type, the ones who get pleasure out of doing good, etc. Well, not everybody in the world is like this. What shall we do with the obsessionals? What shall we do with the schizo-phrenics? What shall we do with the psychopaths who would just love to get in such groups in order to mess them up? Then the people them-selves, the students themselves, were a pretty high-grade group of peo-ple. This was the cream skimmed right off the top of the population. What shall we do with the huge proportion of the population that are reduced to the concrete? They couldn't take anything of the sort and couldn't make anything of it. It would be a waste of time, it would be useless, I *think*. Perhaps the experiment should be tried—if we come to think of these groups in a enlightened way, that is, from the point of view of the United Nations and the future good world and so on, rather than in terms of a little selected group of lucky people who are a frac-tion of a fraction of one percent of the population.

In the same way that individual psychoanalysis is absolutely of no use in changing the world by changing people one by one—for the simple reason that there are just too few psychoanalysts and always will be—just in the same way these few T-groups that are formed here and there throughout the country are no more effective than a spit in the ocean in terms of general social movement in the whole soci-ety, let alone in the whole world. However, be this as it may, the fact remains that the technique can be expanded, that these principles can be used in many, many more situations than they are now being used—for instance, among youngsters in a school situation. I don't know any youngsters any place that are so badly off that they couldn't use this kind of situation, let's say at the age of five, six, seven, and eight, in a very beneficial way.

But, of course, the necessity is to think in large terms, and I must say that all the books I've read on management and organizational theory, etc., simply aren't sweeping enough. They aren't large and great enough; they are not heroic enough. They are written in terms of one particular factory, one particular place, or a particular group of twenty people; this whole group of writers and researchers have to learn to think in terms of two billion people and of twenty generations instead of the little grocery store kind of operations that they are running now. They must become large gauge, more philosophical, more able to see under the aspect of eternity; they must be able to see man as a species, as a race, as a huge unity of brothers who are only slightly different from each other in ways that don't really matter very much. Well, maybe I'll stress this kind of thing.

This reminds me of one of the experiments that I tried in my group therapy experiments (in one group each year for two years). The experiment required each person in addition to participating in a group of about twenty-five people, to become a speaker or unburdener or patient to another individual of the group who was to be a kind of therapist or listener or whatever. Each person then played two roles in relationship to another person. That is, each person was a patient to someone else and a therapist for another someone else. I trained all of the fifty people in the two groups, as well as I could in a quick way, in the basics of good listening in Rogerian style[9] in order to teach them to listen and keep their mouths shut and so on, and then, also, I had lectured them all on the fundamental rule of psychoanalysis, that is, of speaking freely of anything that came into their heads without criticizing it or structuring it or anything of the sort. My Blackfoot Indians did the same sort of thing. They naturally paired off into what they called "specially beloved friends," with whom they were extremely intimate, and for whom they were prepared to lay down their lives in the old days.

I guess what I'm trying to say here is that these interpersonal therapeutic growth-fostering relationships of all kinds which rest on

[9] C. Rogers, *Counseling and Psychotherapy* (Boston: Houghton Mifflin Co., 1942).

intimacy, on honesty, on self-disclosure, on becoming sensitively aware of one's self—and thereby of responsibility for feeding back one's impressions of others, etc.—that these are profoundly revolutionary devices, in the strict sense of the word—that is, of shifting the whole direction of a society in a more preferred direction. As a matter of fact, it might be revolutionary in another sense if something like this were done very widely. I think the whole culture would change within a decade and everything in it.

I've been trying to boil down as much as possible both the techniques and the goals of these therapeutic groups, or personal development groups might be a better name. First of all, and I think most obvious, is learning one's own social stimulus value via feedback from others and after being in an unstructured group where our deepest characteristics are permitted to emerge so that our innermost guts can be seen rather than our external social roles and stereotypes. The point is here, first of all, granted that I can be in a situation where I really expose myself: How do I look to others? How do I affect them? What do they see in me? What do they agree upon seeing in me? How do I affect different kinds of people in different kinds of ways?

Then the second thing that is stressed is what might be called here-now experiencing, or openness to experience as Rogers describes it, or what I called innocent perception, etc. The stress here would be both on experiencing one's innermost psyche and *also* on learning to experience other people carefully and well as they really are, i.e., to become able to really listen, to really look at another person, to really have a kind of a third ear for the music that he's playing as well as the particular notes and words—what he's *trying* to say as well as what he is actually saying in words. This is all a kind of perceptual training, then (94).

Third, separable from these two is the stress on the ability to express honestly, i.e., to be spontaneous; not only to perceive but to be able without inhibition, without vain inhibition or blockage or trouble to say and express honestly what is felt or perceived. This is, of course, a statement on the behavioral side. It amounts to saying, emit honest words and honest behavior. When I tried this statement out on Lubin, he agreed with it and added one more, that is about the group processes themselves. But I think I'll pass this by as being of less direct importance for personal development and personal growth. Maybe I'll come back to this group stuff later. At the moment it interests me much less.

(Another vague thought comes to me here that I'm not really sure about. No, I guess I am sure about it in its general tenor, but only not sure about it in its specific details.) One of the things we need in general is permission to be less structured in our communications. Our world is set up in such a fashion that good thinking and good writing are almost entirely logical, structured, analytic, verbal, realistic, etc. But, obviously, we need to be more poetic, more mythical, more metaphorical, more archaic in the Jung sense. In the appendix to my Being (86) book I think I make a good beginning on calling for this kind of thing and in pointing out how exclusively rational and verbal and how unmetaphorical we are, and I pointed out also how much is lost thereby even in the realm of science.

Well, one impression I think I had, that's coming back to me now, is that these T-groups permitted, among all the other new things that they permitted, a kind of unstructured communication. One could try to express one's feelings, and it was understood by everybody that this was anyway a difficult thing to do and, furthermore, might best be done not by very denotative words but rather by connotative, by a kind of stammering or halting communication which combined the secondary process and primary process in about the way I described in my paper, *Two Kinds of Cognition* (67). Maybe I should go back to that paper again and add this new stuff to it. I think I left out of that paper this recognition that in the therapeutic situation, where one tries to express to another human being feelings and emotions which are about of all things in the world the least susceptible to being put into rational, orderly words, that this kind of group therapeutic experience, this intimacy, this spontaneity about expressing emotions needs new kinds of unstructured communications. And also *permits* new kinds of unstructured communications. Maybe just to watch the kinds of unstructured communications that actually do exist would be a good research project. For instance, I know that there is a lot of stammering and hesitation and picking of words and then rejecting the words and then going back and starting over again and trying out a kind of a statement and then saying, "No, that's not quite what I mean, let me try it again" etc., etc. I think I'll suggest this project to these group boys because I doubt that I'll ever have time or opportunity for it. Well, I think I'll sum it up in this list of goals of T-groups as another goal. Yes, I think I will. And to say it more formally, one of the goals, hitherto unconscious, of T-group training is the acceptance of less

How Unmetaphorical We've Become

Our world is set up in such a fashion that good thinking and good writing are almost entirely logical, structured, analytical, verbal, realistic, etc. But obviously we need to be more poetic, more mythical, more metaphorical, more archaic in the Jung sense. . . . What is it about intellectual meetings, scientific journals, organizations that make certain kinds of truth and certain kinds of expression not suitable or appropriate?

—Abraham Maslow

Nearly 10 years ago, we were in the audience of a large gathering of high technology professionals. The guest speaker was management consultant and author, Tom Peters. His first few statements stuck with us and seem even more appropriate today then a decade ago.

Peters, in his typical unorthodox fashion, looked out at the audience and left us with a point we've never forgotten. He said, "Here's the problem with you guys. Several years ago when I spoke to you I looked out at the audience and saw a very different group. Now you all look alike, speak the same language, dress alike, hang out at the same watering holes, because you are 'professional' and successful now."

The point he was making is similar to one Maslow made. Once a limited amount of success is achieved, we feel compelled by our social framework to structure our ideas, to box them up in neat packages, appear more professional, more in control, more a part of the status quo. In this process, we often homogenize and close the parts of ourselves that bring forth creativity, fun, humor, learning, and innovation. Or, we choose to remain silent withholding our contributions for fear of being ostracized.

We are not advocating that organizations be unruly, unprofessional, unstructured, or nomadic. What we are advocating is a thorough look at what we stand to lose (and are losing) in this process. In looking for examples of the losses, we identified a tremendous one in the diaries of Abraham Maslow. Even this great psychologist, pioneer, and one of the most brilliant thinkers of our time felt the pressure to conform.

In 1960, Maslow was to give an important speech to other prominent colleagues at a professional gathering. He had been grappling with a problem for weeks regarding some of his theories. He said the whole experience was a typical instance of a peak experience and since it was his custom to think on paper, he had written the entire experience out. He wanted

(continued)

to throw out his planned speech and substitute these ideas that he had written. Yet, he was hesitant. He stated:

"There it was, an actual living peak experience, caught on the wing and it illustrated very nicely the various points I wanted to make. And yet, because it was so private and so unconventional, I found myself extremely reluctant to read this out loud in public. . . . It did not fit. The realization that this kind of paper didn't 'fit' either for publication or for presentation at conventions or conferences led me to question 'why?' What is there about intellectual meetings and scientific journals that makes certain kinds of personal truths and certain styles of expressions not 'suitable' or 'appropriate'?"

What was lost in this process to "fit"? We will never know. Yet, if someone as intellectually sophisticated and knowledgeable as Abraham Maslow can be silenced by this process, how will we ever be able to sustain real levels of innovation and creativity in organizations?

structured communications or even unstructured communications, respecting them, valuing them, and thereby teaching people to be able to do them. I'll want to think about this a little more. If my appendix in the *Being* book deserved publication as a separate paper and turned out to be very useful to a lot of people, maybe I should tack this on or get somebody else to tack it on as a kind of going forward with the ideas started to be expressed there. Maybe I should add this as another aspect of the learning about psychic reality that I started to talk about way back at the beginning of this memorandum. I think I'll say a little more about that.

Practically everything that happens in the T-groups could be summarized from the centering point of first confrontations with psychic realities, all of which have been neglected or underplayed or suppressed or repressed by our culture, which insists on being a culture of things and objects, of physicists and chemists and engineers, a culture which almost identifies real knowledge and real science with people who do things with their fingers and hands like physicists and chemists and biologists and a culture which leaves out almost entirely the subtleties of the inner life. Well, all the things I've talked about I suppose are aspects of this world of knowledge or this area of knowledge which most people in our society have got no instruction in except by way of learning how to repress the psychic. Our pragmatic stress on results in the real world, our pure stress on repression and suppression, the doctrines of

original sin and of the human psyche as deeply evil, these are all designed to encourage people to suppress or repress the whole of the psychic life, to keep it under tight control at all times.

Well, no wonder an awful lot of emotion and a great deal of learning and all sorts of consequences arise out of any kind of individual or
group therapeutic experience. Partly it's like being taken into another
world which we knew nothing of before. Or like learning a new science or being shown a whole new set of facts, another side of nature.
Or becoming aware of inner impulses, of primary processes, of
metaphorical thinking, of spontaneity of behavior, of the fact that
dreams and fantasies and wishes are run by a totally different set of
laws than chairs and tables and things and objects in general. This may
be especially so because such a large proportion of these T-groups and
their like are for exactly the least psychic people, that is, engineers,
managers, businessmen, presidents, people of the world generally, the
people who call themselves tough, hard-headed, practical, realistic,
and so on, which usually means absolutely ignorant of all psychic realities. Since such a large proportion of these training groups' students
are "thing" people, this may explain partly why so many startling
things happen so darned fast. It's like a teetotaller being introduced for
the first time to liquor and getting drunk with it.

I may add another consequence or goal of these groups, and this
follows Ferguson, who in his article talks about conceptualization as a
consequence. What he means is certainly very true, that there is a new
kind of conceptualization for many of these people. First of all, about
the simple facts of human life—for instance, a sharp recognition of individual differences, that people really *are* different. But perhaps more
important, many concepts are broken down and restructured in such a
way as to include both the real world of things and objects and the psychic world of sensitivities, fears, wishes, and hopes. New kinds of theories and attitudes then can get built up. And I think I would stress this,
because these attitudes—which I have called "basic character attitudes"
toward *(a)* the self, *(b)* significant others, *(c)* social groupings, *(d)* nature
and physical reality, and *(e)* for some people, supernatural forces—are
about as deep as you can get in anybody's character structure. Any
change in these really mean a change in character, a change in the deepest portion of a person, and I suspect that some of these basic character attitudes are changed around in a pretty radical way in some of the
students in these groups. And, of course, this is a very important change

and a very important consequence, and, therefore, I would say it had better become a conscious goal of the trainers.

Still something else occurs to me now in retrospect. There was a good deal of nonevaluation in these groups, now that I come to think of it. That is, they were taught, I don't know whether consciously or unconsciously, that their feelings did actually exist and that it was a good thing to accept them into consciousness and to express them verbally and that this did not imply approval or disapproval, or action upon, or anything of the sort. For instance, in one session, one man spoke about his feelings of anti-Semitism and, of course, this was the profoundest kind of honesty. He was simply admitting that it was there and wanted help with how to handle it. As I remember it, the group was very good about this. That is, they didn't start arguing in terms of ought or should or what was right or wrong, but they were able to accept the fact that it just was so and then to address themselves to this rather than to being moralistic. Of course, the effects were far better than if they had been moralistic, for this would have turned into a whole business of attack and defense; and the anti-Semitic attitude might simply have been hardened altogether.

In this same group, when the leader called for further examples of personal prejudice, with a little statement about that, this did not imply any approval or justification or anything of the sort. A person might be able to say that something existed and also that he was very much ashamed of it. Then they went around the circle, and a half-dozen people, some of them rather haltingly, admitted, possibly for the first time in their lives, to prejudices about women or Negroes or Jews or religious people or nonreligious or whatever, and everybody was able to take this in a nonevaluative way, just about in the same way the psychoanalyst tries to "accept" in the sense of realizing that such a thing exists. I think of a professor, a patient of one of my psychoanalyst friends, who has been struggling for a couple of years now with his impulse to molest little girls sexually; although he has never actually done this, and although it is now clear that he never will, because he is overcoming the impulse, yet the fact remains that the impulse did exist in the world in just about the same way other unpleasant things do—like mosquitoes and cancer and so on. We certainly couldn't do very much about cancer if we rejected its victims and refused to have anything to do with them because they were evil or bad. A very good attitude to have, as a matter of fact an absolutely necessary one to have for anybody who is going to change psychic things at all is to look at things and see them whether one likes them or not, whether one approves of them or not—just to admit that something actually does exist even if it's bad.

Now, I remember that it occurred to me as this was going on that I should add this to my enlarged definition of love. Certainly I've pointed out that love was nonevaluative. Since love must be considered as different from justice, from judging, from evaluation, from reward and punishment, from deserts in general, then this nonevaluation which is unconsciously learned in group therapy is really a loving act and may be considered an aspect of training in being able to love and in knowing what it feels like. Of course, I had happen to me, and I suppose it happened to others as well, in my therapeutic experience that the more I got to know someone, and the humbler he was about telling me how miserable he felt about his sins and about the nasty things he did, the paradoxical effect is that I got to like him more rather than less. So it happened in these groups. They confessed to all sorts of dirty things occasionally, and yet all it did was to make me like them better rather than less. Perhaps this was because the whole framework permitted nonevaluation, nonjudging, nonpunishment. The framework stressed acceptance rather than rejection. One form of inability to love is censoriousness, moralism, disapproving of a person and trying to make him over, to remodel him, and remold him. This is, of course, a source of great unhappiness in many marriages and a source of many divorces. People, one may say, become good lovers only when they can accept others as they are, and can then enjoy and like them rather than being bothered and irritated and disapproving.

All of this relates to the point that I tried to make in one group that for bosses and leaders, etc., it was extremely desirable to separate two functions: on the one hand the function of judging, punishing, disciplining, and being a policeman or an executioner, and on the other the function of therapy and helping and loving, etc. I pointed out that therapists on our campus, for instance, had better not be teachers if they have to give grades, that is, to approve, disapprove, and punish. Also, that this can be carried to the point, as at the University of Chicago, for instance, where teachers don't give grades at all but only a Board of Examiners does. This would certainly make closer the relationship with the teachers, who would then become pure and simple proponents rather than a mixture of proponent and antagonist. Well, so the trainers in these T-groups are just simply proponents.

They don't give grades or rewards or punish or anything of the sort. They simply accept nonevaluatively.

Similarly, a very good relationship can be seen in the Blackfoot Indian families where the punisher is an old man of the tribe, rather than the parents themselves. When the punisher appears, the parents then intervene for the child; they are on his side. They are his protagonists and his friends rather than his executioners, or punishers, and so these families are far closer than American families where father has to be the love-giver and also the punisher and spanker as well. Perhaps this can be added to the statement of goals and purposes of therapeutic groups.

I remember now that this is something we discussed when Tannenbaum was visiting Non-Linear, and it was generally agreed that this was a very good point. I would like to apply this to the question of the boss in an enterprise who has actual power to hire and fire, to give promotions and raises, and anything of the sort. I would like to point out that it is absolutely impossible for a person in such a position of judge, executioner, etc., to expect the same kind of openness to him, the same kind of trust and love, and so on, that one can give to a person who is not a judge, who doesn't have power over us, and so on.

Yes, I think I will expand this some time, because it's an extremely important point, especially as a critique of all contemporary management policy where my vague feeling about the Pollyannish tendencies comes out again and again. This is certainly one of them—feeling that good managerial policy, good participative management can somehow make the boss and the workers into one big, happy family or into buddies or something of the sort. In the long run this is absolutely impossible. I doubt that it is even desirable. And I know for sure that there are limits upon the degree of friendliness and openness and so on that is possible in such a situation. And the fact remains that it is better for a boss or a judge or an executioner or the man who hires and fires or the policeman, etc., etc., not even to try to get too close, to get too friendly with the people he may have to punish. If the punishing function is important as, in fact, it is and if it is necessary as, in fact, it very frequently is, then this friendliness will actually make the job more difficult both for the judge and for the person being judged. The person being judged will feel betrayed by being, for instance, demoted by this person he thought was his friend. It is very hard for people to understand that one may feel very friendly and yet not push one's friend to run for president, for instance.

Also, the other way about, it makes life much tougher for the boss if he has to execute his friends. Things are likely to get all mixed up, certainly all sorts of guilt feelings can be aroused, and this is a good, fertile source of stomach ulcers. It would be better for a certain amount of detachment and social distance to be maintained here, as between officers and men in the armed forces. As I understand it, there have been many efforts through the world to make armed forces democratic, and it has never worked out well because the fact remains that somebody has to tell this particular person to take a chance on being killed, or even to go to his death. This cannot be decided democratically, because nobody wants to die. Somebody has to choose impersonally, and, therefore, it's better for the general to be a lonely, aloof, detached figure, not to be friendly with any of the people whom he may have to send to their deaths or whom he may have to order to be executed. Perhaps the same thing is true for the physicians, especially for the surgeon who will refuse to operate on his friends. Or for the psychiatrist who will refuse to take on his friends and relatives as patients. This is very sensible in view of the fact that human beings find it very hard to handle the mixture of love and justice in the same person. I know this runs counter to the whole music of the stuff I've read on managerial policy and especially the confusions about participative management. Power is power, and it may even go so far as to be power over life and death, and the person who has power over my life and over my death I certainly cannot love in exactly the same way I love a dear friend where no power is involved.

Kay (Mr. A. Kay, president of Non-Linear Systems) made a very good point here when I discussed this with him, namely that the concept of openness is getting a little confused. He suggested that it have two different meanings, and I thought about it and agreed entirely that this is a very useful distinction. Openness in the boss and in participative management can mean and should mean his openness to any suggestion, to any fact, to any feedback or information that pours in on him, no matter whether it is pleasant or unpleasant. He should be open in this sense, and there's no question about it. He must know what's going on.

But openness in the sense of expressiveness, of dropping of all inhibitions and speaking, I would say is definitely not desirable in the judge, the policeman, the boss, the captain of the ship, and the general of the armies. It is one of the responsibilities of the leader in such a situation to keep his fears to himself often. I know that if I were on an oceangoing ship and the captain were to report all his fears and anxieties and uncertainties and doubts, I wouldn't take that ship again. I would prefer him to take full responsibility for everything, and I would prefer to think of him as capable and competent. I don't want to experience the anxiety of entertaining the thought that he is just a fallible human being and might foul up the compass directions or something of the sort. The same thing is true for the physician. I don't want him to think out loud as he gives me a physical examination; when he is examining me for tuberculosis or cancer or heart disease or god knows what, I'd prefer him to keep his suspicions to himself.

The same thing is true for the general in the army, and, as I have found, for the father or mother in the family. The father or mother loses half his functions as the stable hitching post in the whole family if he comes reporting to his wife and children all his fears, doubts, anxieties, weaknesses, and so on all the time. The fact is that part of his function is to be a confidence-bringer, to be the leader in the sense that he takes responsibility and that they can lean upon him rather than the other way about. I would certainly recommend to any man that though he should be fairly open with his wife and his children and friends and so on, there are situations in which, especially when he has responsibility for leading, he had better keep his troubles to himself and just let them burn out his own guts and not seek the relief of catharting them by expressing them freely.

So also for the boss of an industrial outfit. Certainly, all sorts of human fears, doubts, and depressions, etc., go through his mind; yet he is supposed to keep a firm hand and steady eye on the future and to simply suppress, overcome, or quell all of these perfectly human doubts and fears. He must keep them to himself or at least to express them only outside and not within the organization.

In my early years in teaching, I certainly loved my students and felt very close to them and wanted to be buddies with them. I learned only slowly that while I could keep my smiles and friendliness and so on separated from the grades, i.e., I could certainly love somebody who wasn't a very good student of psychology, *they* rarely could accept and understand this. Normally, when I was friends with students they felt I had betrayed them if they got bad grades. They thought of me as a hypocrite, as a turncoat, etc., etc. Not all of them, of course;

the stronger ones could manage this well enough, but weaker people cannot, I learned. Slowly I had to give it up, until now, especially in large classes, I keep my distance and maintain English-style relationships rather than getting very close and buddy-like. The only times I'll get close is when I prepare them quite specifically for it or explain it to the people involved and warn them in advance that I'll have to give some bad grades, and so on and so on. But all this adds up to not expecting or wanting or recommending an openness of expression in the boss or the leader, even though we certainly can recommend and expect that he learn more openness in the sense of having his ears and eyes wide open as a receptacle for information.

One way of summarizing my impressions of these therapeutic groups in relationship to individual psychotherapy is to come back to the old conclusion that many have come to that it's senseless arguing about group therapy versus individual therapy. For one thing, there are many kinds of each serving different purposes, different kinds of people, and so on. Secondly, they do have different functions in certain respects, and so our question then transforms itself into for what problems, under what kinds of circumstances, for what kind of people, for what kinds of goals, should we use what kind of group therapy or what kind of individual therapy and in what combination or alternation.

Another general summarizing statement is that it is quite clear that these T-groups can be growth-fostering, personality-developing, psychogogic (as contrasted with psychotherapy which makes sick people well, psychogogy makes well people better). These groups, with the rules by which they run, are good growing soil. The parallel here is with farming. The good farmer simply throws out seeds, sets up good growing conditions, and then gets out of the way of the growing seeds most of the time, helping them only where they really need help. He doesn't pull up the sprouting seed to see if it's doing all right; he doesn't twist it, or train it or shove it around or put it back in the soil, or whatever. He just leaves it alone, giving it the minimum necessary help. Well, there's little question that the group conditions at Lake Arrowhead were good growing conditions in this sense. Of course the parallel can be made also with the good trainer, or the good leader in general, that the good leader is again like the farmer, not so much in training or molding or forcing or shaping people, but in offering them good growing conditions and in either supplying them with seeds or bringing out their own inner seeds and then permitting them to grow without too much interference.

Another problem just occurred to me which I'd almost forgotten about, and this is the whole question of privacy. I have felt in half-a-dozen points in my recent reading, and certainly I felt at Arrowhead, that this question of the desirability and even the need of privacy is almost totally overlooked by the workers in this field. Certainly, the training groups are in part a learning to drop privacy in the pathological sense, that is, in the compulsion sense. This kind of spontaneity training teaches these people to be private or self-disclosing, as they themselves *wish*. Most of these people learn that their so-called privacy is just a matter of fear, compulsion, inability, inhibition, and so on. As a matter of fact, if my studies on the self-actualizing people are any decent guide here, we may expect that people as they get more healthy will have more desire for real privacy of the noncompulsive, enjoyable sort, and will have *less* need for neurotic privacy and keeping of unnecessary and silly secrets and of hiding one's scars and of trying to fool people and to keep up masks and fronts of all sorts.

Partly my thoughts up at Arrowhead on this point were stimulated by Bertha, who is an exceptionally private person and who would shudder at the thought of unburdening herself about private things in front of a group of twenty people. This is certainly not a neurotic privacy, because she is perfectly able to unburden herself and to be very intimate with her intimate friends—but with them only. Certainly, there are many people with a normal need for privacy, and the self-selection process guarantees that they will never show up at Lake Arrowhead. They would find the prospect so unpleasant a priori that they would simply never want to come and even if they're forced to come, I'm not sure how it would work out for many of them. They might remain guarded and retain their distaste for the process of public nudism, even while going through the groups. What I'm saying, I guess, is that we have to distinguish between healthy, desirable privacy and neurotic, compulsive, uncontrollable privacy and that these are very, very different things. In our effort to break down neurotic privacies—which are really a set of inhibitions and which are stupid, silly, irrational, undesirable, and unrealistic, etc.—we're apt to forget that there is such a thing as desirable privacy. And, also, we're apt to forget about individual differences here. In my own personal experience alone, I've known that it was possible to rate people on a continuum from being easy self-disclosers to people who preferred to be private in a healthy way, that is, in an unneurotic way.

I suppose, for the sake of making the point, I could even go so far as to say that learning to break down neurotic privacy was a prerequisite to getting up to the level of being able to be healthily private, and certainly to be able to enjoy privacy and being alone (which most neurotic and even most average people cannot do—certainly not in the United States). In this sense the breaking down of neurotic privacy is a trend toward health, but health itself includes, as a subaspect, the need for privacy, the enjoying of privacy, the ability to stand privacy, and the like.

This relates a little to the remarks up above of the requirement in the boss that he not expose himself totally at all times. There are certain things which he had better keep private, depending upon the particular situation. When the general has made up his mind about a particular plan of action, he had better not run around expressing uncertainties and doubts and wringing his hands and showing his fears because in this way he will undercut the morale of the whole group. He has to learn to keep this to himself. Well, in the same way I suppose healthy privacy can include this kind of keeping things to oneself and keeping one's mouth shut and being able to keep secrets when this is factually, objectively the better thing to do.

This relates to another point that I made a note of in the course of one of the group discussions, where there was a real confusion about the desirability or undesirability of defenses, just as there is confusion on this point among practically everybody. I remember what I wanted to say if I had wanted to butt in was that there was a difference between neurotic defenses and healthy defenses or desirable defenses. We should keep in mind that the neurotic defense is neurotic because it is uncontrollable, ego-alien, compulsive, irrational, stupid, disapproved of, and the like. There are many kinds of controls on our impulses, i.e., defenses, which are very desirable and even necessary. Certainly, we are now aware, as Freud was not, that in our day, in our culture, many disorders are really disorders of *lack* of control, the disorders, i.e., of impulsivity. Frequently, people will make wisecracks about this and say what somebody needs is to acquire some inhibitions. This is regarded as a joke, but I don't regard it as a joke; I think it's perfectly true and sound that we cannot and should not and ultimately don't really want to give expression to our impulses of any kind whatsoever at any moment whatsoever and in any circumstances whatsoever. We do control them, we have to control them; not only reality demands it, but our own personal organization and continuity and values demand it. The fact is that ultimately there are many existential conflicts in human life; there are many insoluble problems; there are many situations in which we have to give up something in order to give up something else, and this is in the very essence of the human condition. This always means a certain conflict, it always means that while we go forward in one direction, we give up something else, and, therefore, we mourn over it and have to control ourselves.

Very frequently a choice means a commitment to one and an exclusion of the other. We can't wobble back and forth choosing now one thing and now the opposite. The whole system of monogamy, for instance, depends upon this final kind of choice and consistent kind of commitment, and, therefore, necessarily involves controls and defenses of desirable, healthy, and necessary sorts. The word "defense" has become too much of a dirty word. I supplemented it with the concept of "coping mechanisms" (22) and this has been a help. Anyway, the social philosophers will have to stress and stress again that Freud lived in 1910 and that the world was different then. Then, we might say, they were suffering, all of them, from too many inhibitions. Now, partly due to Freud, these unnecessary inhibitions have been weakened and destroyed. Now very frequently what we need is controls on the impulses and even some desirable inhibitions. I now think of one example: there was one woman in one of the groups who just kept flapping her mouth whenever she felt like it, right in the middle of anybody else's talk; she had to be slapped down, and she was attacked very vigorously by half-a-dozen people in the group. In essence, what they were saying was, "Control yourself, shut your mouth, we want to talk too; regulate the flow of words, talk when other people are not talking, don't interrupt, etc." Well, this kind of thing is an example of a desirable defense or coping mechanism or control.

I thought so frequently that the T-groups or the various other names that are used, e.g., sensitivity training, human relations, leadership groups, etc., were all pseudonyms for group therapy. Now I think I've changed my mind a little, for some of the reasons I've given above, but also for other reasons as well. For one thing, it occurred to me that the word therapy is anyway too darned condescending and implies something which isn't true necessarily in these situations, that people are sick in a psychiatric sense. But my impression is that most of the clients or customers in these groups are not sick in the ordinary psychiatric sense but are sick only in the normal, average sense, that is, they are ordinary, average citizens. Therefore what they need is not so much personal therapy of the psychiatric sort, which implies psychiatric sickness, but rather personal development or psychogogy or self-actualization training or something of the sort. These words are actually more accurate than psychotherapy.

Another point that dawned on me is that if you call it psychotherapy, this is very distasteful to whole portions of the population even though they may need psychotherapy. For instance, all these pseudonyms and synonyms make it far more acceptable to mesomorphs, to obsessionals, to tough-minded people, to thing-minded people, to people who hate psychology and distrust it, and so on and so on. Therefore I think I will keep some such term (that doesn't imply curing an illness) although I think it ought to be a better term than training, which is also condescending. The term trainer for the leader of these groups is as condescending as the word therapist, which implies that I, the god, healthy, perfect, way up here, will reach down, way down there, to you, poor worm, unhealthy, helpless, and I will help you. This kind of thing must be avoided. Even any faintest whisper of this kind of thing must be avoided as in the name—training group. Here the stress of the existential psychotherapists, as I interpret them, would be helpful, i.e., of brother human beings who are in the same boat, in the same human condition, helping each other as an older brother helps a younger brother out of love rather than out of condescension. We must certainly give up here in these groups any taint of the old medical paradigm in which a healthy man treated sick people, in an authoritative way.

An additional goal is "learning to trust," letting down the guards and defenses (especially counterattack and counterhostility, and especially giving up the paranoid kind of making yourself the target—see Laura Huxley, *You Are Not the Target*[10]). This is different from the learning of expressiveness or spontaneity. Also, it can be seen to some extent as a training in realism and objectivity, because it is a training in a current truth which is different from a childhood truth. That is,

[10] (New York: Farrar, Straus, 1963).

it is a childhood truth which has become a current unreality or false expectation. This makes it parallel to the Freudian stress on freedom from the past. Therefore, I think that it might be phrased better if we say "learning to trust"—when trust is warranted realistically; and "learning to *mistrust*"—when *that* is warranted by reality.

Another partial goal is learning to tolerate emotion. The calm of the leader (I refuse to call him trainer which reminds me of training bears, dogs) the way in which he can tolerate hostility perhaps, or remain calm when someone weeps, is going counter to the American mistrust of, and discomfort with, emotion, especially deep emotion, whether negative or positive. Part of this, possibly, or possibly something warranting separate treatment, is that the people in a T-group are apt to learn that the other people are not so hurtable after all, as some commonly think. It seems to be common in the reports of T-groups that somebody is criticized (however, objectively), or someone weeps or is a target of anger or whatever, and there is always someone else in the group who springs to his rescue because he is being hurt. In the long run such groups should teach by simple experience that people don't collapse under criticism, that they can tolerate a good deal more criticism than they are given credit for, i.e., if it is realistic and given in friendship.

Perhaps again separate, perhaps not, is learning to discriminate personal remarks which are objective and friendly from personal attacks. In the few group sessions I saw, this was very quickly apparent.

The learning to tolerate the lack of structure, ambiguity, planlessness, the lack of future, the lack of predictability, the lack of control of the future, all this is extremely therapeutic and psychogogic. Or to put it another way, it is a very desirable aspect of personal development, for instance, especially a necessary prerequisite for creativeness.

I think it is quite necessary to stress the selectivity of the T-groups, especially up on top of the mountain there in Lake Arrowhead or in other isolation cultures. In such a group, there are no real bastards, no real rattlesnakes, no real maliciousness and venom. These are decent people, in general, or at least people trying to be decent (or is that the same thing?). It is certainly an easy mistake to make if one generalizes from these selected T-groups on top of the mountain to cover bad conditions as well. Perhaps I'd better say it this way, that one of the reasons that these T-groups on top of the mountain function is because they work under good conditions. It is a real question whether they would work under bad conditions, that is, with really authoritarian people, or paranoid people, or quite immature people, or the like. This is especially true because the trainers or leaders are highly selected also. My impression was that every person in the staff group was a decent person; certainly, the group average was far above the average for the general population. But this again is a kind of selectivity. There aren't enough nice people in the whole population to make thousands and thousands of T-groups instead of the few dozen that there are in this country. It is especially necessary, therefore, to regard this as a kind of limited experiment under especially good conditions and, therefore, to watch out for dogma, piety, ritual, formulas, etc.

This is even more true when I ask the questions of a staff on top of a mountain, "Where is the evil? Where is the psychopathology? Where is the amount of Freudian pessimism and grimness which is realistically warranted?" I smelled up on top of the mountain there just a little too much of the Rogerian optimism about all people being good under all conditions and all people responding to good treatment, etc., which is simply not true. Under good conditions *many* people will respond well with growth—but not all. I also had this same lurking doubt about the leaders. It is clear that, in the long run, one cannot rely on self-selection for supplying leaders and therapists. Why do I not see in this literature more stress on personal therapy for the would-be leaders? Certainly, I would recommend it very strongly.

The whole discussion of hostility ought to be opened up much more richly by the sensitivity-training people—much more explicitly, with much more detail. For instance, it could certainly be said, even in the few days that I was there, that I saw people getting practice in expressing hostility openly. This is a huge problem in our society. Some people think that this is even the main problem confronting the psychoanalyst rather than what Freud took to be the main problem in 1890–1900 of repressed sexuality. Sexuality is no longer repressed in that same way nor so widely; now, hostility and aggression are repressed as sexuality used to be. There is more generally in the society a fear of conflict, of disagreement, of hostility, antagonism, enmity. There is much stress on getting along well with other people, even if you don't like them. Not only was hostility expressed more openly in these groups (in one group I saw the whole gang trying to help one rather mild man work himself up to the point of being able to criticize and counterattack), but also there was training in receiving hostility, in being the target of it, without falling apart. I saw in several groups transcendence of our normal American "politeness" in which people who were already accepted as affectionate friends now offered unpleasant comments, critical statements about a person with a very friendly air, so that the recipient was able to take it without feeling attacked, but simply as an act of affection, as a wish to help. Most people in our society can't do this; any criticism is an attack upon the whole person. But in the Arrowhead groups, there was an effort to teach the lesson that out of love and out of friendship, and out of the impulse to help, critical remarks may come, and these should be differentiated from deep-lying hostility or attack.

This also relates to the learning in the groups that people are more tough and more resilient and can absorb more pain than is implied by our system of politeness. This would undoubtedly leave behind as a permanent acquisition the ability to say no, the ability to criticize, the ability to disagree without assuming catastrophe was going to result.

Now all of this would be especially important for the men. If masculinity is a moot problem in our society, and if American men in general are not aggressive enough or forceful enough or decisive enough, then this kind of sensitivity group training could be considered as a kind of training in masculinity or at least this aspect of it. We have in our society such a huge proportion of appeasing, ingratiating males, men who avoid all disagreement, all fight, all sharp conflict of differences, who try to smooth over everything, try to be diplomatic, to make compromises always and not to make waves, not to rock the boat, and who give in easily when there is a majority against them, rather than holding out stubbornly and disagreeing. The characteristic picture is of the castrated male in the Freudian sense acting like a kind of a puppy dog who fawns and who wags his tail in order to curry favor in the face of disapproval, rather than one who is able to bite when necessary.

I would think here that a careful study of the Freudian stuff on aggression and destruction and even on the death wishes would be a good basis for trying to see this problem clearly. This does not mean that the whole Freudian business has to be swallowed; it means only a kind of a training in looking very deeply into the human psyche.

Still another point somewhat related to this, but over in a slightly different direction is that I was reminded often enough of the whole dominance-subordinates relationship, of the pecking order of the dominance hierarchies, for instance, as seen in my monkeys and apes (10, 9, 20). This variable apparently is *not sufficiently known to the group dynamics people.* I think I'll recommend to them that they read up on the monkey materials, etc. What I smell here is again some of the democratic dogma and piety in which all people are equal and in which the conception of a factually stronger person or natural leader or dominant person or superior intellect or superior decisiveness or whatever is bypassed because it makes everybody uncomfortable and because it seems to contradict the democratic philosophy (of course, it does *not* really contradict it). This is an additional research variable in the whole process of group dynamics and should be consciously perceived. In the stuff that I read, there were no references to this huge literature, just as there were practically no references to the whole Freudian psychoanalytic literature.

Notes on Creativeness

Creativeness is correlated with the ability to withstand the lack of structure, the lack of future, the lack of predictability, of control, the tolerance for ambiguity, for planlessness.

We can learn from the T-group experiences that creativeness is correlated with the ability to withstand the lack of structure, the lack of future, lack of predictability, of control, the tolerance for ambiguity, for planlessness.

Here-now creativeness is dependent on this kind of ability to forget about the future, to improvise in the present, to give full attention to the present, e.g., to be able fully to listen or to observe.

This general ability to give up future, structure, to give up control and predictability, is also characteristic of loafing, or of the ability to enjoy—to say it in another way—which itself is also essentially unmotivated, purposeless, without goal, and therefore without future. That is to say, in order to be able to listen totally, in order to be able to immerse oneself, to be all there in the here-now, one must be able to give up the future in the sense of being able to enjoy, to loaf, to saunter instead of purposefully walking, to take one's ease, in a word—to play (94).

Note, also, that the self-actualizing subjects can enjoy mystery, futurelessness, ambiguity, lack of structure. They can be contrasted with Kurt Goldstein's brain-injured subjects as well as with the obsessional neurotics in whom there is such a tremendous and compulsive need for control, for prediction, for structure, for law and order, for an agenda, for classifying, for rehearsing, for planning. In other words, it is as if these people were afraid of the future and also mistrusted their own ability to improvise in the face of an emergency, of something that would come up unexpectedly. This is then a combination of a lack of

INTERVIEW WITH MICHAEL RAY

What is the cause of creativity? What is the most important single thing we can do? Shall we add a three credit course in creativity? I half expect to hear someone ask soon "Where is it localized or try implanting electrodes with which to turn it off or on. I also get the strong impression that industry keeps looking for some secret button to push, like switching a light on and off. My feeling is that the concept of creativeness and the concept of the healthy, self-actualizing, fully human person seem to be coming closer and closer together, and may perhaps turn out to be the same thing.

—*Abraham Maslow, 1952*

In the early 1950s, Abraham Maslow began to acquire a national reputation for his work and research in the area of creativity. In his book, *Motivation and Personality*, Maslow noted that the world of psychology had yet to even scratch the surface in understanding the creative process of human beings. Today, creativity and innovation are considered to be among a company's greatest attributes. We sought out one of the leading scholars in the area of creativity to discuss Maslow's work.

Michael Ray is the John G. McCoy Bank One Corporation Professor of Creativity and Innovation at the Stanford University Graduate School of Business. He is a founding partner in the consulting firm Insight Out Collaborations. Ray is a social psychologist with extensive experience in advertising and marketing management, and is a fellow of the World Business Academy.

For the past 20 years, Ray has taught one of the most popular courses in the Stanford Graduate School of Business. Entitled Personal Creativity in Business, the course has shepherded hundreds of Stanford students through the process of gaining practical, long-term tools for accessing and applying creativity in their chosen professions. Guest lecturers in the class have been a who's who of American business leaders such as Charles Schwab (Schwab Investment), Steve Jobs (Pixar and Apple Computer), Tom Peters (author and consultant), Phillip Knight (Nike), Regis McKenna (McKenna Inc.), Vice Admiral James Stockdale, and others.

Several years ago, Michael decided to take the proven content and delivery method of his class into the corporate setting. He and several colleagues launched Insight Out Collaborations in an effort to assist employees and organizations in recapturing the creativity which Michael

(continued)

believes we are all born with. Michael Ray and his colleagues say that when creativity is stifled, individual performance is compromised, and the organization cannot function at full capacity. By leveraging the creative potential that already dwells within each individual, the organization can bring about dramatic improvement.

We spoke with Michael and his colleague, Jackie McGrath at their company headquarters in Menlo Park, California, regarding Abraham Maslow's research and his own work in the area of creativity.

★ ★ ★

Dr. Ray, consistently your class has been among the most popular in the business school. Twenty years should be some sort of a track record! Why do you think there is such immense interest?

Michael: What this course is about is what Maslow was writing about in his journals. We call it creativity but the content is about the most important things in life and the students sense this. We have had close to 200 speakers who have stories to tell about being creative. About 15 or 20 of the speakers are people who have taken the course and have distinguished themselves in business. They come back to speak to the students to share their experiences. One speaker in particular told the class that the course was not about business and not about creativity. He said it's about being yourself in life. We try to help students and executives answer two very important questions: Who am I and what is my life's work? So in the spirit of Maslow, we help them uncover the thing that is their "peak experience" or the work that is exactly right for them. It's the kind of work where, for example, there is an earthquake and the ceiling tiles could fall down around you and you wouldn't even notice because you are so absorbed. It is similar to what athletes call being in the zone. I think that is the basis for the popularity of the course.

Yet Maslow stated creativity is not something one can cause or instill. One can only help a person unleash their own inherent creativity. Would you agree?

Yes. Our creativity and innovation, that which we are born with, is five or six layers beneath the surface. When we observe children, we see a glimpse of what we've lost in the process of maturing. Children are totally honest, living very much in the moment, and very creative. Our ability to contribute in the world can be enormous if we access that part of ourselves we lose due to society's pressures to conform, to fit in.

There was a study conducted at Harvard University several years ago which set out to measure IQ, spatial, visual, social, and emotional intelligence of infants and young children. The researchers found that up to age 4, the young children were up to the genius level. After age 4, through the development process, their scores were lower. What I take from this research is that after age 4, mainly from parents and society, we get messages which cover up our own natural tendencies to creativity. We get messages that we shouldn't approach a problem in this way, we shouldn't do this and we shouldn't do that. Even the best of parents send these messages. As a result, by the time we are 35 or 40 our creativity is completely covered over. This voice which really isn't you but tells you the way the world works is a direct attack on creativity. We have to work to remove it. Observe how many times a day that voice keeps you from doing something. We attempt to help people expand their world, to see beyond the structure and the order.

Jackie: In our society now, with the stress, rapid pace, and amount of mistrust and distrust, it is really a challenge to live this way. Maslow stated that creativity comes from ambiguity, uncertainty, living in the moment, lack of predictability. He believed that in fact these qualities caused creativity to flow. These seem to be the very qualities we tend to fight. What does he mean?

Michael: It's really self-trust that Maslow is talking about. Having faith in your own creativity is self-trust. We're saying it's evidence of things unseen or the substance of things hoped for. It's so qualitative. In the scientific paradigm we live in, the only thing we are supposed to believe and trust in are the things we can measure and see. However, what we are speaking about can't be measured or quantified. Creativity is not just idea generation, problem solving, or the next innovative product. The process of creativity contains joy, wisdom, faith, intuition, compassion. It's having so much faith in the creativity you are born with that you know you can have it at your disposal all the time.

Jackie: I think in corporations we need to help individuals become comfortable living with ambiguity and lack of structure. Yet, these very things we fight can lead to high performance and the ability to sustain ourselves. We talk about organizational whitewater within organizations but the truth is that we are all in the whitewater. We still live under this illusion that we have control. We do not.

Michael: This is a direct frontal attack on this issue of the need for order and predictability. We need to get away from the order and the structure to unleash our creativity.

(continued)

How do you assist students and executives in reclaiming their creativity and innovation?

Michael: There is no seven-step or nine-step processes to finding your way back to your creative nature. We begin by introducing a concept we call a "live with." The live with is asking executives to go for one week with no expectations, no mechanisms of control, no walking into a situation with a plan or vision of the future. We also suggest they become comfortable with saying "I don't know." This approach helps them to begin to rely and to trust their own creative nature. Creativity is idiosyncratic. So, we use many different things in bringing about creativity. We refer people to meditation, the martial arts, drawing, music, singing, writing. We try to help them re-connect with that part of themselves which is creative. Our concept of "the absence of judgment" has an interesting effect on corporate executives. A re-occurring theme we see is the sadness they speak of when they are cognizant of the voice of judgment they bring to almost all situations in their lives. Therein lies our comfort zone because it's our way of structuring a problem or situation. When we learn to silence the inner voice that judges yourself and others, there is no limit to what we can accomplish, individually and as part of a team. Absence of judgment makes you more receptive to innovative ideas. You look for information in places you wouldn't normally think about.

Would you give us some examples of what happens when people take these steps?

Michael: One large consumer products company enrolled 180 people in our program. The vice president of the division told us one of the employees was a fellow who was very quiet, had never really accomplished high levels of performance, and had very low self-esteem. After the course, this fellow decided to become involved in one area of the company and through his work he was responsible for developing a particular product that ended up giving them a two to one advantage over any other product in that market category. The facts were undeniable. We were able to help him unleash his creative potential. Another executive was seeking approval from the federal government for a particular product. The response from the government was a two-year delay in the product cycle. He said that in the past he could have simply packed up his bags and accepted the response from the government. He decided to apply some of the concepts he had learned in unleashing the creative process and was able to turn a two-year mandate into a span of six months. Another executive ran into a labeling problem with a particular product. He and his team learned to trust their creative abilities. They solved the labeling problem and patented the process for solving it. A group of employees from a research and development lab had always taken an hour of set-up time just to begin a project. They took the creative process they had learned and cut the hour set-up time back to one minute which resulted in an annual savings to the company of nearly $300,000.

Jackie: The creative process allows for a new way for people to relate to one another. They naturally move to more self-directed teams and to what has been referred to as a community. It's a team of people that is inclusive, where diversity is celebrated, where one learns to fight gracefully, where people can be vulnerable with each other, and where trust flourishes. Recalling our natural creative process shows us a new way of working together that will produce break-away levels of performance.

Michael: One of the things Maslow was saying we see in our work. When people are creative, they are sensitive to all types of possibilities. When they are not operating from a creative base, people block out the possibilities and operate from a control base or control mechanism. That control base prevents us from reclaiming our creativity.

Jackie: It was interesting to me in reading Maslow's journal entries that he was really telling us to be in the moment, to be present. A lot of these techniques we use are to bring people into the present. Why is it we run through our day, shutting out much of what is going on? When you get stressed out you start to cycle through. We teach people to learn to cycle through and be fully present.

Michael: Maslow also talks about fear. We do a lot of work around this issue. We refer to the concept as our voice of objective intelligence. It is that voice that sees the world, pointing out what really is. We talk about deep fears and give people the opportunity to anonymously air their deepest fears with other executives in the organization. It's amazing what happens. People begin to see similarities in their fears. Their fears bring them closer together. Executives soon begin to question that if their own fear is high, what is the level of fear throughout the organization. How is that fear crippling creativity? Another assumption we hold is that any strong emotion (fear, anger, hurt, sorrow) can be tracked back to its source. That same source holds joy, happiness, and so on. As Maslow states about human nature, and we believe, for every vice we have there is a virtuous side. Uncovering the source helps us find the virtuous side. One of the typical breakthroughs people have in the creative process we've outlined is the power of being in the moment. When you see something really beautiful and you are taken by it, everything stops and you are really accessing

(continued)

something about yourself which is profound. That is a tiny glimpse into who you are and your core of creativity. A tiny glimpse of what your creativity is all about.

Jackie: We really encourage people to write daily about being in the moment. It's about paying attention. It's so important because a Type A person like me doesn't want to reflect. As executives we've been taught not to reflect. Especially in the high technology area. We are conditioned to move fast. In these industries you have very bright people moving very quickly who never have time for contemplation or reflective moments. They don't stop to think about what they're doing. They know the game, how the game is played and they really play the game. However, they spend no time in contemplation with questions such as "Is there a different way to play?" "Do I want to play at all?"

Michael: We need to be determined to assist people in experiencing a creative life. It all begins with the individual. As individuals contribute more of their unique talents, the business reaps the rewards in the form of innovative products, reduced time to market, more efficient planning strategies, and dramatically improved decision making.

---

trust in one's self, a kind of fear that one does not have the ability or the capacity to face anything which is unexpected, which is not planned for, which is not controllable and predictable, and so on. Give the examples here of the geometrizing of time and space of the brain-injured people.[1] I think I can also use my article, "Emotional Blocks to Creativity" for good obsessional examples (68).

Point out that these are all safety mechanisms, all fear and anxiety mechanisms. They all represent lack of courage, lack of confidence in the future, lack of confidence in one's self. It takes a certain kind of courage, which is simultaneously a kind of justified trust in one's self and a justified trust in the goodness of the environment and of the future, to be able to face an unexpected, an unknown, unstructured situation without any guards or defenses, and with an innocent faith that one can improvise in the situation. Perhaps, for communication purposes some simpler examples may be necessary, for instance, like pointing out to an audience how commonly in a conversation, when the other person is talking, they are not really

[1] E. Strauss in Rollo May, et al. (Eds.), *Existence* (New York: Basic Books, 1958).

listening but are rather planning and rehearsing what they are going to say as a response. Then point out how this means lack of confidence in their ability to improvise, that is, to think up words to say without preparing beforehand, without planning.

I think another good example might be actual motion pictures of the way in which a little toddler or perhaps an infant shows in actual behavior total trust in the mother or the father. Get pictures of a kid jumping off a height into his father's arms with total fearlessness and total trust. Or into a swimming pool.

I think that it would be useful to add this to my discussion of safety science contrasted with growth science or self-actualizing science.[2] Compare with Kurt Goldstein's brain-injured patients[3] and with the symptoms of the obsessional neurotics (22). Let's compare, in a parallel column, B. F. Skinner's (83) stress again and again and again in his lectures and written papers on predictability, on control, lawfulness, structure, etc. Then make an actual count of how infrequently the words creativeness, improvising, spontaneity, expressiveness, autonomy, and the like, occur. Then do the same for Carl Rogers or for other similar, "humanistic" writers. It occurs to me that this would make a very nice experiment that even an undergraduate student could do easily enough. It would make the point I'm trying to make very neatly and easily and unmistakably. In any case this would also make the parallel with two kinds of psychopathology and at the very least dramatize the point that I am trying to make that these words may be psychopathological. (Of course, it's also necessary to stress that they can be quite healthy. But then, the question is how to make the differentiation between neurotic need for predictability and the normal pleasure in predictability, control, lawfulness, orderliness in the world, and so on.)

I guess here it would be useful, especially for the laymen, to make a little discussion of just what the differences are between the neurotic needs and normal or healthy needs. At the moment I can think of the facts that the neurotic needs are uncontrollable, inflexible, compulsive, irrational, independent of good or bad circumstances; that their gratification does not bring real pleasure but only momentary relief; that their frustration brings, very quickly, tension, anxiety, and

[2] Forthcoming book on *Psychology of Science*.
[3] Kurt Goldstein, *The Organism* (Boston: Beacon Press, 1963).

finally hostility and anger. Furthermore, they are ego-dystonic rather than ego-syntonic; that is, they are felt as alien or as something overcoming one, rather than as one's own autonomous self-willed coming-from-within desires or impulses. The neurotic person is apt to say, "Something comes over me," or "I don't know what came over me," or "I have no control over it."

Run through all of this creativeness stuff and apply it to the managerial situation, the leadership and fellowship situation. In every discussion about these things in any enterprise of any kind whatsoever, there is certainly going to come up from those who need more structure, whether for good reasons or bad, the questions about anarchy and chaos and the like. It is necessary to meet these not only on a rational level but also to understand them as possibly neurotic or irrational or deeply emotional. Sometimes the proper way to handle this is not to argue logically but to interpret psychoanalytically. It's very easy to point out without too much offense in such groupings that this is a demand for a set of laws and rules and principles which are all written down in the book, that this is a demand for controlling the future and for anticipating anything that might come up in the future. Since this latter is realistically impossible, that is, since the future is, after all, unpredictable to some extent, then trying to make a "book of rules" which will anticipate any possible contingency in the future is a futile effort; and then one can go on to ask, Why can't we trust ourselves to be able to handle these unexpected contingencies in the future? Why must we prepare for them so? Can't we handle exceptions; don't we trust ourselves to have good judgment, even in an unanticipated situation? Why can't we wait until we have experiences piling up in the situations and *then* make whatever rules are necessary as a kind of formulation of actual experience in the actual situation. In this way one comes to a minimum of rules rather than to a maximum of rules. (But it may be necessary to concede, as I have had to do in the past, that in extremely large organizations like the Army and the Navy it is necessary to have a Book of Rules.)

Addition to the Notes on the Creative Person

It is as if these people were afraid of the future and also mistrusted their own ability to improvise in the face of something that would come up unexpectedly. This is then a combination of a lack of trust in ones' self, a kind of fear that one does not have the ability or the capacity to face anything which is unexpected, unpredictable.

Since so much of the trouble with mechanical and authoritarian organization, and with old-fashioned treatment of the worker as an interchangeable part, seems to be the inability to shift and change, the obsessional need for a planned-out future, for schedules, for sameness, and the like, it seems to me that it would be basically quite important for the philosophy of democratic management to study more carefully the psychodynamics of creativeness.

It is desirable to stress, in this context particularly, the ability to be imprecise. The creative person is able to be flexible; he can change course as the situation changes (which it always does); he can give up his plans, he can continuously and flexibly adapt to the law of the changing situation and to the changing authority of the facts, to the demand character of the shifting problem.

This means, to say it in a theoretical way, that he is able to face a changing future; that is, he does not need a fixed and unchanging future. He seems not to be threatened by unexpectedness (as the obsessional and rigid person is). For the creative person who is able to improvise, plans are definitely no more than heuristic scaffoldings and can be cast aside easily without regret and without anxiety. He tends not to feel irritated when plans change or schedules change or the future changes. On the contrary, my impression is that he is sometimes

apt to show *increased* interest, alertness, and engagement with the problem. Self-actualizing people are attracted to mystery, to novelty,
change, flux, and find all of these easy to live with; as a matter of fact,
these are what make life interesting. These people, that is, the self-
actualizing people and also the creative people and the good improvi-
sors tend, on the contrary, to be easily bored with monotony, with
plans, with fixity, with lack of change.

Of course, this is all seen from another angle—the ability of the
matured personality, the strong personality to be *all there,* to be totally
here and now, to be able to pour himself totally into the current situation, to be able to listen perfectly and to see perfectly, etc. This, I
have pointed out, can be phrased in terms of giving up the past and the
future, or of pushing them aside from the present situation. That is,
the person viewing a present problem does not see it merely as a matter of shuffling over every problem he has ever had in the past to see
which past solutions fit this present problem. Nor does he use the
problematic situation as a period in which to prepare himself for the
future, to rehearse what he is going to say, to plan his attack or counterattack, etc. He is totally immersed in the here and now, thereby
implying considerable courage and trust in himself, the calm expectation of being able to improvise when the time comes for him to solve
new problems. This means a particular kind of healthy self-respect,
self-trust. It also implies freedom from anxiety and from fear. This, in
turn, means a certain appraisal of the world, of reality, of environment,
which permits him to trust it, not to see it as overwhelmingly dangerous and powerful. He feels that he is able to manage it. He is not
afraid of it. It does not look monstrous or frightening. Self-respect
means that the person thinks of himself as a prime mover, as the responsible one, as autonomous, the determiner of his own fate.

Notes on the Entrepreneur

The main point that I could make in communication in this area would be to point out the difference between the great and the good societies and the regressing, deteriorating societies is largely in terms of the entrepreneurial opportunity and the number of such people in society.

T he entrepreneurial function is too much underplayed and undervalued. The entrepreneurs—the managers, integrators, organizers, and planners—themselves undervalue the worth of their own function and are still apt to think of themselves in the older terms as exploiters, as superficial, as not really working, not really contributing. Therefore, as a group they are apt to feel a little guilty about their rewards.

Partly, I think, this is tied in with the notion of work as *only* sweating and laboring, and partly it is a consequence of misunderstanding of the nature of inventions.

As for inventions, our tendency is to think that they result from a great flash of insight in which in one instant darkness becomes light and ignorance becomes knowledge. This is the notion of the brand-new discovery which never existed before, and it is obviously wrong in most cases, since any invention, however novel, has its history. It should be seen anyway as the product of collaboration and division of labor; that is, invention may result from a sudden integration of previously known bits of knowledge not yet suitably patterned. The flash of discovery is most frequently the closure of a Gestalt rather than the creation of something out of nothing.

If this is so, then the distinction between the invention and the administrative arrangement fails. The administrative arrangement or the managerial invention, e.g., the use of interchangeable standard parts at Winchester Arms Company or on Henry Ford's assembly line, etc., are also the putting into collocation of pieces of knowledge which were lying there available for anyone but which suddenly become potent and important in this new constellation or pattern.

We might, if we wished, differentiate social inventions from technological inventions, but it does not really matter in principle very much. Discovering a way in which the husband and wife could communicate with each other better is an invention in this sense.

I should say also that the entrepreneurial plan or vision, the recognition of a need which is being unfulfilled and which could be fulfilled to the profit of the entrepreneur and to everyone else's benefit as well, had also better come under the general head of invention.

The main point that I could make in communication in this area would be to point out that the difference between the great and good societies and the regressing, deteriorating societies is largely in terms of the entrepreneurial opportunity and the number of such people in the society. I think everyone would agree that the most valuable 100 people to bring into a deteriorating society like, for instance, Peru, would be not 100 chemists, or politicians, or professors, or engineers, but rather 100 entrepreneurs.

Phrased in this style, the guilt of the self-devaluating entrepreneurs can be allayed. He can then see how important he is, even how crucial.

My own opinion is that this need not get tangled up with the question of monetary rewards exclusively. There are other kinds of rewards. It is true that an entrepreneur may be worth huge sums of money to a society, but it is also true that great disparities of income may breed their own problems. If only for theoretical purposes, it is well to recognize that the entrepreneur, the organizer, the spark plug, the active leader upon whom everything depends, can be rewarded in other ways than by money. In the synergic society, like that of the Blackfoot Indians, the leader, or organizer was paid off in public honors of various sorts, in the respect and the regard of everybody in the tribe, in his being welcomed wherever he went, etc. The point is that this worked in spite of the fact that this great leader frequently was penniless. That is part of the picture of the great leader—his total generosity. His wealth there was defined in terms of how much he could afford to earn and give away. So also, in England knighthood is considered a great reward. I think we might one day go so far as to single out the great entrepreneur or inventor or leader and honor him by

THE HUMAN SIDE OF ENGINEERING

What is then the correct way of teaching people to be engineers? It is quite clear that we must teach them to be creative persons, at least in the sense of being able to confront novelty, to improvise . . . and if possible (because best of all) even be able to enjoy novelty and change. Education can no longer be considered essentially or only a learning process; it is now also a character training, a person-training process and it will become truer and truer year by year . . . Since, in essence we are talking about a kind of person, a kind of philosophy, a kind of character, then the stress shifts away from stress on created products, and technological innovation and aesthetic products and innovations. We must become more interested in the creative process, the creative attitude, the creative person, rather than the creative product alone.

—Abraham Maslow, 1963

Professor Tom Kosnik of Stanford University's School of Engineering plays an integral role in educating some of the best and brightest leaders in the United States. His students will graduate from this prestigious university into leadership roles within a variety of corporations. They are the cream of the crop as future business executives go. Dr. Kosnik not only teaches them the basic concepts of engineering but the human components of leadership. As in the quote from Maslow, Kosnik seems to know that their personhood, their character, their internal operating philosophy are as important as their technical training.

Spending time with Dr. Kosnik brings one quickly to the realization that we've spent decades perfecting the technical, numerical, scientific, and statistical goals in the halls of our business and engineering schools. Yet, Kosnik realizes that those who will be the great managers and leaders will embody not only the technical tasks but an understanding of the importance of the human side of the enterprise. He knows that greatness is much more than technique or skill. Thus, the elements of integrity, core values, unrelenting optimism, and contribution to society play as large a role in Kosnik's repertoire as the quantitative topics. He manages to blend both worlds with the finesse of a symphony conductor.

Yet, Dr. Kosnik's philosophy is still a rarity in the halls of business and engineering schools. Take, for example, the lack of emphasis on such subjects in our schools. However, things may be changing. Recently the associate dean of a rather large and prestigious school of business said,

(continued)

"Companies are scrambling to keep employees. They realize that a company is the people doing the work—a relatively new trend. So we are adding courses to our curriculum to address the people side of business." Another comment from a business school administrator paints the picture when he said *"I think within the last 10 years managers and executives of companies finally realized that people are the real assets, so we are responding with changes in our curriculum."*

Perhaps we can all learn from Dr. Kosnik as he is able to help his students discover the richness behind economics, accounting, marketing, and engineering by uncovering the sacred and the human elements of organizations. He did just that with us when he offered us the opportunity to give his class a reading assignment from Maslow's journals. We joined Dr. Kosnik for a lecture and dialogue on a variety of subjects from Maslow's journals. We made one mistake. We expected to do the teaching. Yet, the students did most of that! Here is what they told us:

"Although money is certainly important, I want to go to work for a firm that understands some of the things Maslow talks about. I want to work in an environment that will allow me to make a difference."

"My father worked for a large corporation all of his life. Although he had all of the trappings and the accomplishments, I never believed he was happy. I think somehow the environment sucked away all of his spirit. I will not allow that to happen to me."

"I realize that issues such as leadership, values, and managing people will be core to my success. Yet, we never really seem to focus on those issues for any lengthy period of time. I suppose we just all assume that we somehow have those skills or will get them. I don't think that's a very wise strategy."

"This was one of the best lectures we've had. I was excited by it and I loved reading Maslow's work. This is what life is about. I sometimes think we focus too much on the processes and procedures and forget about the joy in work."

"I'm on a fellowship with a large corporation. As I was reading Maslow's book I kept thinking, "Why can't we have an organization like this?" Actually, we are a fairly good organization, one of the best, but we could do much better when it comes to some of these issues."

"I just want to tell you that Maslow's book and your lecture touched me deeply. I loved the section on leadership."

"I wish more CEOs and upper level managers could have heard this discussion today. Perhaps it would make life better for those in the trenches."

"Thanks for making me think. These are profound questions you raise."

giving him absolute simplicity as in the Catholic church. Conferring a robe of gray monk's cloth perhaps would have the same meaning and the same psychological rewarding power as great sums of money, perhaps even more, depending upon the way in which the society looked at it. If such a man were greatly admired, respected, appreciated, approved, applauded, welcomed, then he would need no money.

It would help keep the point clean and uncontaminated if I were to point out that it holds in principle for any society and for any economic system, whether capitalist, socialist, communist, or fascist. The initiator, spark-plug, coordinator type of person is equally necessary, equally valuable in each of these societies (even though this will conflict with the desire to stagnate and not change, which may exist simultaneously). It is true that other determinants are also involved, e.g., is the society synergic or not, exploitative or not, caste-stratified or not, etc.

McClelland's work is very important in this connection.[1]

---

[1] D. McClelland, *The Achieving Society* (Princeton, NJ: D. Van Nostrand Co., Inc., 1961).

Memorandum on the Redefinition of Profit, Taxes, Costs, Money, Economics, etc.

There are many people who cannot be won away from their present jobs except by offering all sorts of higher need and meta need satisfactions . . . if I take into account all these other higher need intangibles which nobody puts into the contract nor on the balance sheet, but which are nevertheless very, very, real to any sensible person . . . Why should a necessary and valuable person stay in a job rather than move to another one?

The redefining of the concept "profit" necessarily involves the redefining of the concept "cost." Also it requires the redefining of the concept "price." Maybe I can approach the whole business from a different angle altogether, that is, from the angle of the critique of classical economic theory. In the textbooks I've seen, this is based almost entirely on an obsolete motivation theory of lower basic needs exclusively (leaving out higher needs and metaneeds); furthermore it assumes that these can be phrased in interchangeable terms, which in turn implies that any accounting deals entirely with objects or qualities or characteristics that can be phrased in terms of money and therefore put into a money accounting balance sheet.

But all this is today absolute nonsense. This is true only because we now know so much more about the higher basic needs and also the metaneeds beyond them (which will be far from important motivators in the affluent, automated society). One way of showing this is to stress the fact that money no longer is a very important motivation. There are now many people in our society who cannot be won away to another job by offering more money unless it is a *huge* increase in money. Or say it still another way. Suppose that money becomes unimportant because everybody has enough, or anybody can get enough rather easily in order to satisfy his basic needs. As labor of any kind gets higher and higher priced it becomes possible to earn a minimum subsistence with less and less work. Anybody who really wants to be a hobo can rather easily be one these days. It's very easy to earn what used to be called "a living." (The trouble is when most people talk about earning a living these days they really mean earning an automobile, a fine house, landscaped garden, and so on and so on.)

If this is so, as it indeed seems to be, there are many people who cannot be won away from their present jobs except by offering all sorts of higher need and metaneed satisfactions. Furthermore, many people are influenced more by nonmonetary than by monetary considerations. For instance, I pointed out to Andy Kay that when anybody offered me a job I tried to put some rough money value on all sorts of intangibles, like for instance, giving up a friend, or beautiful surroundings, or giving up warm relationships at my place of work, or the simple fact of familiarity with everything and everybody, or going to the trouble of moving from one city to another, or even such things as having to learn my way around a new city. I have asked myself how much money is it worth to me to give up my friendship with my best friends. At my time of life it is difficult to develop this kind of intimacy in a short period of time. Is my best friend worth $1,000 a year or $500 a year or $5,000 or what? Anyway, it's quite clear that he is worth *something* which I had better take into account. If, for instance, I arbitrarily assign a value of $1,000 a year to having an intimate friend (which is certainly a modest figure), then this new job which has been offered at a raise, of let's say $2,000 or $3,000, or $4,000 a year simply is not what it looked like at first. I may actually be losing value, or dollar value, if I take into account all these other higher need intangibles which nobody puts into the contract nor on the balance sheet, but which are nevertheless very, very real to any sensible person.

But something of the same sort is true of industry. Why should a necessary and valuable person stay on a job rather than move to another one? Well, is it not that he likes the house he lives in or that he has a pleasant boss to work with or pleasant colleagues or that the secretary that he works with is cheerful rather than surly or that the janitors are obliging rather than nasty or even such a thing as that the place is attractive or beautiful rather than ugly? Certainly the questions of climate and weather and education for the children, etc., are all taken into account by any sensible person.

The old concept of taxes is that they are like the fees which the robber barons arbitrarily imposed, or which some group of bandits squeezed out of passersby under threat of military oppression. The "protection money" which the gangsters used to impose in Chicago is very close to this original meaning of the word "tax." The word today still carries some of this connotation, that of arbitrary, greedy people who are demanding some money for which they return nothing, just simply because they're in a position of power, and you have to grind your teeth and give in. But, under good circumstances and under eupsychian theoretical conditions, taxes are a very different kind of thing and must be seen in a very different way, that is, as payment for necessary services at a bargain rate, because otherwise the healthy long-term enterprise would have to replace all of these services on a private basis, which would cost a great deal more. This is true for water, police services, medical services, fire services, general sanitation services and the like. Practically all of these represent terrific bargains, and the taxes for them should be considered to be part of the necessary costs of any long-term enterprise, an indispensable *sine qua non* of enterprise. This is also as true or almost as true for the huge chunk of local taxes which goes for education and schools in general. From the point of view of an enterprise, this can be seen as preparation by the community of skilled workers and managers of all kinds. If the community did not teach reading, writing, and arithmetic, then the enterprise itself would have to do this. If there were no school system, then this would have to be created by the enterprise itself. So this, too, is a great bargain.

(Of course this all assumes enlightened managerial policy in which the more developed the human being is, the more evolved, the more fully grown, the better for the enterprise. Under Theory X conditions the opposite would be true, because authoritarianism rests upon ignorance and fear rather than upon enlightenment, autonomy, and courage.)

Sooner or later we will have to deal with the questions of higher-need economics and of metaneed economics in a serious theoretical way. I cannot foresee how many modifications of economic theory and practice would be needed because of this, but certainly some can be seen now. One is this; in a prosperous society and under fairly good conditions and with fairly good people, the lowest creature needs would be taken care of very easily; it would take rather little money to be able to barely eat and sleep and have shelter and so on. Perhaps it will even be cheaper to give them away. Then as we rise higher in the hierarchy of basic needs, we find that money gets to be less and less important in buying them. Of the highest needs we can say that they come free or almost free. Or to say it another way, the higher need satisfactions of belongingness, of love and friendliness and affection, of respect given, and of possibility of building self-respect—all these are largely outside the money economy altogether; e.g., they can be given to the poorest family just so long as it is well organized.

These higher needs are precisely what enlightened management policy points itself toward. That is to say, enlightened management policy may be *defined* as an attempt to satisfy the higher needs in the work situation, in a nonmonetary way, that is, to have the work situation give intrinsically higher need satisfaction (rather than to give the money and expect the money to buy these satisfactions outside the work situation). We can go pretty far with this because it's actually possible to distinguish between Theory X management and Theory Y management simply on this basis; that is, Theory X is a theory of motivation which implies all the lower needs and Theory Y is a more inclusive and more scientific and realistic theory of motivation because it includes the higher needs and considers them to be factors in the work situation and in the economic situation. Or to say it still another way, authoritarian economics or Theory X economics and managerial policy proceed on the assumption that there are no instinctoid higher basic needs. (Since there is so much evidence that there are such needs, Theory X is not only distasteful in a democratic society on moral principles, but it is also scientifically false.) (I think the high and low grumble experiment [see below] will prove that metaneeds are also part of the economic situation or the work situation and of managerial Theory X. That is, we may turn out to have a lower-need economics, a higher-need economics, and also a meta-need economics, in a kind of hierarchy of prepotency.) I wish Walter Weisskopf could be permitted to teach others about these points as he has taught me.[1]

[1] W. Weisskopf, *The Psychology of Economics* (Chicago: University of Chicago Press, 1995); also "Economic Growth and Human Well-Being," *Manas*, August 21, 1963, *16*, 1–8.

The trouble is how to put these on the balance sheet, how to put them into the accounting system, how to give them weight in the actual calculation of salary for a particular man or of the worth to the organization of the personality development of the people in it, for instance. Try to put it this way, for one example: if a particular man who is twenty-five years old is working in an organization at a particular level X which is not terribly good, and then for some reason goes into psychotherapy for a long period of time and becomes a better person and as a result comes out able to work at a higher level Y, then it is very clear that attaining this higher level of efficiency in productivity and managerial skill cost him a great deal of money. Is this part of his "wealth"? Where in his accounting system does this gain get written down? (The same question is true for higher education of any other kind.)

Still another question here: assuming that in one factory Theory X prevails and in another factory Theory Y prevails, and that naturally the latter one is better for the personal growth of any individual in it, how can this gain be put into the accounting system? Certainly it all costs some money. The cost of training enlightened managers is greater than the cost of training unenlightened managers. How shall this gain be represented in a numerical fashion in the balance sheet? Certainly it must be considered some kind of fringe benefit, that is to say a non-money benefit, and any sensible man, of course, would realize that this was a benefit, an economic benefit, a higher-need economic benefit, even though it would be hard to put into numerical terms or monetary terms.

Another question: the fact that an enlightened factory undoubtedly will be discovered to make all sorts of differences not only in the intrinsic work situation, that is, by way of turning out better products and so on, but also in helping its people to become better citizens, better husbands, better wives, etc., etc. This is an asset or a benefit to the population at large in exactly the same way that a schoolhouse is or college or hospital or a therapeutic institute. That is, how could an accounting system build into itself the benefits that an enterprise gives to the community? Certainly, even in the money economy, this makes a certain amount of sense, because this costs a certain amount of money to the enterprise, e.g., for education within the company, for enlightened services of various sorts, for education in the broadest sense, etc.

Sometime in the future we will have to deal with more subtle aspects of long-term, enlightened management, democratic holistic society economics, in at least this sense: A healthy business assumes all sorts of things that we haven't yet spoken about. For instance, it really assumes a kind of an open and free market, perhaps we can use the word "open competition" here. It is better for the long-term health of an enterprise that it be able to compete, that there be rival factories turning out similar products which can be compared with each other, that other factories keep on pressing for improvement, etc. This is in contrast with, let's say, the Franco-Spain situation in which a monopoly is arbitrarily given to some relative, who thereafter, for instance, will produce all the matches in Spain or all the automobiles or whatever it may be. What happens inevitably in the monopoly situation of this sort, since there is no pressure to keep up quality or certainly none to improve, is that everything will most likely deteriorate steadily. The people involved must inevitably become cynical as they realize that they are crooks and liars and evil people in general who have been forced into an evil situation. They will almost inevitably tax the helpless population, i.e., set a higher price on the products than they would be worth in an open market, and furthermore, since the product itself will most likely deteriorate, the enterprise will certainly not be healthy.

To use a slightly different parallel a child who is brought up in a germ-free environment, is carefully protected against all bacteria and viruses and so on, loses entirely, sooner or later, the ability to resist disease. That is to say, he must thereafter, for the rest of his life be artificially protected because he cannot protect himself. By contrast, the child who is permitted to take his own chances and to live in the world of dangers and is only ordinarily and reasonably protected against the dangers will, because he gets these dangers in small doses, build up antibodies and resistances so that he can walk freely through all the germs and viruses thereafter for the rest of his life without fear and without getting disease. I think this is indication enough that some new theory of competition or of free market or of free enterprise in this sense will have to be worked out. It should be kept separate from cold war talk, or political talk of any kind, because precisely the same thing is true of any other kind of social or economic system. That is, a healthy enterprise in the socialistic economy would depend upon the same conditions of exposure to stress, exposure to competition that would be required in a capitalistic economy. That is to say, this is not simply a political economic or moral consideration; it follows very simply from the intrinsic necessities of an enterprise which is to last for a couple of centuries, and which is to remain alive homeostatically and also to grow. A good boxer needs a good sparring partner or he will deteriorate.

Furthermore, if we assumed, as I think it could be demonstrated that we *must,* that rationality, truth, honesty, and justice in this free market, in this free competition of similar products, should prevail in order to keep up the health of all the enterprises and of all the people in these enterprises and of the society in general, then it is very desirable (and perhaps even theoretically necessary), that cream be able to rise to the top of the milk. The best product should be bought, the best man should be rewarded more. Interfering factors which befuddle this triumph of virtue, justice, truth, and efficiency, etc., should be kept to an absolute minimum or should approach zero as a limit. Here I'm talking about the salesman's winning smiles, personal loyalties, favoring your relatives, or fake advertising which stresses the wrong thing (like the beautiful design of a car on the outside without regard to the lousy motor inside).

If all these things can be demonstrated to be true for the healthy enterprise and the healthy system of enterprises, i.e., society, then many things will follow. And one of these things is that the consumer, the buyer, the customer must be assumed to be rational, that is, that he will want the best product for his purposes. This means also to think that he will look for factual information, examine specifications, read the labels, get indignant over being swindled instead of taking it for granted, and shudder with disgust when he meets a crook or liar and thereafter stay away from him, etc., etc. Now, all these qualities are characteristics of higher psychological health, growth toward self-actualization. Therefore, any determinant that increases the health of a particular person, making him therefore not only a better manager or better worker or better citizen but also a better consumer, must be considered to be good for the health of any particular enterprise, even though in a tiny, tiny way. Anything that will enable the consumers to select out on the basis of facts and of truly good workmanship, etc., is good for everybody else or everything else in the whole society, including the single, long-termed enlightened enterprise. Therefore, the enlightened factory which helps people to grow is thereby helping every other factory in the whole society in principle. And, in principle at least, this should be valued by all the other factories, just as anything else should be valued that turns out better, more realistic, "higher" customers. Now the question is, can this somehow be put on the balance sheet: can an accounting system take account of fringe benefits to other factories from having an efficient, enlightened scientific factory setup.

Another way to try to say these various things is to start with the conception of the "good customer or the enlightened customer." Everything that has preceded and everything in the management literature rests on assuming that the customer is rational, prefers good quality, will choose the better product for the purpose, will choose the lesser price if quality is equal, will not be seduced by irrelevancies, will prefer virtue and truth and justice and so on, and will get indignant or insulted or disgusted or angry when someone tries to swindle him. This assumption is also necessary because the main basis upon which enlightened management policy so far rests is that productivity is improved both in quantity and quality. *But* what good will it do to turn out a better product at a cheaper price if betterness and cheapness mean nothing to the consumer? That is, if he cares less about these than about other things which are irrelevant, then the whole argument for more efficient factories, managers, and supervisors falls to the ground entirely. If people like being fooled, if they like being swindled, if they prefer being seduced, if they prefer being bribed, then enlightened management is bad, rather than good for economic survival. Therefore, the theory of the good and efficient factory has as an absolute prerequisite, the good and rational customer armed with good taste and with righteous indignation. It is only when people value honesty that honesty pays. It is only when people value good quality that good quality pays. It is only when people get righteously indignant over being swindled, that people will tend to stop swindling. If swindling pays, then it will *not* stop. The definition of the good society is one in which virtue pays. I can now add a slight variation on this; you cannot have a good society *unless* virtue pays. But here we get very close to the whole subject of metaneeds, and also of the synergy theory, which in turn is a by-product of B-psychology—the B-psychology of ideal conditions where dichotomies are resolved and transcended. (Put all this together with the other memorandum on the good enlightened salesman and the good enlightened customer and stress that a "good customer" is both a necessity and a virtuous, desirable person, because he wishes the system to work. As soon as he stops caring, the whole system will collapse.)

Additions to the
Notes on Profits

I am reminded here of the parallel between the accountant's necessity for having everything down in numbers and those authoritarian organizational theorists who have to have all the human and interpersonal relationships in any organization reducible to a chart on the wall with simple lines and simple geometric forms.

Observe that much of the difficulty in the conception of profit, taxes, costs, and so on, can be seen to come from the professionalization of the accountants as a group. They are the ones who force upon the industrial situation the concern with numbers, with exchangeable money, with tangibles rather than intangibles, with exactness, with predictability, with control, with law and order generally, etc. Andy Kay pointed out that the accountants have the lowest vocabulary scores of any of the professional groups. I added that the psychiatrists think of them as being the most obsessional of any group. From what I know of them, they also attract to the schools of accounting those who are number bound, those who are interested in small details, those who are tradition bound, and the like.

In the colleges and the universities, with all their educational policies and intellectual goals, the accountant types and other obsessional types somehow manage to force an overemphasis upon the interchangeability of credits, of grades, of diplomas, of degrees, of scores, and of arithmetizing the whole of the educational venture, even though this is entirely alien and antagonistic to it. Clearly, in this same way the new kind of industry and enterprise philosophy will certainly need a different type of accounting, and, therefore, probably a different accountant character structure.

So much of this accountant's philosophy of life ultimately boils down to a mistrust of self. These are the people who will make budgets for their households, put certain sums of money in one bottle or another bottle or another envelope or whatever and not touch it. These are the people who earmark funds for particular purposes. These are the people who will not touch their savings which are drawing 4 percent interest and prefer instead to borrow money at 12 percent interest, just because it is their habit or philosophy to "not touch your savings ever." These can be considered to be people who fool themselves, in a way like the ones who arbitrarily set their alarm clocks ten minutes ahead so as to fool themselves into getting a little more sleep, but not too much sleep, etc. The whole thing is ludicrous because, of course, they know that the alarm clock is set ten minutes ahead. This is a little like the mild form of pathology that we see in the confusion of daylight savings time. Instead of passing laws to make offices open an hour earlier in the summertime, everybody has to fool himself by making believe he is getting up at the same hour by changing the clock time.

This is all the opposite of the creative personality. The creative person trusts himself sufficiently to face a new problem or a new situation without any preparation, to improvise a solution in the new situation. The more obsessional person tends to classify the whole of the future, to prepare for every contingency, to have schedules and plans which he will not break, and the like. Some obsessionals make themselves a promise about the future and then stick to it through thick or thin. For instance, if they have planned to go to a party or a picnic or a trip on a certain date, they will do it even if they have broken a leg or even though they feel very depressed or unhappy or whatever. It's as if they cannot change their minds, as if this throws them into anxiety, into a panic. Of course, this kind of scheduling of the future, of geometrizing the future, of making everything arithmetical, exact, predictable, controllable and so on, this is all a big set of defenses against the anxiety which comes to such people from having to meet something unexpected, something they're not prepared for. It's as if they want to avoid getting into any situation without being prepared for it in advance. They can't improvise. They don't trust themselves to find the solution on the spur of the moment.

For such people, for such accountants, the giving up of careful controls and checks is going to be an anxiety-producing situation. They must know everything that is going on at all times, even if it's trivial or unimportant, and even if it involves mistrusting other people. Probably also, this accounts for the tendency in our accounting systems to deal only with tangibles and only with qualities or characteristics that can be translated into money exchange. Obsessional people in general tend to mistrust emotions, chaos of any kind, unpredictability of any kind, human nature in general. I am reminded here of the parallel between the accountant's necessity for having everything down in numbers, and those authoritarian organizational theorists who have to have all the human and interpersonal relationships in any organization reducible to a chart on the wall with simple lines and simple geometric form.

Statistics, schedules and other external cues can serve as a substitute for the lack of inner voices and certainties. The person who is decisive because he *knows* experientially is the one who can use these external aids in a healthy way.

Additions to the Notes on Redefinition of Profits, Costs, etc.

We might ask the accountant: in which company would you prefer to invest your savings—one which had a high amount of human assets in the organization or one which had a low amount of human assets in the organization, quite irrespective of the profit picture for the last twelve months. In which company would you invest, one that had consumer good will or one that had used up its consumer good will? One which had good morale among the workers or one which had bad?

The problem for the accountants is to work out some way of putting on the balance sheet the human assets of the organization: that is, the amount of synergy, the degree of education of all the workers in the organization, the amount of time and money and effort that has been invested in getting good informal groups to work together well like a good basketball team, the development of loyalties, the cutting down of hostilities and jealousies, the reduction of the tendencies to restrict production, the lowering of the tendency to stay away when mildly sick, etc. This is quite apart from the values of these human assets to the town or city, state, or country, or to the human species.

I think this point is drawn very well in Likert's book, in the experiment described on page 64 in which it was possible to increase productivity for a time by authoritarian and hierarchically controlled pressure programs. Direct pressure produced a substantial increase in production during the time of the experiment, somewhat larger than the increase in productivity which was achieved in a participative management program. However, as soon as we take a look at the other human consequences of this experiment, we see that the picture is a little lopsided when we concentrate only on productivity. To sum it up, the experiment, while it increased productivity, it decreased loyalty, interest, involvement in the work, and so on, and caused attitudes to worsen. To put it briefly, all the human assets which are not seen on the balance sheet were cut very considerably, so that in fact, the welfare of the business to some extent was injured in the long run in favor of increased productivity in the short run. But I am told that this is very easy to do in any business situation—that it is easy to show a profit for a particular short period by using up assets, by not building for the future, by throwing away all sorts of human assets which are not counted by the accountants—loyalties, good attitudes toward the supervisors and toward the managers, and the like.

This again brings up the importance for all managerial philosophy of sharply differentiating the short run from the long run. Enlightened management really works best for the long run; it may not work best for the short run. This is somewhat like the way in which the body can use up its future resources for a short period of time in an emergency. The adrenal glands, for instance, may rise to an emergency and keep on producing for the duration of the emergency period, but in the long run this may actually result in death or permanent damaging of the organism. The same kind of thing is true for using up other reserves like the body fat or the oxygen reserve or the glycogen reserve in the liver and the like.

Perhaps here also we could add an equally obvious point about consumer attitudes. Consumer good will can also be used up in the short run in order to show a higher profit, in a way which is suicidal in the long run. For instance, a new management taking over an old, respected, and trusted company can gut the assets of the company and can trade on the trust among consumers by putting out a cheaper or fake product. For a period of time, the consumers will not notice the difference and, of course, a much greater profit can be made in this way. But the customer good will, the consumer loyalty, will be lost thereby in the long run. For any business that wants to last for a century, this is suicidal.

The question to put to the accountant is, Where do you put consumer good will and consumer loyalty in your balance sheets? There is absolutely no question about the economic reality of this factor. The problem is one of translating it into numbers or qualities of some sort which can be taken account of in the statements of assets and liabilities of any organization. We might ask the accountant himself: In which company would you prefer to invest your savings, one which had a high amount of human assets in the organization or one which had a low amount of human assets in the organization, quite irrespective of the profit picture for the last twelve months? And then another: In which company would you invest, one that had consumer good will or one that had used up its consumer good will? More questions to the accountant: In which company would you rather invest your savings, one which had good morale among the workers or one which had bad morale among the workers; one which had heavy turnover or one which had low turnover; one which had high sickness absences or one which had low sickness absences, etc., etc.?

The Good Enlightened
Salesman and Customer

*A good sales person is the eyes and ears of the company . . .
he is the ambassador of the enterprise . . . He is the company at a distance . . . any enterprise ought to have a very
steady feedback about consumer demand, about needs of markets, about satisfaction and dissatisfaction of product and the
salesperson is exactly the person to collect this information
and feedback. He is the V.P. in charge of innovation and development of future products as well as just the guy who sells
something.*

I f we start with our standard assumption of the enterprise persisting over a long period of time and remaining healthy, both in the
homeostatic sense and in the growth sense, and if we include all
the things that we have deduced such an enterprise needs in order to
remain healthy, then this will also make a difference in the definition
of the salesman and of the customer. The way things stand now, the
current conceptions and definitions of salesmen and customer are only
slight modifications in principle from that of the snake-oil salesman
and the sucker. The relationship is seen very clearly in the language
which is used, which implies that either the customer screws the salesman or the salesman screws the customer, and there is much talk about
who gets screwed, who gets raped, who gets exploited, or who gets
taken advantage of. Or, it is as if the customer is sometimes spoken of
as a sheep with plenty of blood which is there to be sucked by the
smarter mosquitoes or leeches or whatever, i.e., he is simply a host
animal who is not respected but who is there only to be used or taken
advantage of.

The current stereotype is that the salesman is a short-range-in-time kind of person. That is, the salesman wants a quick score or quick success; he wants to make this particular sale and doesn't think too much of what will happen next week; nor does he think too much of what will happen to the enterprise in general or to other sales offices in other sections of the country, etc. He is focused on the here and now; he is not only short range in time but in space as well. This is the kind of person considered to be the salesman type; the successful, good salesman; he is simply the one who can sell a product today, all other conditions being equal, and the worse the product or the worse the conditions, the better salesman he is considered to be if he manages to sell.

But, realistic management and the healthy enterprise, of course, need a different kind of person and a different kind of relationship between salesman and customer. First of all, the salesman must be longer range in time and longer range in space and wider thinking in terms of causes and effects and holistic relationships. Why is this? Well, in general it's because the relationships between the healthy enterprise and its customer are very different when these customers are supposed to be kept for a century or two. A good customer, under ideal conditions or in eupsychia would be the person who wants the best product, who is intelligent, realistic, rational, virtuous and moral, etc., and who will choose in a rational way the best product, the cheapest price, the highest quality, but who also will tend to judge the product and the enterprise and everything connected with it in terms of the morality and integrity of the salesman and the enterprise in general. That is, he will get angry if he is swindled or lied to, or if something is palmed off on him that is not quite what it was supposed to be.

For instance, I can use the example of the way in which I tried to make my life simpler when I was the manager of a small plant. I told the suppliers that I did not want to spend time inspecting carefully whatever they brought to my plant; I wanted to be able to trust them. I told them that I would give them an order but not inspect the material supplied. Then, if I were swindled, I would make up for the swindle, certainly, and get my money back, but, also, I would never have anything to do with them thereafter, and they would lose the possibility of a profitable relationship. With one of these men this is exactly what happened. In a very stupid way he sent over some completely inadequate products. I had to go to the trouble of sending them back and getting my money back, and I told him never to deliver anything to me again, that I would never accept his products no matter what price he put on them. Thereafter he did try to underbid other people, but I refused to take advantage of this, and in fact, never had anything more to do with him. What he did, in effect, was to lose a customer. He behaved as if his business were going to run for only two weeks and then close up shop. He didn't care for my good opinion. The salesman who does this kind of thing, will, in the long run, destroy the enterprise that he is representing (and since we're dealing with long-run enterprise, this becomes essential). That is to say, a "good eupsychian customer" is one who doesn't like being fooled, one who appreciates it if his interests are kept in mind by the enterprise and its representative.

On the other hand, taking the customer's interests seriously and actually trying to serve him or to help him prosper, even though this sometimes means willingly and knowingly getting him to buy a rival product rather than one's own, is in the same way helpful because it builds in him a feeling of trust, and guarantees that if this enterprise eventually turns out a better product, it can assume that the customer will buy it.

All of this implies a kind of a virtue which certainly cannot be expected to most human beings today; that is to say, an enterprise manager would *want* the customer to buy the best product, even if it were produced by the rival factory. That is, he would see that this represents a kind of justice and virtue, and even if it hurt him at the moment, it would in the long run help him and everybody else—at least at the higher need levels and the metamotivational levels. This, of course, demands a very great deal of objectivity and detachment. The fact is, however, that we do get it once in a while in our society; for instance, a priest who has lost his religious faith, even though it is entirely private and within his own head, will do the gentlemanly thing and resign from his post. This is also expected from people in a political situation, that is, in certain kinds of government, anyhow: if they do not agree with the government, they give up their jobs voluntarily and resign. If good conditions were to prevail for some length of time, we would expect that more and more of this kind of objectivity and gentlemanliness and honesty would spread more and more. Very rarely today, but still sometimes, do we see this in the lover relationship.

I suppose it would be too much to ask for many or most businessmen and salesmen to point out to the customer that there is a rival product which he should try out and which might be better for his purposes, and yet, I think it can be shown that in a healthy, long-term enterprise exactly this will pay off; that is, this kind of virtue will pay under these good conditions. It also follows that what Andy Kay was trying to change over to is desirable as a kind of ideal condition, for instance, not bothering to curry the favor of, to bribe, to buy lunches for, or to mimic personal friendship with, all sorts of unlikable people, just in the hope that this might induce them to buy the product. It is quite reasonable to ask, as Kay did, What kind of life is this? What kind of a life will I be leading if I am forced to be a hypocrite and pretend to be friends with people that I actually don't feel friendly with? What's the good of being in business then, and controlling my own fate, if I don't have the freedom not to have lunch with the people I dislike?

This policy carries over also in the system of not giving budget credit for this kind of bribery, which is essentially a befuddling of the customer, a confusing of the issue, trying to get him, by implication, to buy a second-rate product out of personal gratitude or loyalty and the like. Here too, it can be pointed out that if the customer is a rational person, precisely this sort of thing is going to make him doubly suspicious about the worth of the product. A good product does not need this kind of contamination or befuddling or bribery. And just in the same way that an honest man will be repelled by the offer of bribery, so an honest man will be repelled by the necessity for offering the bribe.

Under ideal economic conditions all that any enterprise can ask or *should* ask is that the best product should win. This is fair, free and open, and desirable competition. Therefore, it follows that these same people who feel that the best product should win should find distasteful any factors in the situation that would confuse this basic issue (in any systematic presentation of this point of view it would be very desirable here to pile up the examples of instances in which true service to the customer paid off not only for the customer but for the enterprise itself).

The salesman for the enlightened enterprise, then, has functions which are different from the old conventional ones. For one thing, he should know his product as well as is necessary, he should be a knowledgeable man about the state of the market, about his customers needs, about the whole business, the whole section of industry he is involved in. Facts, candor, honesty, truth, efficiency—these should be his mottos. (Remember to point out that this is said not only on moral grounds, or on merely moral grounds or a priori grounds of any kind, but on the grounds that this will pay for the enterprise, that under these conditions in the long run virtue of this sort will actually pay off in selfish terms as well. But it is best to make the final statement in terms of synergy, that is, of teaching the reader that at a high level of good conditions and of good humanness, selfishness and unselfishness, private interest and public interest are not polar-opposites, or are not mutually exclusive, but do come together into a new kind of unity.) Another way of saying this is that the salesman then must be a man of integrity, a man who can be trusted, a man whose word will be believed, a man whose word is his bond, a man of honor, a gentleman (in clear contrast with the standard conventional stereotype of the old-time salesman, who is the opposite of all these things).

Finally, another thing has to be strongly stressed which is missing from the stuff on salesmanship that I've read, namely, that the salesman has another function entirely besides just selling. He is the eyes and ears of the company, and furthermore, he is the representative or the ambassador of the company. He is the company at a distance. For one thing, in good marketing situations, any enterprise ought to have a very steady feedback about consumer demands, about the needs of the market, about the satisfaction or dissatisfaction the product it giving, and the field representative or the salesman is exactly the person to collect this information and feedback. This implies, furthermore, that the salesman or the diplomat or the field representative or the marketer, whatever we will finally choose to call him (the word "salesman" is really not very good anymore), takes on himself every single function of anybody in the whole enterprise back home, insofar as these functions are important in his particular situation and in the particular moment: for instance, he is, let's say, the vice president in charge of innovation and future products as well as being just the guy who sells something.

Another way of looking at the future type of marketer is to shear away from the concept the overtone of manipulation. The way things are now, the average salesman considers himself to be a manipulator, considers the psychologist, for instance, to be a manipulator and a

BUILDING RELATIONSHIPS
ONE CUSTOMER AT A TIME

Those serving customers must be longer range in time and longer range in space and wider thinking in terms of causes and effects and holistic relationships. Why is this? It's because the relationships . . . are very different when these customers are supposed to be kept for a century or two . . . instead of for the short term.

—Abraham Maslow

We were guests in the Industry Thought Forum at Stanford University's School of Engineering. Ken Morris, cofounder of PeopleSoft, a high technology company with phenomenal records of growth, was the guest lecturer. The picture he painted of the firm's passion for customers fits well with Maslow's thoughts.

PeopleSoft has grown from $1000 to $1.3 billion in 10 years. Currently it employs 4452 people and an astonishing 42 percent of those employees are focused on customer service and customer management. Predictably, PeopleSoft is the fastest growing competitor in its industry.

Ken Morris attributed his firm's success to their core values. He said the first value was dedicated to their employees. People were important. They say it, they mean it, try to live it, and will not compromise on this value. PeopleSoft has several internal sayings which speak volumes about the culture: no bureaucracy equals no B.S., think big, manage small, dress casual, and work smart, seek forgiveness and not permission. The firm intentionally tries to change its systems and procedures and work teams, not only for innovation purposes, but to keep bureaucracy from setting in. Bureaucracy, they believe, kills the spirit of people. As Morris said, "We have a very strong democratic workplace. At PeopleSoft there is no hierarchy because everyone has access to everything."

The firm's second core value is an unending and unrelentless focus on the customer. Although we have heard this before from company leaders, what surprised us was the firm's approach to customer partnerships. PeopleSoft approaches each customer with the belief that employees will work with customers for 10, 15, 20 years or more. As with any long-term relationship, PeopleSoft lets their customers know that at the end of the day, through good times and bad times, the firm will be there to serve their needs. PeopleSoft doesn't look for short-term ventures with their customer partners but long-term, enduring relationships.

The final core value at PeopleSoft concerns profitability. As Morris says, they believe that if they have lived their core values about employees and customers, profitability just naturally takes care of itself.

controller, that is, someone who functions partly on the basis of *hiding* information and truth. But, in principle, the new enlightened salesmanship or marketing must, like all the other aspects of any good enterprise, rest on full disclosure of facts, on candor, honesty, and truthfulness. Well, this takes a particular kind of character to be able to do. The stereotyped present-day salesman is not this kind of character. Therefore, there must be a change in the selection policies; the salesman who is hired now to work in an enlightened enterprise toward the future must be trained in a different way and must be the kind of personality who is capable of picking up these new requirements.

Further Notes on Salesmen and Customers . . .

We should be able to institutionalize all the democratic, communicative, respecting, loving, listening, customer satisfaction kinds of things in the future by using the advantages of technology. In other words, keeping all the benefits of smallness but also capitalizing on the benefits of bigness.

The enlightened–type salesman and the enlightened customer are both based on the assumption of a good and worthwhile product. If the product they turn out is not good, then this Y type of management will destroy the whole enterprise, as truth generally will destroy untruth and phoniness and fakery. Another way to say this is that Theory Y management works only for virtuous situations, where everybody trusts the product and can identify with it and be proud of it. Contrariwise, if the product is not good and must be concealed and faked and lied about, then only Theory X managers, customers, and salesmen are possible. Countrariwise, if Theory X is actually used, then this indicates possible mistrust of the product and a mistrust of the rationality of the customer (assuming that he doesn't have sense enough to pick the best product, and assuming he is stupid enough to be fooled and swindled by irrelevant data). Actually, this suggests that the measurement of the level of the customer rationality would give us an indication of what type of management to use that would be most successful. Low rationality would indicate that a successful business would have to use Theory X philosophy. High customer rationality would indicate that it would be better and more successful to use Theory Y management.

Memorandum on Salesmen
and Salesmanship

This is on the grounds that any enterprise which wishes to endure over a long period of time and to remain in a healthy and growing state would certainly want a non-manipulative trusting, relationship with its customers rather than the relationship of the quick fleecing, never to see them again.

One characterological difference that seemed to show up very quickly was that the characteristic salesman was much more a short-range person, wanting quick results, wanting a steady and quick flow of rewards and reinforcements. This is a little like saying that he is a more "practical" person, and then it occurred to me that this contrasts with the more "theoretical" kind of person. And this contrast, in turn, may possibly be phraseable in terms of short range in time and space versus long range in time and space. The "practical" person in this sense has less ability to delay. He needs quick success and quick wins. This should mean that he works within a shorter time span, and I think this would be testable. That is, for him the next few hours, the next few days, constitute the present, in contrast with the more theoretical person for whom the present may spread over into several years hence.

Then, what I mean by short range or narrow range in space is something like this: The characteristic salesman type gets his eyes focused on a particular deal on Thursday afternoon in Philadelphia, perhaps, with customer Jones and gets eager about consummating that particular sale. He is less cognizant than a theoretical person would be of the reverberation effects, the echoes, of this one isolated transaction upon what might be happening a year from that time in Philadelphia, in the same place, or in the same space. He cares less about what the effect might be on other parts of the sales organization or of the engineering organization of his enterprise. That is, the practical type is less apt to think of the consequences, of the regularities, of the consistencies and inconsistencies, and of the cause/effect chain at a distance across the country. It's like the holistic way of thinking, not so much in chains of causes and effects, but rather in terms of concentric circles or rings of waves spreading out from center, or of a nest of boxes in the syndrome hierarchy. The more theoretical person is much more aware of all the far consequences both in time and space, of anything he does. The person we call more practical is probably less aware of these reverberating consequences in time and in space.

Perhaps another angle on this, also I think testable, is that the more practical type, the salesmen type, is also more concrete (rather than abstract). He tends to be preoccupied with what's before his nose, with what he can see and touch and feel and what is right here and right now, rather than that which is unseen and which is distant and delayed.

Partly, I suppose, in any society there will be such individual differences in practicality, in concreteness, in here-nowness, and it will be well to use these differences in character for different kinds of purposes. And yet I can't help feeling that the move toward more enlightened management would encourage less rather than more of this particular kind of salesmanship and of practicality and concreteness. That is, I expect the characterological differences would remain but would be diminished. I expect that these characterological differences also would be used, but that extreme practicality would be less usable and less needed. It involves too much cutting off from other people: it involves too much isolation of the person; it involves too much isolation of the particular interpersonal relationship of selling. After all, an enlightened society is more holistic than a nonenlightened society. As a matter of fact, these statements are almost synonyms. Atomistic can describe the nonenlightened society. It's more split up, more dissociated, less bound together, less tied together, less integrated.

There certainly is one useful theoretical point here for characterological descriptions. Our tendency certainly is to contrast in a dichotomous way the practical person and the theoretical person, in the sense that we expect the theoretical person to be not practical. That is, he is all theoretical, he is very high in theory and very low in practicality. But one lesson that we have learned from the study of healthy people is that the healthy person is apt to be *everything*. In this instance the healthy theoretical person would be both healthy and practical, depending upon the particular situation and the objective needs of that situation. Also, the healthy practical person or in this case, the healthy salesman type, would certainly be more practical in the above sense, but not exclusively so. He would also be able to be theoretical when the objective requirements of the situation called for it. These characterological differences would be differences simply in balance and in degree, rather than in all or none, present or absent.

This is all to say that even under enlightened conditions, a salesman type, a practical kind of person, would be needed. The salesman type ought not to be regarded, therefore, as unneeded or useless or pathological. All we have to do is, for enlightened purposes, modify and correct some of the overemphasis, the overdichotomized quality that we now find in what we consider to be the typical salesman, who characteristically is supposed not to give a damn about what happens the day after tomorrow or at a distance from the particular job he is involved in, nor to worry about the far consequences of what he does. This stereotype needs correcting, of course.

One thing that occurs to me, also as testable, is that this kind of here-and-now focus on the present sort of salesman type probably, therefore, is less affected by his past, and particularly by his past successes. For the average person a success of a year ago still is active in bolstering his self-esteem. Probably this is much less so for the here-and-now type of salesman. He needs a continual supply of successes. He's the one who might say in Hollywood, "You're only as good as your last picture." The salesman might say, "You're only as good as your last sale or your last account book" or something of the sort.

I think there *is* something in the picture of the ideal salesman type, whether under good social conditions or under bad social conditions, of the dominance and cockiness and manipulative quality and controlling quality that has been so much mentioned in the literature. A certain amount of self-esteem and self-confidence is a *sine qua non* for a salesman. In order to like the clash of battle, in order to regard a balky customer as a delightful challenge, one would have to have a stable and deep self-confidence and self-esteem, that is, to have the feeling that success is probable. This means on the negative side that the salesman type ought to have few inhibitions and self-doubts. Certainly he ought to have *very* little of the masochistic tendency, of the fear of winning, of the "tendency to be a loser." He mustn't want to bring about his own destruction; he mustn't want to bring about his own punishment; he must not feel guilty about winning; he must not feel exposed to punishment if he wins. This I think is all testable.

It is doubtful that the surface sociability of the salesman type, of the liking for company, of the immersion in groups of people, etc., represents any true liking for people. If the phrasing is correct that the salesman type sees himself as a kind of an elk or a moose running out to do battle with other elks, and enjoying the clash of battle but especially enjoying the success in battle, then certainly there must be a rather low impulse to help other people, to be parental, or especially maternal, to be the nursing type, or the doctor or psychotherapeutic type who gets a great kick out of curing other people or of relieving pain, or who gets a great kick out of watching the self-actualization of others. There should be a pretty narrow range of love-identifications, of the circle of brotherhood. There should also be rather less feeling of synergy in the salesman type than in other types of human beings. It all really adds up to a kind of jungle philosophy to some extent, even though the good salesman is apt to see this as a very pleasant jungle, all full of fun and nice battle and sure successes. It is all very pleasing, because he has great confidence in himself and in his ability to overcome the others in the jungle whom he tends to see as weak, not as good as he is, not as bright, not as strong (and perhaps therefore as a little contemptible, as people to be condescended to rather than loved or identified with).

It will be immediately useful in trying to figure out what is a "good" salesman today if we recognize that these are different kinds of people for Theory X and Theory Y. That is, the good Theory X salesman is different from the good Theory Y salesman. And certainly this is important in the selection of personnel and in the training of personnel if the enterprise which the salesman represents is Theory Y rather than Theory X type. A good Theory Y salesman today would certainly be more aware of his ties to his enterprise, more identified with it, more identified with all the people in it. I think he would have a self-image more as a kind of ambassador or representative of the whole enterprise than as a lone wolf, who simply pursues his own interests, or even as an intermediary between the enterprise and the customer. Certainly the elements of manipulation would be less in the Theory Y salesman. For various reasons this would be so, but probably the most important one would be that the best kind of Theory Y salesmanship comes much closer to complete honesty and candor than does Theory X type salesmanship. This is on the grounds that any enterprise which wishes to endure over a long period of time and to remain in a healthy and growing state would certainly want a nonmanipulative, trusting relationship with its customers rather than the relationship of the quick fleecing, never to see them again. This is one of the reasons why a longer range in time is required of a Theory Y salesman than of a Theory X salesman.

Another kind of change needed in the Theory Y salesman is that he would have to regard himself not only as an overcomer and winner and conqueror of the customer, but also as the sense organs of the enterprise for getting feedback from the customers. The Theory Y salesman not only sells, but tries to have good objective factual relationships with the customer, and the salesman in this context should be perceived as a highly valuable source of feedback of information which is absolutely necessary in order to keep on improving the product or to keep on correcting its shortcomings. This kind of conception of the customer and of the salesman requires a different conception of the relationship between them and also the relationship of the salesman to his enterprise. He is part of it, with at least two kinds of specialized functions which only he does, rather than any other members of the enterprise and which he cannot do very well if he regards the customer as a sheep to be fleeced.

I suppose the whole question of mutual good will is involved here. Certainly one can expect from any customer of any type that he will complain when the product is no good. But one can expect only from a customer with good will that he should actively try to pass on information to the salesman and the enterprise which is not a complaint but which is a positive suggestion about improving the product and of expanding the enterprise. What I think of here is the example of the customer going beyond the call of duty, that is actually of taking some trouble to help the salesman and the enterprise. For instance, the local radio station KITT is now announcing that it would like its hearers, if they have any loyalty to the station, to let their advertisers know what they like or dislike about KITT programs. They explain this will make it easier for the radio station to sell advertising time. Well, this is a request beyond the call of duty and would require a very positive feeling for the radio station. This is the kind of example I mean which would be absent from any jungle relationship between the salesman and the customer.

All of this thinking about the long-range and short-range types reminds me that general organismic theory can be used more than it has been in managerial policy. I consider that one of the strongest long-time supports, empirical and theoretical supports, for enlightened management policy is that it is more likely to guarantee maintenance and positive growth in the company if one thinks over a really long-time span of perhaps a century. There are many qualities of enlightened management which become very, very clear and are very easy to understand if one asks the manager, "Do you want this company to grow even after you're dead?" Any man, for instance, who wanted to pass on his privately owned business to his son or to his grandson would certainly function differently from the way he would act if he didn't give a damn about what happened to the whole business when he died or retired. One of the most obvious consequences of a really long-range attitude is the demand it makes for a completely different relationship to the customer. Honesty, candor, good will, nonconcealment, a synergic relationship—all become imperative in such a long-run case.

Something similar is true of a real application of organismic theory, especially in its holistic aspects. That is, if one recognizes the fact that one's enterprise is really related to the community, to the state, to the nation, and to the world, that this is more so under good conditions, then there would be really easily understood consequences of such an attitude. Such an enterprise would behave differently from an enterprise which regarded itself as totally independent and autonomous and beholden to nobody else and really not connected with anybody else, or even *against* everybody else, an enterprise, for instance, involved in swindling some customer who simply passes by on the sidewalk as in a tourist trap or which caters to a transient who will never come by again. Swindling such people is easier for the concrete or short-run kind of person. The fact remains that if one wants a healthy enterprise in the long run and with healthy connections to the whole society, then one cannot be this kind of swindler and let the morrow take care of itself. Again here the example might be the treatment of the Orientals in California from the beginning of the century on, which as can easily be demonstrated, had *some* influence in bringing about Pearl Harbor on the one hand and on the other hand the present Chinese hatred for the United States which may yet help to bring on a war.

All of this discussion about Theory X salesmen and Theory Y salesmen can be compared with the new synergic conception of the law, which it is possible to contrast with the present conception of the law as a kind of duel or trial by combat, or clash between a defense attorney and a prosecuting attorney, in which each one is supposed not to think of justice or truth or anything of the sort, but simply of trying to win under the rules that are available. In a more synergic society, certainly, there would be defendants and prosecutors and so on, but I'm sure it would be far more suitable, far more congruent with such a society that the prosecuting attorney and the defense attorney not only have the obligation to put their client's best foot forward or to make the best case possible, but that this would be embedded in the *larger* duty which they all would have of justice and truth for everybody concerned.

So also, even under enlightened conditions, we are going to want good salesmen (or perhaps we'll call them marketers rather than salesmen to stress the different attitudes and the additional functions). In any case the good marketer will certainly want to put his best foot forward and to stress all the good aspects of his product and not necessarily be totally neutral about it. And let it be stressed that to do this would serve a real function in the society. In any society, by the way, whether socialist or capitalist or anything else, there ought to be someone to point up the best aspects, the great desirability of the particular product. (This is possible in a socialist or a communist society as well as a capitalist for the simple reason that if they ever get really intelligent about it, they are going to decentralize their industries and give a great deal of local autonomy to a particular factory management, and also they are going to retain all of the advantages of competition by having not just one centralized industry turning out bicycles but four or six relatively autonomous factories each of them turning out bicycles, thereby getting the best of both the socialist and capitalist world.)

Theory Y salesmanship would obviously foster less graft and dishonesty in the business world than Theory X management would. This would be not only for moral and ethical reasons (which certainly increase in motivating value as individuals and organizations get healthier), but also in simple pragmatic terms like what was mentioned above in the Theory Y relationship with the salesman to the customer. The building of good will, of trust, of integrity, all have very pragmatic business consequences which are very desirable in relation to customers. I know for myself that if some salesman offers me a crooked deal, I have learned to have nothing to do with him or the enterprise; I simply get away from that situation and have nothing to do with it. It never pays to deal with crooks, especially in the long run and especially if one keeps in mind psychological rewards and punishments as well as financial ones. From this point of view it doesn't pay to swindle on one's income tax or to steal. Taking into account guilt feelings, shame feelings, embarrassment feelings, and inner conflict and the like, this is factually pragmatically true as well as being abstract, ethically desirable—that is to say, it's a practical, hard-headed kind of a statement as well as a soft-headed or tender-minded kind of a statement.

This brings to mind that one consequence of Theory Y salesmanship will be actually to lose some customers, but these will be the bad customers, who I think had better be lost if the enterprise can possibly afford this. These are the customers who would not be loyal anyhow; they would be the ones who would keep on trying to swindle and to lie and to cheat, etc. Unless the company badly needs sales at a particular moment, it is really wise, over the course of a century, to have nothing to do with such customers for the sake of momentary profits because in the long run they will be trying to swindle. On the other hand, Theory Y honesty in salesmanship is going to be a positive attraction to the people that we may call *good* customers, the ones who would be loyal, who would stick, who could be trusted, etc. Talk here about the theory of the semipermeable membrane which lets the good ones through and keeps the bad ones out.

All of these considerations bring up the question of selection: selection of salesmen by management, selection of customers and salesmen by each other. It raises the question of who is the best selector of men, who would be the best personnel officer to hire and to fire. In general we can say that the healthier people are better selectors because they will select more objectively, that is, in terms of the objective requirements, of the objective situations, in contrast with neurotics who are more apt to pick in terms of a satisfaction of their own neurotic needs. Another way of saying this is that the healthier people are the larger, more widespreading. That is, they can see farther and more objectively in time and space than can less healthy people. This amounts to saying that they are more realistic. This in turn amounts to saying they are more pragmatic, that is to say, more successful, hard-headedly successful, if one takes into account the long range in time and space.

On Low Grumbles, High Grumbles, and Metagrumbles

If the level of complaints is studied in the industrial situation, it can be used also as a measure of the level of health of the organization, especially if one has a large enough sampling.

The general principle from which the whole thing proceeds is something like this: People can live at various levels in the motivation hierarchy, that is, they can live a high life or a low life, they can live barely at the level of survival in the jungle, or they can live in an enlightened society with good fortune and with all the basic needs taken care of so that they can live at a higher level and think about the nature of poetry or mathematics or that kind of thing.

There are various ways of judging the motivational level of life. For instance, one can judge the level at which people live by the kind of humor that they laugh at. The person living at the lowest need levels is apt to find hostile and cruel humor very amusing, e.g., the old lady who is getting bitten by a dog or the town moron who is being plagued by the other children, etc. The Abraham Lincoln type of humor—the philosophical, educational type of humor—brings a smile rather than a belly laugh; it has little to do with hostility or conquest. This higher type of humor cannot be understood at all by the person living at the lower need levels.

The projective tests also can serve as an example of the way in which the motivational level at which we are living expresses itself in all kinds of symptoms and expressive acts. The Rorschach test can be used to indicate what the person is actively striving for, what he wishes, needs, and craves. All the basic needs which have been fully gratified tend to be forgotten by the individual and to disappear from consciousness. Gratified basic needs just simply cease to exist in a certain sense, at least in consciousness. Therefore, what the person is craving and wanting and wishing for tends to be that which is just out ahead of him in the motivational hierarchy. Focusing on this particular need indicates that all the lower needs have been satisfied, and it indicates that the needs which are still higher and beyond what the person is craving for have not yet come into the realm of possibility for him, so he doesn't even think about that. This can be judged from Rorschach tests. Also, this can be judged from dreams and dream analysis.

In the same way it was my thought that the level of complaints—which is to say, the level of what one needs and craves and wishes for—can be an indicator of the motivational level at which the person is living; and if the level of complaints is studied in the industrial situation, it can be used also as a measure of the level of health of the whole organization, especially if one has a large enough sampling.

For instance, take the workers living in the authoritarian jungle industrial situation in which fear and want and even simple starvation are a real possibility, and determine the choice of job and the way in which bosses will behave and the submissiveness with which workers will accept cruelty, etc., etc. Such workers who have complaints or grumbles are apt to be falling short of basic needs which are low in the hierarchy. At this lowest level this means complaints about cold and wet and danger to life and fatigue and poor shelter and all of these basic biological necessities.

Certainly, in the modern industrial situation, if one runs across complaints of this sort, then this is an indication of extremely poor management and an extremely low level of living in the organization. In even average industrial situations, this kind of complaint, this sort of low grumble hardly ever comes up. On the positive side, that is, those complaints which represent a wish or craving out ahead of what is now available—these are at this same low level approximately. That is, the worker in Mexico might be making positive grumbles at the security and safety level, at such things as being fired arbitrarily, of not being able to plan his family budget because he does not know how long the job will last. He may complain about a total lack of job security, about the arbitrariness of the foreman, about the kinds of indignities that he has to take in order to keep his job, etc. I think we can call low grumbles those grumbles which come at the biological and at the safety level, perhaps, also, at the level of gregariousness and belonging to the informal, sociable group.

The higher-need levels would be mostly at the level of esteem and self-esteem, where questions would be involved of dignity, of autonomy, of self-respect, of respect from the other; feelings of worth, of getting praise and rewards and credit for one's accomplishments and the like. Grumbles at this level would probably be mostly about something that involved loss of dignity or the threat to self-esteem or to prestige. Now, so far as the metagrumbles are concerned, what I have in mind here are the metamotivations which hold in the self-actualizing life. More specifically, these can be summed up as the B-values which are listed in my book on *Religions, Values and Peak-Experiences* (102). These metaneeds for perfection, for justice, for beauty, for truth, and the like also show themselves in the industrial situation where there might very well be complaints about inefficiency (even when this does not affect the pocket of the complainer). In effect, then, he is making a statement about the imperfection of the world in which he lives (again not a selfish complaint but an impersonal and altruistic philosopher's complaint, one might almost call it). Or he might complain about not being given the full truth, all the facts, or about other blocks in the free flow of communications.

This preference for truth and honesty and all the facts again is one of the metaneeds rather than one of the "basic" needs, and people who have the luxury of complaining at this level are strictly living a very high-level life. In the society which is cynical, which is run by thieves or by tyrants or by nasty people, one would get no such complaints as this—the complaints would be at a lower level. Complaints about justice are also metagrumbles, and I see plenty of them in the protocols from the workers in a well-managed place. They are apt to complain about an injustice even where it is to their personal financial advantage. Another kind of metagrumble is the complaint about a virtue not being rewarded, and about villainy getting these rewards, i.e., a failure of justice.

In other words, everything above implies very strongly that human beings will always complain. There is no Garden of Eden, there is no paradise, there is no heaven except for a passing moment or two. Whatever satisfactions are given to human beings, it is inconceivable that they should be perfectly content with these. This in itself would be a negation of the highest reaches of human nature because it would imply that no improvements could be made after this point—and this, of course, is nonsense. We cannot conceive of a million years of further development bringing such a perfection to pass. Human beings will always be able to tuck in under their belts whatever gratifications, whatever blessings, whatever good fortune are available. They'll be absolutely delighted with these blessings for a little while. And then, as soon as they get used to them, they'll forget about them and start reaching out into the future for still higher blessings, as they restlessly perceive how things could be even more perfect than they are at this moment. This looks to me like an eternal process going on into the future forever.[1]

Therefore, I am concerned to stress this point very heavily because I see in the management literature a considerable amount of disappointment and disillusionment, and an occasional giving up the whole philosophy of enlightened management and going back to authoritarian management, because the management has been sharply disappointed by the lack of gratitude, by the continuation of complaints when the better conditions came to pass. But we should, according to motivation theory, never expect a cessation of complaints; we should expect only that these complaints will get to be higher and higher complaints, i.e., that they will move from the lower-grumble level to higher-grumble levels and finally to metagrumble levels. This is in accordance in principle with what I have written about human motivation being never ending and simply proceeding to higher and higher levels all the time as conditions improve. And it also conforms with my concept of frustration levels. That is, I repudiated the simple acceptance of frustration as being always necessarily bad; I assumed that there were hierarchies of frustration and that moving from a low-frustration to a high-frustration level is a sign of blessedness, of good fortune, of good social conditions, and of good personal maturity, etc. To complain about the garden programs in the city where I live, to have committees of women heatedly coming in and complaining that the rose

---

[1] Recently I have run across an important discussion of a very similar thesis. Colin Wilson, in his *Beyond the Outsider* (London: Arthur Barker, Ltd., 1965), has made me aware of even more profound philosophical consequences than I have set forth here. This is in his discussion of what he calls the "St. Neot margin."

gardens in the parks are not sufficiently cared for, is in itself a wonderful thing because it indicates the height of life at which the complainers are living. To complain about rose gardens means that your belly is full, that you have a good roof over your head, that your furnace is working, that you're not afraid of bubonic plague, that you're not afraid of assassination, that the police and fire departments work well, that the government is good, that the school system is good, that local politics are good, and many other preconditions are already satisfied. *This is the point: the high-level complaint is not to be taken as simply like any other complaint; it must be used to indicate all the preconditions which have been satisfied in order to make the height of this complaint theoretically possible.*

If an enlightened and intelligent management understands all the above deeply, then such a management will expect that improvement in conditions would raise the complaint level and raise the frustration level as outlined above, *rather than expecting that improved conditions will make all complaints disappear.* There will then be little danger that they will become disillusioned and angry when much trouble and money and effort goes into making some improvements in work conditions and then the complaints continue. What we must learn to look for is, Have these complaints gone up in motivational level? This is the real test and this is, of course, all that can be expected. But furthermore, I suppose this means that we must learn to be very happy about such a thing, not merely to be contented with it.

Some special problems do emerge here. One such problem is the question of what to call justice and injustice. There are certainly going to be many petty complaints about comparisons between others and one's self—maybe that someone has a better light, or a better chair or somewhat better rate of pay or something of this sort. Such things can become extremely petty, with people comparing the size of the desks that they'll have in their offices or whether they'll have two flowers or one flower in the vase and that sort of thing. Frequently, we will have to make an *ad hoc* judgment in the particular sense as to whether this is at the level of justice in the metaneeds or whether it is simply a surface indication of dominance hierarchy and of elbowing forward in this hierarchy, and trying to go up the ladder in terms of prestige. Or even it could be, as in Dalton's book where there are several examples of this sort of thing, that one could tell from the context that this was clearly referring to a safety need. One example I remember is that it

INTERVIEW WITH GARY HEIL

I think that I could make a generalization that the health or the level of development of the organization can in theory be judged by the rating of the complaints and grumbles.

—Abraham Maslow

Gary Heil, founder of the Center for Innovative Leadership and a published author, has spent nearly 25 years listening to the stories executives tell. He learned early in his career that stories gathered inside companies contain powerful information which, if studied, can paint an accurate picture of how well the organization is serving customers, empowering employees, and bridging the gap between what is perceived and what is reality. Gary turned his story gathering into a process which he refers to as anecdotal assessments. Such assessments have helped many companies improve their processes and people practices. We wanted to learn more about his notes on grumbles.

★ ★ ★

What is the purpose of most of the anecdotal assessments that you have conducted?

Most have attempted to create a glimpse of how "reality" is perceived throughout the organization. You can't deal with reality if you don't see it. When you identify the stories that people tell about the company, you begin to see how they truly feel about their environment.

You have spent considerable time helping organizations design processes for capturing the organizational stories that reflect people's feelings and thinking. Are these methods reliable?

The stories that people tell each other describe important events and are consistent with their feelings about the subject being described. This is true even when an interviewee relates a set of circumstances using someone else to make his or her point. When people choose to answer broad questions about life in organizations, they tend to pick issues that are important to them at that time. As Maslow taught us, by comparing the information obtained with a theoretical construct (Maslow's hierarchy of needs), we can reliably make some inferences about how "developed" the organization might be in certain areas.

Can you give me an example?

(continued)

Let's say people are asked to describe the obstacles that they encounter in performing their jobs. Some might choose to focus on the amount of information available to them to serve their customers and how frustrated they become when that lack of information prevents them from doing the best job possible. On the other hand, others might seem preoccupied with their supervisor because he or she is overly controlling in performance areas or treats people within the work group disrespectfully. In another work group, the prepotent issues might be fear of downsizing or fear of being fired. When combined with other information, each of these circumstances could describe organizations at a very different level of development. The information gives people in leadership positions better data from which to plan future efforts.

Don't we get much of this information from "culture surveys" which are used extensively within organizations?

Certainly, we get much helpful information from quantitative surveys. I believe, however, that we have rejected the use of anecdotal data gathering techniques too quickly, and in doing so, we have failed to capture data that can more fully explain much of what we read in the surveys we conduct. For example, one question that is often asked in culture surveys is, "To what extent do you get the information that you need to do your job?" In most good companies the answer to this question approaches 5 (to a great extent) on a 6-point scale. However, when you interview people about the information they get, you often find that they don't understand the amount of variation that exists in the process in which they work nor do they understand the causes of that variation. Rarely do they understand how many customers are choosing to do business with other organizations instead of theirs—and why. And so on. The point is that people often say they feel good about the information they receive but don't have a fraction of what they need. Without the interview, the answer to the question in the survey can be misleading.

Perhaps the most important, unrealized benefit of anecdotal data gathering is that it gives the interviewer an opportunity to ask why the person feels as they do and to ask for specific examples of the types of interactions that engender these feelings. The purposes of the quantitative survey and the anecdotal survey are similar. Both attempt to create a body of information that will engender creative, candid dialogue in the company.

Who should conduct the interviews?

We have found that we get the best data when we use a team of both outsiders—consultants trained in the collection of anecdotal data—and insiders—leaders in the company who have good interpersonal and analytical skills. The outsiders will see things that the insiders won't and the insiders know more about the organization than the outsiders can learn in any short period of time.

How do you answer the people who say that these interviews create too much negativity and give people an invitation to complain?

As Maslow noted, people's environment needs are deficit needs. That is, they don't feel or talk about them unless there is a deficit. Only then are people motivated to address these concerns. So, it should not be surprising that when people are interviewed, they want to talk about the issues they are most frustrated with at that time. Leaders should look at such discussions as gifts. People are communicating how they feel and why they feel as they do. As in all relationships, understanding the feelings of others is key to creating stronger relationships. Unfortunately, we do hear people describe these interviews as complaining. Too often, these leaders choose to defend past actions and present culture instead of trying to see the world through the eyes of the people who work with them.

was noticed that if the boss's secretary behaved in a friendly fashion with one person and in a neglectful fashion with another person, that this meant that the latter person was about to be fired. In other words, one must make a guess in the particular instance about the motivation level.

Another one perhaps more difficult is to try to make some analysis of the meaning of money in a motivational way. Money can mean practically anything in the motivational hierarchy. It can mean low or middle or high values or metavalues as well. When I've tried to specify the particular need level, there were certainly some instances in which I simply failed—in such cases I just let them slide altogether and considered the instances unrateable, and pushed them aside without attempting to rate them in the motivational hierarchy.

There will certainly be other instances that will be difficult to rate. Probably the most cautious thing to do is simply not to try to rate them, to put them aside as unusable data. Certainly, if one were making a huge and careful and personal study, then one could go back and reinterview the persons to see just exactly what they did mean in a motivational sense by a particular complaint, e.g., about money. But in the present study this is not feasible or possible or even necessary. This is especially true if we use the same criterion of rating for the two outfits which are being used for experimental purposes, that is, the well-managed plant and the poorly managed plant.

THE MEANING OF REALLY BAD CONDITIONS

Let us keep in mind what bad conditions really are at the extreme. In the management literature we don't have any instances of really bad conditions of the kind that any casual or nonprofessional laborer is used to, where conditions come close to the verge of civil war. Perhaps we could take as an example for the end of the scale something like a prisoner-of-war camp or a jail or a concentration camp. Or else within this country we could take the small one- or two-man business in a highly competitive and cutthroat activity where nickels and dimes are important; where the boss can survive only by bleeding his employees to the last drop, to the point of desperation where they simply have to quit; where he tries to make a living by hanging on to them as long as possible, squeezing out as much profit as he can before they quit. Let us not fall into the delusion of thinking of a relatively less well-managed large corporation as having "bad conditions"—these are not bad at all. Let us remember that 99 percent of the human species would give several years of their lives to get a job in the worst-managed large corporation we have in the whole country. We must have a wider scale for comparison. I think it would probably be desirable for research such as this to start making a collection of really bad instances in our own experience.

ANOTHER COMPLICATION

One characteristic of good conditions that is emerging to view these days for the first time, and certainly surprised me when I first ran across it, is that good conditions, though they have a growth effect on most of the population, nevertheless also have a bad, even catastrophic, effect on a certain small proportion of the population. Freedom and trust given to authoritarians, for instance, will simply bring out bad behavior in these people. Freedom and permissiveness and responsibility will make really dependent and passive people collapse in anxiety and fear. I don't know much about this because I started noticing it only a few years ago. But it's a good thing to keep in mind in this kind of work. We should accumulate more naturalistic instances of this before we try making any theories about it and certainly before we try making any experiments. Put it this way: A fair proportion of the population at the psychopathological end are, for example, very easily tempted to steal but perhaps never realize this because they work in a situation where they are watched all the time, so that the temptation hardly ever comes up to consciousness. Suppose, for example, that a bank suddenly goes "liberal," takes off all the controls, fires the detectives, and so on, and trusts the employees; then, certainly one employee in ten or in twenty—I really don't know what proportion—will be assailed for the first time in his conscious life with temptations to steal. Some of them may give in if they think they can get away with it.

The big point here is not to think that good conditions inevitably make all human beings into growing, self-actualizing, people. Certain forms of neurosis don't respond in this way. Certain kinds of constitution or temperament are much less apt to respond in this way. And finally, the little bit of larceny and sadism and all the other sins which you can find in practically any human being on the face of the earth may be called forth by these "good conditions," when the person is trusted and put completely on his own honor and the like. I am reminded of the way the honor system worked when I was an undergraduate student at Cornell University in 1926 and 1927. It was really amazing that about 95 percent (or more) of the student population, I would estimate, were very honored, very pleased by this system, and it worked perfectly for them. But there was always that 1 or 2 or 3 percent for whom it didn't work, who took advantage of the whole business to copy, to lie, to cheat on examinations, and so on. The honor system still cannot be used generally in situations where the temptations are too great, where the stakes are too great.

All of the above ideas and techniques could in principle be applied to many other social-psychological situations. For instance, in the college situation, we could judge the level of enlightenment in which the whole community was living by the grumbles, by the height of the grumbles of the faculty, of the administration, and of the students. There can be in such a situation a whole hierarchy of complaints, of gratifications being sought for. The same thing is true for a marriage and might even turn out to be a way of judging the goodness of the marriage, or its health, one might say, i.e., by the level of the complaints and grumbles in the marriage. A wife who complained about her husband forgetting to bring her flowers once, or taking too much sugar in his coffee, or something of the sort is certainly at a different level from the wife who complains that her husband broke her nose or knocked her teeth out or scarred her or the like. In general the same thing could be true for children's complaints about their parents. Or for children's complaints about their school or their teachers.

I think I could make a generalization of this, that the health or the level of development of any human interpersonal organization can in theory be judged by this same technique of rating the height in the hierarchy of the complaints and grumbles. The one thing to remember is that no matter how good the marriage or the college or the school or the parents, there will be perceived ways of improving the situation, i.e., there will be complaints and grumbles. It should also be taken for granted that it is necessary to divide these into the negative and positive, that is, that there will be very quick and sharp complaints about any more basic gratifications which are taken away or threatened or jeopardized, even though the person doesn't notice these gratifications or takes them for granted entirely when they are easily available. That is, if you ask a person what's good about his place, he won't think to tell you that his feet didn't get wet because the floors aren't flooded, or that he is protected against lice and cockroaches in his office, or the like. He will simply take all of these for granted and won't put them down as pluses. But if any of these taken-for-granted conditions disappears, then of course you'll hear a big howl. To say it another way, these gratifications do not bring appreciation or gratitude, even though they do bring violent complaints when they are taken away. Then, on the other hand, in contrast, we must talk about the positive grumbles or complaints or suggestions about improvement. These are generally comments about what is just higher in the hierarchy of motivation, what is just out ahead, what is the next wish wished for.

I suppose that, in principle, an easily possible extension of this research on grumbles, would be, first of all, to collect real instances of bad bosses in the extreme sense and of bad conditions in the extreme sense. For instance, one upholsterer that I know—who feels murderous about his boss but who simply cannot get a better job because in that industry no better jobs are available—is made perpetually angry by the fact that his boss whistles for him instead of calling him by name. This insult is chronic and deliberate and makes him angrier and angrier over the months. Another instance occurred in my own experience in working in hotel dining rooms and restaurants when I was in college. I signed up for a summer job at a resort hotel as a waiter (around 1925), and then paid my way up to the hotel and was made a busboy instead at much lower wages, and as it turned out, without any tips at all. I was simply swindled in this situation—I didn't have the money to go back with, and anyway it was too late to get another job for the summer; the boss promised he would make me a waiter very soon, and I took his word for it. As a busboy without tips I was working at the rate of about $10 or $20 a month. This was a seven-day-a-week job, about fourteen hours a day, with no days off. Also, this man asked the staff to take on the additional task of preparing all of the salads because he said the salad man, whose job this was, was delayed for a day or two. After a few days of the staff doing this additional work, we asked him where the salad man was, and he said he was coming the following day. This kind of thing kept up for about two weeks, but it became very clear that the man was simply swindling us all and trying to snatch an extra dollar or two out of the situation.

Finally, for the July Fourth holiday, there were three or four hundred guests in the hotel, and we were asked to stay up most of the night before preparing some very fancy dessert which looked pretty but which took a huge amount of time. The staff all got together and agreed to do this without complaint; but then after we had set the first course of dinner on the Fourth, the whole staff walked out and quit the job. This was, of course, a great sacrifice financially to the workers because it was already late to get good jobs and possibly too late to get any job, and yet the hatred and the desire to retaliate was so great that the satisfaction of doing so remains with me to this day, thirty-five years later. This is what I mean by really bad conditions and what I mean by civil war.

Well, anyway, collecting this sort of treatment, this sort of instance, might be the basis for making up a check list in order to make well-managed workers more aware of their blessings (which normally they won't even notice, which they will take for granted, as normal). That is, instead of asking them to volunteer complaints, it might be desirable to have a check list of really bad conditions and ask them if any of these things happen; for instance, if there are any bugs or if it's too cold, or too hot or too noisy or too dangerous or if corrosive chemicals spatter on them or if they are physically hurt or attacked by anybody or if there are no safety precautions on dangerous machines, etc., etc. Any man presented with a check list of 200 such items could then realize that the absence of all these 200 bad conditions was itself a positive good.

The Theory of Social Improvement;
The Theory of the Slow Revolution

It is true for now that the rapid spread in this country of the philosophy of enlightened management, which will surely change the whole society toward improvement and therefore, must be considered to be revolutionary.

Since I take holistic theory quite seriously, not only with individual persons, but also with societies and cultures, and any other organismic wholes, the theory of social improvement must also be holistic. What this means mostly is to proceed on the assumption that the society changes as a whole or as a unit, and that everything within the society is related and tied to everything else in the society. One thing that this means is that you can't improve any society by pushing a single button or by making a single law or changing a single institution or having a particular kind of change in regime or leader or president or dictator or whatever the case may be. I know of no single change that will automatically transform the whole society. (Although it is holistically true that *any* single change will have an effect on the whole society, even though this may be minute.) In turn, what this means is that the way to change a society must necessarily be to change it simultaneously on all fronts, in all its institutions, ideally even, in all its single individuals within the society (granted of course, that change is permitted and is possible, i.e., that it is not a tyranny).

Article No. 1 would be then that societal change comes about by attack along the total front, by efforts to change simultaneously every single institution and subinstitution within the entire society. It's true that we might argue about some institutions being more important or more basic than others. And I certainly think it's true that in the American culture the most potent or most basic or most powerful single institution would be industry in general; yet this is only practically true rather than theoretically true. As a practical politician I would certainly feel that changes in industry would have wider repercussive effects than changes in any other institution, and yet I would not like to lose sight of the principle that all the other institutions have to be changed, if only to make it possible to change industry itself. As an instance, it is clear that enlightened management as a force in industry cannot spread unless the society is ready for it, unless managers are ready for it, supervisors are ready for it, workers are ready for it, the politicians are, the schools are, etc., etc. Enlightened management is quite impossible today in any really authoritarian society. The authoritarianism would have to be modified considerably before one could even begin to think of enlightened management. This is just one example; there could be others.

Article No. 2 accepts the necessity and the inevitability of slow rather than rapid social change. If any institution can be changed only by changing all the other institutions sufficiently to permit this change in the crucial institution, then this attack along the total front must inevitably be a slower process than the revolutionaries have hoped in the past. We may be revolutionaries, and as a matter of fact we are whenever we think of social betterment, even though the word has a bad flavor; yet the people who work at social betterment must be a very different kind of revolutionary from any that have existed. They must accept fully and understand fully and even approve of the necessity for slow rather than rapid change. (This could be worked out with all sorts of examples, within institutions or within individual people to show how it is necessary to lift them up to a certain level before something else is possible.)

Article No. 3 says that it follows necessarily from the above two articles that change by knowledge, by conscious control, by conscious design and planning, by science is necessary (and is the only sensible possibility). This becomes so as soon as we take up the complicated theory of social betterment rather than the simple pushbutton theory of social betterment. It's very easy for anybody to believe or to think he understands that the whole society is going to change if only you pass some particular law or change a particular article in the

Constitution. One reason why these pushbutton theories of revolution have taken hold throughout history is that they can be understood by stupid or uneducated people. They are therefore preferred to the more complicated, because more correct and more true, theories of social change. The very fact that social change must be holistic, practically guarantees that it must also be very complex, which practically guarantees that it is not going to be easily understood by an uneducated man, and that it certainly cannot even be quickly understood by *any* man, however intelligent, and however learned. Perhaps it can *never* be totally understood by any one human being; perhaps it has to be a colleague-hood or a joint effort with division of labor among a fairly large group of specialists each of whom can understand well his own sector of the society. This means as one of the underlying necessities of social betterment or of slow revolution science, research, education, learning, teaching, etc., etc. This is a shiftover from the traditional revolutionary requirement of people who are ready to fight and to kill. Soldiers may be needed in any social improvement, if only to keep law and order, but social scientists are more needed, at least for any directed, conscious social improvement.

Article No. 4 is the practical, political item of feasibility and practicality. Obviously, situations will be different in different societies and in different eras within the same society. The best way to change a society is certainly not to waste one's efforts, but rather to use one's energies in attacking or trying to change or to improve or reform that institution or subinstitution which is most ready for reform, which is calling for it. For instance, in our society, there are several institutions which are practically begging for change and will soon change anyhow or are now in the process of change, without any particular antagonism from anybody. Most people do not realize, for instance, that the spreading of nursery schools and trained nursery school teachers with a particular growth philosophy that they practically all have, is a revolutionary social change. The same is true for kindergarten policy, for the progressive education of the sensible and practical type, for particular kinds of family education, training of mothers, well-baby clinics, and the like. It is true for the now rapid spread in this country of the philosophy of enlightened management, which will surely change the whole society toward improvement, and therefore must be considered to be revolutionary. That is, this sums up to a recommendation to add to the aforementioned articles: "The slow holistic revolution by simultaneous attack along the total front, with conscious and controlled knowledge, and infiltration at the weakest or readiest points."

The next article (5) says that there is hope of change. If only we accept the necessity for slowness of change and are quite content with this (or if we get wise enough and insightful enough to *prefer* slowness of change for good technical reasons), then we will not be disillusioned and disheartened and lose self-esteem and feel hopeless and powerless when we realize that we can make only a small change in the society as a single person. If we understand the situation well enough, we can feel quite proud of the amount of change which a single person can make, because if everything above is true, that single person is the best there is. That is, one cannot do any more than a single person can do. Or better say it this way: A single person can do no more than a single person can do. This can make the single person feel as powerful as (and no more powerful than) he should feel, rather than weak and helpless, rather than a puppet totally weak and useless and helpless before overwhelming and powerful social forces which he can do nothing about.

This is the real danger that I see, especially in our younger people in the teens and in the twenties and thirties, that they feel helpless in the face of atom bombs and huge international conferences and cold wars and the like. They are then apt to turn to a truly selfish and private life, what Reisman has called "privatism," just simply getting the best they can out of life for themselves selfishly and without too much regard for other people, squeezing out as much fun as possible before they all get killed and before the world ends. Colin Wilson[1] talks about the choice between being a hero or a worm; so many choose wormhood. They have a hopelessness, a lack of regard for what one person can do, an adolescent disillusionment because the whole world doesn't change when one new law is passed, or when people get two cars instead of one car, or when votes are given to women, or the labor unions are given power to organize, or there is direct election of senators, or there is a graduated income tax, etc., etc. It is this disillusionment that has so often taken the heart out of social reformers and do-gooders and men of good will generally, so that as they grow older

[1] C. Wilson, *The Stature of Man* (Boston: Houghton Mifflin Co., 1959).

they get tired and hopeless and glum and go into privatism instead of conscious social betterment.

Instead we must learn as a people to thrill with pride, to get excited, to have a strengthened feeling of self-esteem, to have a strong feeling of accomplishment when one particular little reform or improvement takes place that we have had a part in (i.e., when our *team* wins). For instance, if we manage to elect a better representative to the state senate or to the local library committee or to the local school board or if more money is allotted to the library, or if we manage to get better teachers for the local high school or whatever the case may be we should feel victorious.

The next fundamental article (6) is to recognize the necessity for total commitment and hard work at particular local tasks without demanding great cosmic tasks. It is another source of disillusionment that one man can do so little in the face of huge world problems. For instance, I can take the example of a person I was listening to on the radio. This is a young man, a Quaker who went down to Mexico for the Friends Service Committee and who worked for years simply in digging deep wells to bring pure water to Mexican villages to replace the contaminated water that they were using. In all the time that he was there he managed to dig three wells and in each case it took a huge amount of time to teach the villagers to use the pure water rather than the contaminated water. This meant education of various kinds, it meant in some cases building paths and roads. One very good example I can use is that this young man spent a full year tinkering with a well-drilling rig which was in very bad condition, which belonged to the Mexican government, and which he finally managed to bring into condition to dig a *lot* of wells. But this took him almost an entire year. He must have wondered as he read the newspapers just how much good he was doing. But the point is that this is absolutely necessary.

All sorts of jobs at this level are prerequisite before other higher jobs can be done in the world. It's perfectly true that in the United States we can be working at much higher levels, for instance in the colleges, but in Mexico, let alone in such places as the Congo, all sorts of prerequisites are necessary before we can start thinking of colleges and high schools—such things as building roads, digging wells, building hospitals, and simply having a good civil service, and the like. Anybody who wants to improve the world is improving it exactly as much by spending a year fussing around with a well-drilling machine in Mexico as he could be at a much higher level in a much more advanced society. The strong tendency to think that such work is a waste of time or is hopeless is to some extent overcome by a full recognition of the articles of faith above, that is, of the absolute necessity of a whole hierarchy of steps in social improvement. One can then feel as patriotic about helping to build a particular road over a mountain pass in a backward country as one could in performing at a much higher level in another country. I guess the full realization that it is an *absolute* prerequisite that nothing higher can happen before the lower needs get satisfied may do the trick, at least for intelligent and insightful people. They may then be able to pour their energies into a task at any level of social betterment, high or low.

Applied to the industrial situation the same kind of thing is true, that is, a multitude of little steps, little committee meetings, and little conversations are necessary before a particular plant can make its transition over from a lower-need motivational level, or authoritarian level to a higher basic need level or to democratic or enlightened management level. Each of these little steps is absolutely necessary and each of them is doing a big job. Or to say it in another way, any big job like improving American industry, translates itself down to millions of little jobs. There is no big job other than the total sum of all these little jobs. This, too, had better be stressed, especially with younger people who sit around waiting for some huge cause to enlist themselves in, for something worthy of them, for some great patriotic effort which will command their enthusiasm. They are generally willing to give up their lives for their country, but they are not willing to wash dishes for their country, or to run a mimeograph machine. Part of the job of teaching here is to teach that big, noble-sounding, resounding words like patriotism and democracy and social betterment and the like translate themselves down into the hour-to-hour, day-to-day slugging away at tasks which are means to the end. The thing to do here is to be very acutely aware of the goal or end of all the work, after making sure that all the means are going in the proper direction toward the proper end. This was exemplified during the war when people could feel quite patriotic while drilling holes some place or putting in rivets some place, or doing the most dull work like peeling potatoes or scrubbing floors or whatever. People understood far better then that all these little tasks added together to make the big task. In principle it should be possible to do this during peacetime too.

Another article of faith (7) in the holistic theory of social better-ment is that no one man can do everything. We have to give up for-ever the notion of a god or of a Messiah or of some great leader who will take care of everything and do everything. No human being can know enough or can be in enough places at once in order to do this total job of social betterment. The best a leader can do is to bind to-gether and to coordinate into a good organization all the various spe-cialists and theorists, etc., who are needed for the job.

This implies another article of faith (8) that there must be a divi-sion of labor in the task of changing a society, that is to say, there must necessarily be many people and many kinds of people to do the job. And this means in turn that each of these people is as necessary as any of the other individuals. Every kind of character, every kind of skill, every kind of talent, every kind of genius can be used and must be used, as a matter of fact is a prerequisite to total social change. This means that chemists must respect sociologists because they are both necessary. This means that chauffeurs and garbage collectors and clerks and machine operators and typists and god knows what else, *everybody* else as a matter of fact, are each of them and all of them necessary. This means then that any one person can be self-respecting in his task. It is not that people are divided into leaders and followers. In ideal so-cial change everybody knows exactly what the goal is and is doing his best and making his own best contribution toward this goal. He is, therefore, as much a general as anybody else. In ideal social change everybody *is* a general. Every kind of skill being needed, it then be-comes quite possible and feasible for any person to do anything that needs doing and feel good about it.

It becomes clearly understood then (9) that every person can be and should be healthily selfish. That is to say that, according to the-ory, since every kind of character, every kind of person can be help-ful and indeed is needed because he can do things that other kinds of character cannot do, therefore the most unique contribution that he can make is the best contribution that he can make. This means that he must look within himself, know his own talents and capacities well, and then offer for the common pool his own unique identity—that at which he can be better than anybody else in the whole world. This healthy selfishness is a wonderful thing because it permits us to be both altruistic and selfish at the same time. Or to say it another way about, being selfish is the most altruistic thing we can do ultimately in social betterment (if both of these words are very carefully defined). And also, if somebody asks about the best way to be altruistic or the best way to help the society, then the answer must be, first find out what you can do best and then offer yourself to do that. And since that which we can do best is self-actualizing, self-fulfilling, joy-producing, happiness-producing, then here is an excellent instance of the transcendence of the dichotomy between selfishness and altruism at this level of B-psychology, or of synergy. This permits us to do exactly what we want to do, which is what we can do best, which is what will bring us most fun and pleasure and joy, which is best for the society, which will permit us to feel virtuous, and permit us to have fun, and permit us to do our duty—all of these at exactly the same time simultaneously.

This implies another article of faith (10), namely the feeling of brotherhood and colleague-hood. If we really understand the foregoing, then we must also understand that we are all enlisted in the same army, all members of the same club or of the same team, that we have the same goals, and that therefore we must appreciate not only what we ourselves can give, but also appreciate the fact that what others are giving, they can give better than *we* can give. That is to say, we should be thankful and grateful for the fact that other people are different from ourselves. This is on the principle that if there were not enough mesomorphs, then ectomorphs like me would have to do the jobs of the mesomorphs. But since I am an ectomorph, I cannot do the mesomorph's job very well and anyway I don't enjoy them. They would be a miserable duty for me, although a great pleasure for the constitutional mesomorph. Therefore, if I have any sense I should be very happy about the fact that there are mesomorphs in the world, and I should be very grateful to them for being constitutionally equipped so as to desire to do the jobs that I don't like doing, but which must absolutely be done. If I deeply appreciate this then I will love mesomorphs, on just about the same principle that men and women who really deeply understand how they supplement each other can love the other sex instead of grudgingly cooperating with them. Every man should be profoundly and deeply grateful that there are such things as women in the world; and every sensible woman should be deeply and profoundly grateful that there are such things as men in the world.

So also should lawyers be grateful that there are doctors in the world, and doctors be grateful that there are machinists in the world, etc., etc. If this all goes deep enough, we come to the point even of being grateful (and therefore affectionate) to the morons in the world, people who are willing to do the garbage collecting, the dirty work, the repetitive work, etc., the work that must absolutely be done but that we would hate to do. The whole conception of rivalry and competition, of course, must be totally redefined against such a background of colleague-hood.

We may usefully consider that one group of people who have more of this feeling of colleague-hood than any other group in the world, namely the scientists. Their laws and rules and folkways are, of course, an example for other people. Science is very profoundly a division of labor and a colleague-hood, a brotherhood. But even here a careful analysis of the foregoing will show that the colleague-hood and division of labor and brotherhood of scientist is even so not as good as it might be. Rivalry and competition and the feeling of mutual exclusiveness, the feeling of hierarchies of respect and contempt, the feelings that some physicists have, for instance, that biology is not *really* a science and therefore worthy only of contempt, or the feeling that some sociologists have that engineers are only little boys who are still playing with toys and are not really doing the important work of the world—such feelings should fade away before a real understanding of the above articles of faith. Of course, all of this needs as a supplement a very widespread understanding of the definition of synergy and of the transcendence of dichotomies which result in synergy.

Perhaps a different article (11), perhaps only an extension of the above, follows from the above, namely, that each person must pick himself for his own job, that is, that there must be only volunteers for particular jobs. Each person must place himself in the society. This is so because each person must know his own identity and find out his own identity, meaning his own talents, capacities, skills, values, responsibilities, etc. Of course, each person can be helped by guidance workers, personnel workers, and clinical psychologists, etc., who can pass on to him information about himself via tests, or pass on to him economic information about what the society needs in the way of vocations, etc. And yet the final decision has to rest with the person himself, perhaps except in emergency situations.

Another fundamental article (12) which must be taught as part of this whole theory of revolutionary change or social betterment is the necessity for self-development, for self-actualization, for discipline and hard work in the fullest development of one's own talents or capacities, one's own genius. This is crucially necessary today because so many young people are making a distorted interpretation of the pervasive psychology of growth and self-actualization. More dependent, more indulged, more oral, more passive people are interpreting this philosophy of self-actualization to mean "waiting for inspiration," waiting for something to happen, waiting for something to grab them, waiting for some peak experience which will tell them automatically and without effort what their destiny is and what they should do. Part of this feeling of self-indulgence is that anything which is self-actualizing should be enjoyable.

Now, while this is in principle ultimately true, it is not always immediately true. Cultivating one's capacities can be hard work, can be distasteful in itself (even though it may simultaneously be enjoyed by those who understand it as taking a necessary step toward the ultimate goal of self-actualization by a commitment to a particular destiny). This attitude of the young is to some extent paralleled by the attitude of their parents and elders of not interfering with people, of letting them drift, of waiting for them to make up their own minds, or to find themselves, etc. Now, while this undoubtedly does happen and while this regime undoubtedly works well with some people, especially those with very strong and unmistakable talents or drives or wishes or devotions, it does not work nearly as well with more passive people, with confused and conflicted people, and especially with quite young children.

This whole philosophy of waiting for things to happen instead of making them happen, of loafing and loitering during this waiting period instead of regarding talent as requiring teaching, exercise, rehearsal, training, hard work, and the like, has to be counteracted. This means more research than we now have on the good effects of discipline and the bad effects of indulgence, the good effects of frustration, the good effects of hardship, the good effects of challenge, etc. Also it requires a careful theoretical and empirical working out of the way in which self-actualizing people in my study have *all* been hard workers, have *all* been dedicated and devoted people who poured themselves into their own vocations, or duties or the work with which they have identified themselves. Of course, all of this means a considerable improvement in parent education and parent behavior. It means combatting the present wave of child centering, interpreted as giving everything to any child whenever he wants it, and of fearing to hurt him by saying "no," or by frustrating him or making him delay his gratifications (see some very good examples here in the book by Richard Gordon and others, *The Split-Level Trap,* especially the chapter on children in the suburbs).[2]

A final article of faith (13), which is necessary to all the others and which is implied by all the others, is that the American type of revolution or social betterment differs from the traditional type of revolution in being not eternal, fixed, final, but rather in being open and experimental and even humble in a scientific way. Since not all information is in, and since knowledge is growing, and since especially we know so little about social things by comparison with what we need to know, any premature certainty, any overconfidence is not only unbecoming but is anti-scientific in this arena. All the rules of science, especially of a beginning science, are demanded by this general theory of social change.

John Dewey is the type of hero to be admired in this context, rather than the fiery, bloody, war-bringing revolutionaries of the past. The scientific attitude that is needed is, and must be, very pervasive and very deep. That is, every suggested improvement ought to be considered a hypothesis or an experiment to be tested and confirmed, always with the implication that it may turn out to be untrue or false or unwise, and even more universally, with the expectation that even though it may work well, it is going to bring up all sorts of new and unforeseen questions.

Thus we may point to the example of the affluence of our society which has been sought by mankind for many centuries and which was expected to bring not only possibilities of higher development for human beings but immediate happiness as well. This affluence has brought all sorts of virtues, advantages and steps forward, and yet it has also brought all sorts of totally unexpected problems, bad results, and booby traps. This kind of experimental attitude can and should be taken in another very explicit way. For instance, if we believe on the basis of all the evidence available that a particular kind of change in the style of teaching arithmetic is desirable for the goals of the society at large, then this can be instituted in various ways. One way is

[2] R. Gordon, K. Gordon, and M. Gunther, *The Split-Level Trap* (New York: Dell Books, 1962).

to believe that one has had a divine inspiration of some sort, to be absolutely certain and decisive about the whole business, to predict confidently that it will work perfectly, to scorn and despise and attack those who are skeptical or who disagree, etc. The other way of doing it is to assume that the probabilities are on the side of it working, but that there are real chances that it will not work, and in any case success has to be confirmed. The whole thing can be set up then as an experiment in advance with the possibility, for instance, of control groups so that we can know if there is a real effect or not, with before-and-after testing, with careful attention to the best experimental design possible under the circumstances, etc. Furthermore, there is no reason why a half-dozen experiments shouldn't be done simultaneously. If there are two or three or four equally reasonable possibilities for improvement, why not try them all simultaneously? Under the old system of certainty, of being the true believer, and of having been converted totally once and for all to the true and only and eternal faith, this kind of experimentation of course would not be possible. (See Eric Hoffer's book, *The True Believer*[3] for the characteristics of this older type of revolutionary or convert.)

One task implied by this article of faith is a redefinition of the concept of certainty. It should be shown in its various dictionary senses, and these should be sharply differentiated. The search for absolute certainty of the mathematical sort or of the old-fashioned religious sort must be given up once and for all. The only trouble is that once this kind of supernatural certainty is given up, many people tend to give up all notions of certainty altogether and they go in for a total relativity. This is not necessary. Show how the scientist can be very sure of himself and yet be perfectly aware of the probable errors involved in a particular statement. Making a statement on the basis of an accumulation of empirical evidence gives a "scientific certainty," even though not an "eternal and perfect mathematical certainty." These are different and should be differentiated.

Of course, many other changes in the theory, philosophy, and method of science would be made necessary by this use of Dewey type experimental method in social betterment. For instance, the whole question of participant observers must be worked out very carefully. The identification of science with laboratory experimentation

---

[3] E. Hoffer, *The True Believer* (New York: Harper & Bros., 1951).

must be given up once and for all. The notion of the observer affecting what he is observing just by observing it must be worked out more carefully. The Dalton kind of study in his book *Men Who Manage* could serve as a case example (especially with the addition of his new chapter, "Preconceptions and Methods," that he has written for a book called *Chronicles of Research,* edited by Phillip Hammond).

This kind of study needs duplication in dozens of different areas of social life. The whole question of the spurious and impossible separation of scientific objectivity and values must be given up permanently. This also requires a lot more fact and a lot more philosophizing than we now have available. Finally, one consequence of this article is an increased emphasis on slowness of social change, even of necessary slowness. We must have the patience of the scientist who waits until the data are in before he draws his conclusions.

The Necessity for Enlightened Management Policies

The more evolved people get, the more psychologically healthy they get, the more will enlightened management policy be necessary in order to survive in competition and the more handicapped will be an enterprise with an authoritarian policy.

People are growing and growing, either in their actual health of personality, or in their aspirations, especially in the United States, and especially women and other underprivileged groups. The more grown people are, the worse authoritarian management will work, the less well people will function in the authoritarian situation, and the more they will hate it. Partly this comes about from the fact that when people have a choice between a high and a low pleasure, they practically always choose the high pleasure if they have previously experienced both. What this means is that people who have experienced freedom can never really be content again with slavery, even though they made no protest about the slavery *before* they had the experience of freedom. This is true with all higher pleasures; those people who have known the feeling of dignity and self-respect for the first time can never again be content with slavishness, even though they made no protest about it before being treated with dignity.

Treating people well spoils them for being treated badly. That is, they become much less contented and willing to accept lower life conditions. This means in general that the better the society grows, the better the politics, the better the education, etc., the less suitable will the people be for Theory X management, or for authoritarian politics, or for gangster rule, or for prison-type colleges, and the more and more they will need and demand eupsychian management, growth-permitting education, etc. For this they will work well; for the authoritarian hierarchical management they will work badly and will be rebellious and hostile. This should show up in pragmatic ways, that is, in terms of production, quality, identification with the managers, etc.

Giving people good conditions spoils them for bad conditions.

Now what all this means so far as the competitive situation is concerned in the U.S. is that considering the level of personality development in this society that eupsychian or enlightened management is already beginning to become a competitive factor. That is, old-style management is steadily becoming obsolete, putting the enterprise in a less and less advantageous position in competition with other enterprises in the same industry that are under enlightened management and are therefore turning out better products, better service, etc., etc. That is to say that old-style management should soon be obsolete, even in the accounting sense, in the business sense, in the sense of competition, just in the same way that any enterprise will become obsolete and take a bad position in respect to competition if it has obsolete machinery.

The same is true for obsolete people. The more evolved people get, the more evolved psychologically, the more psychologically healthy they get, the more this will be true—the more will enlightened management policy be necessary in order to survive in competition and the more handicapped will be an enterprise with an authoritarian policy. This means all sorts of other theoretical things: for instance, the better our schools get, the greater the economic advantage for enlightened management. The more enlightened the religious institutions get, that is to say, the more liberal they get, the greater will be the competitive advantage for an enterprise run in an enlightened way. Etc., etc.

This is why I am so optimistic about the future of eupsychian management policy, why I consider it to be the wave of the future. The chances are that general political, social, and economic conditions will not change in any basic way; that is to say, I think we are in a stalemate of a military-political kind. Therefore, I expect that the present rates of growth and directions of growth in religion and industry, politics, education, etc., will continue in the same way. If anything, the tendency toward favoring eupsychian management should increase, because the tendency is toward more internationalism rather than less, which, in turn, will force all sorts of other growth-fostering changes in our society and in other societies as well. The same thing is probably true for the development of automation, although this, too, will bring all sorts of huge transitional problems along with it. The same thing is true for the possibility that we may shift over to a peace economy, laying much less stress on defense and military expenditures. This tendency will, I think, also favor enlightened management or democratic management over authoritarian or old-style management.

It looks as if it might be desirable eventually to coordinate, under one ninth vice president (in addition to Drucker's eight), what we might call the eupsychian tendency, the fostering of growth, the increasing of the personality level of all the employees of an enterprise including the managers. It is perfectly true now that this could be included and probably is included in enlightened plans under department seven of "worker-attitude and performance" and also under Drucker's department six, "managerial performance and development." I don't know that this ninth department is necessary *today,* but it may one day become professionalized and demanding a different kind, a different constellation of training, than either Drucker's department-six manager or Drucker's department-seven manager. For instance, a wide philosophical, psychological, and psychotherapeutic and educational training would certainly be very heavily involved in this ninth department.

This ninth department may soon turn out to be especially important and may be precipitated into action because of the requirement of the cold war. The way things are now, it looks as if there has been a military stalemate and a stalemate in the usefulness of physical, chemical, and biological weapons. These are no longer useful at all in the cold war except to prevent an open outbreak of war. The way in which the cold war will be won or will tip one way or the other will be in terms of the human products turned out by the Russian society and the American society. Since the cold war now really consists of all sorts of political, social, educational, and personal maneuvering before the neutral nations—that is, the effort is to win over *their* good opinion—then clearly all sorts of nonmilitary things come into account. One is race prejudice, in which the Russians have such a tremendous advantage over the Americans now, especially before the African nations.

But this will probably all add up ultimately in terms of the kind of person, the kind of average citizen, that is turned out by the two cultures. This is getting steadily more and more important as international travel gets easier and easier. It's the tourists, the visiting businessmen, the visiting scientists, the cultural exchanges that are now making a big impression and will get to be more and more important. If the Americans can turn out a better type of human being than the Russians, then this will ultimately do the trick. Americans will simply be more loved, more respected, more trusted, etc., etc. If this is so, then the establishment of growth-fostering tendencies in industry becomes a matter of high national policy and even of crash programs of the atom bomb sort. If we were to put into this the kind of money that we put into the atom bomb and are now putting into missiles and the space program, we might get a hell of a lot more for our money in the political sense. It may yet become national policy to have this ninth psychological vice president in every industry, partly as a public service, partly at the request of the government, the state department, etc.

(This is still another instance of increased interrelatedness, both in theory and in practice, plus the increased synergy and symbiosis of any industry and of the whole society. Furthermore, this kind of thing guarantees that this symbiosis will increase year by year rather than decrease, that the ties between government and industry will be greater rather than less. Any industry represents the whole society. Any industry has also the function of making good citizens or bad citizens in a democracy.)

The quality of product turned out also has international, cold war status as well as personal, local, and national status. That this is a practical everyday kind of consideration is already very clear, even though America doesn't realize this as much as other countries do. The stereotype in most of the world is that an American fountain pen is more likely to be a good, workable, efficient fountain pen than if it comes from another country. And we have the recent example of the self-conscious cooperation between the government of Japan and its industries in deliberately shifting over to higher-quality products. The stereotype of Japanese products before the war was that they were shoddy and cheap or low-quality imitations. But already, we are getting to think of Japanese products in about the same way that we used to think of a German product in the old days, that is, as being of very high quality and of excellent workmanship. Countries to some extent get judged by the quality of automobile or camera that they turn out. I am told that German quality has gone down. If this is so, then the status of West Germany in the eyes of the whole world will go down. It will be considered in an unconscious way to have less status, to have poorer quality as a nation. This, of course, since every West German tends to identify with his country and tends to introject it, means a loss of self-esteem in every single citizen, just as the increased Japanese quality and the general respect for their products means an increase in the self-esteem of every Japanese citizen. The same thing is true for the United States in a very general way.

Bibliography

A. H. Maslow, Brandeis University

1932

    1. (With Harry Harlow and Harold Uehling) Delayed reaction tests on primates from the lemur to the Orangoutan. *Jour. Comparative Psychol.*, 13:313–43.

    2. (With Harry Harlow) Delayed reaction tests on primates at Bronx Park Zoo. *Jour. Comparative Psychol.*, 14:97–107.

    3. The "emotion" of disgust in dogs. *Jour. Comparative Psychol.*, 14:401–07.

1933

    4. Food preferences of primates. *Jour. of Comparative Psychol.*, 16:187–97.

1934

    5. (With Elizabeth Groshong) Influence of differential motivation on delayed reactions in monkeys. *Jour. Comparative Psychol.*, 18:75–83.

    6. The effect of varying external conditions on learning, retention and reproduction. *Jour. Experimental Psychol.*, 17:38–47.

    7. The effect of varying time intervals between acts of learning with a note on proactive inhibition. *Jour. Experimental Psychol.*, 17:141–44.

1935

    8. Appetites and hungers in animal motivation. *Jour. Comparative Psychol.*, 20:75–83.

    9. Individual psychology and the social behavior of monkeys and apes. *Int. Jour. of Individ. Psychol.*, 1:47–59. Reprinted in German translation in *Internationale Zeitachrift für Individual Psychologie*, 1936, I, 14–25.

1936

    10. The role of dominance in the social and sexual behavior of infra-human primates. I. Observations at Vilas Park Zoo. *Jour. Genetic Psychol.*, 48:261–277.

    11. (With Sydney Flanzbaum) II. An experimental determination of the dominance behavior syndrome. *Jour. Genetic Psychol.*, 48:278–309. Reprinted in

W. Dennis (Ed.), *Readings in General Psychology* (Englewood Cliffs, NJ: Prentice-Hall, 1949).

12. III. A theory of sexual behavior of infra-human primates. *Jour. Genetic Psychol.*, 48:310–38.

13. IV. The determination of hierarchy in pairs and in groups. *Jour. Genetic Psychol.*, 49:161–98.

1937

14. The comparative approach to social behavior. *Social Forces,* 15:487–90.

15. The influence of familiarization on preferences. *Jour. Experimental Psychol.*, 21:162–80.

16. Dominance-feeling, behavior and status. *Psychological Review,* 44:404–29.

17. Personality and patterns of culture. In Stagner, Ross, *Psychology of Personality* (New York: McGraw-Hill, 1937). Reprinted in S. Britt (Ed.), *Selected Readings in Social Psychology* (New York: Rinehart, 1950).

18. (With Walter Grether) An experimental study of insight in monkeys. *Jour. Comparative Psychol.*, 24:127–34.

1938

18a. *Cases in Personality and Abnormal Psychology* (New York: Brooklyn College Press, 1938).

1939

19. Dominance-feeling, personality and social behavior in women. *Jour. Social Psychol.*, 10:3–39.

1940

20. Dominance-quality and social behavior in infra-human primates. *Jour. Social Psychol.*, 11:313–24.

21. A test for dominance-feeling (self-esteem) in college women. *Jour. Social Psychol.*, 12:255–70.

1941

22. (With Bela Mittelmann) *Principles of Abnormal Psychology: The Dynamics of Psychic Illness.* (New York: Harper and Brothers, 1941). Recorded as Talking Book for the Blind.

23. Deprivation, threat and frustration. *Psychol. Review,* 48:364–66. Reprinted in T. Newcomb and E. Hartley (Eds.), *Readings in Social Psychology*

(New York: Holt, Rinehart & Winston, 1947). Reprinted in Marx, M., *Psychological Theory: Contemporary Readings* (New York: Macmillan, 1951). Reprinted in C. Stacey & M. DeMartino (Eds.). *Understanding Human Motivation* (Cleveland: Howard Allen Publishers, 1958).

1942

24. Liberal leadership and personality. *Freedom,* 2:27–30.

25. *The Social Personality Inventory: A Test for Self-Esteem in Women* (with manual). (Palo Alto, Calif.: Consulting Psychologists Press, 1942).

26. The dynamics of psychological security-insecurity. *Character and Personality,* 10:331–44.

27. A comparative approach to the problem of destructiveness. *Psychiatry, 5* 517–22.

28. Self-esteem (dominance–feeling) and sexuality in women. *Jour. Social Psychol. 16* 259–94. Reprinted in M. DeMartino (Ed.), *Sexual Behavior & Personality Characteristics* (New York: Citadel Press, 1963).

1943

29. A preface to motivation theory. *Psychosomatic Medicine, 5,* 85–92.

30. A theory of human motivation. *Psychological Review, 50,* 370–96. Reprinted in P. Harriman (Ed.), *Twentieth Century Psychology* (New York: Philosophical Library, 1946). Reprinted in H. Remmers et al. (Eds.), *Growth, Teaching and Learning* (New York: Harpers, 1957). Reprinted in C. Stacey & M. DeMartino (Eds.), *Understanding Human Motivation* (Cleveland: Howard Allen Publishers, 1958). Reprinted in W. Lazer & E. Kelley (Eds.), *Managerial Marketing* (Homewood, Ill.: Richard D. Irwin, Inc., 1958). Reprinted in W. Baller (Ed.), *Readings in Psychology of Human Growth and Development* (New York: Holt, Rinehart & Winston, 1962). Reprinted in J. Seidman (Ed.), *The Child* (New York: Holt, Rinehart & Winston, 1958). Reprinted in L. Gorlow & W. Katkowsky (Eds.), *Readings in the Psychology of Adjustment* (New York: McGraw-Hill Book Co., Inc., 1959). Reprinted in R. Sutermeister (Ed.), *People and Productivity* (New York: McGraw-Hill Book Co., Inc., 1963). Reprinted in J. A. Dyal (Ed.), *Readings in Psychology: Understanding Human Behavior* (New York: McGraw-Hill Book Co., Inc., 1962). Reprinted in H. J. Leavitt & L. R. Pondy (Eds.), *Readings in Managerial Psychology* (Chicago: University of Chicago Press, 1964). Reprinted in J. Reykowski (Ed.), *Problemy Osobowsci I Motywacji W Psychologii Amerykanskiej* (Warsaw: Panstwowe Wyndawnictwo Naukowe, 1964). Reprinted in T. Costello & S. Zalkind (Eds.), *Psychology in Administration: A Research Orientation* (Englewood Cliffs, N.J.: Prentice-Hall, 1963). Reprinted in P. Hountras (Ed.), *Mental Hygiene: A Test of Readings* (Columbus, Ohio: Charles E. Merrill Co., 1961). Reprinted in I. Heckman &

S. Huneryager (Eds.), *Human Relations in Management* (Cincinnati, Ohio: South-Western Publishing Co., 1960).

31. Conflict, frustration and the theory of threat. *Jour. of Abnormal and Social Psychology, 38,* 81–86. Reprinted in S. Tomkins (Ed.), *Contemporary Psychopathology: A Sourcebook* (Cambridge, Mass.: Harvard University Press, 1943).

32. The dynamics of personality organization I. & II., *Psychological Review, 50,* 514–39, 541–58.

33. The authoritarian character structure. *Jour. of Social Psychol., 18,* 401–11. Reprinted in P. Harriman (Ed.), *Twentieth Century Psychology; Recent Developments in Psychology* (New York: Philosophical Library, 1946).

1944

34. What intelligence tests mean. *Jour. of General Psych.,* 31:85–93.

1945

35. (With Birsh, E., Stein, M., and Honigman, I.) A clinically derived test for measuring psychological security-insecurity. *Jour. of General Psychology,* 33:21–41.

36. A suggested improvement in semantic usage. *Psychological Review,* 52:239–40. Reprinted in *Etc., A Journal of General Semantics,* 1947, 4, 219–20.

37. Experimentalizing the clinical method. *Jour. of Clinical Psychology,* 1:241–43.

1946

38. (With I. Szilagyi-Kessler.) Security and breast-feeding. *Jour. of Abnormal and Social Psychology,* 41:83–85.

39. Problem-centering vs. means-centering in science. *Philosophy of Science,* 13:326–31.

1947

40. A symbol for holistic thinking. *Persona,* 1:24–25.

1948

41. "Higher" and "lower" needs. *Jour. of Psychology,* 25:433–36. Reprinted in C. Stacey & M. DeMartino (Eds.), *Understanding Human Motivation* (Cleveland: Howard Allen Publishers, 1958). Reprinted in K. Schultz (Ed.), *Applied Dynamic Psychology* (Berkeley: University of California Press, 1958).

42. Cognition of the particular and of the generic. *Psychological Review,* 55:22–40.

43. Some theoretical consequences of basic need-gratification. *Jour. of Personality,* 16:402–16.

1949

44. Our maligned animal nature. *Jour. of Psychology,* 28:273–78. Reprinted in S. Koenig and others (Eds.), *Sociology: A Book of Readings* (Englewood Cliffs, N.J.: Prentice-Hall, 1953).

45. The expressive component of behavior. *Psychol. Review,* 56:261–72. Condensed in *Digest of Neurology and Psychiatry,* Jan., 1950. Reprinted in Howard Brand (Ed.), *The Study of Personality: A Book of Readings* (New York: John Wiley & Sons, 1954).

1950

46. Self-actualizing people: a study of psychological health. *Personality Symposia:* Symposium #1 on Values, 1950, pp. 11–34 (New York: Grune & Stratton). Reprinted in C. Moustakes (Ed.), *The Self* (New York: Harper & Row, 1956). Reprinted in G. B. Levitas (Ed.), *The World of Psychology* (New York: George Braziller, 1963). Reprinted in C. G. Kemp (Ed.), *Perspectives on the Group Process* (New York: Houghton Mifflin Co., 1964).

1951

47. Social Theory of Motivation. In M. Shore (Ed.), *Twentieth Century Mental Hygiene* (New York: Social Science Publishers, 1950). Reprinted in K. Zerfoss (Ed.), *Readings in Counseling* (New York: Association Press, 1952).

48. (With D. MacKinnon.) Personality, in H. Helson (Ed.), *Theoretical Foundations of Psychology* (New York: D. Van Nostrand Co., 1951).

49. Higher needs and personality, *Dialectica* (University of Liege, 1951), 5, 257–65.

50. Resistance to acculturation, *Jour. of Social Issues,* 1951, 7, 26–29.

51. (With B. Mittelman) *Principles of Abnormal Psychology* (Rev. Ed.) (New York: Harper & Row, 1951). Recorded as Talking Book for the Blind. Chapter 16 reprinted in C. Thompson et al. (Eds.), *An Outline of Psychoanalysis* (New York: Modern Library, 1955).

52. Volunteer-error in the Kinsey study. (With J. Sakoda.) *Jour. Abnormal & Social Psychology,* 1952, 47, 259–62. Reprinted in J. Himelhoch and S. Fava (Ed.), *Sexual Behavior in American Society* (New York: W. W. Norton Co., 1955).

53. *The S-I Test* (A measure of psychological security-insecurity.) (Palo Alto, Calif.: Consulting Psychologists Press, 1951). Reprinted in Spanish translation, Instituto de Pedagogia, Universidad de Madrid, 1961. Polish translation, 1963.

1953

54. Love in Healthy People. In A. Montagu (Ed.), *The Meaning of Love* (New York: Julian Press, 1953), pp. 57–93. Reprinted in M. DeMartino (Ed.), *Sexual Behavior & Personality Characteristics* (New York: Citadel Press, 1963).

55. College teaching ability, scholarly activity and personality. *J. Educ. Psychol.*, 1953, *47*, 185–189. (With W. Zimmerman.) Reprinted in *Case Book: Education Beyond the High School, 1* (Washington, D.C.: U.S. Department of Health, Education, & Welfare, 1958).

1954

56. The instinctoid nature of basic needs. *Jour. of Personality*, 1954, *22*, 326–47.

57. *Motivation and Personality* (New York: Harper & Row, 1954). (Includes papers 23, 27, 29, 30, 31, 32, 39, 41, 42, 43, 44, 45, 46, 49, 50, 54, 56, 59.) Spanish Edition, 1963, Sagitario, Barcelona.

58. "Abnormal Psychology" (National Encyclopedia.)

59. Normality, health and values, *Main Currents,* 1954, *10,* 75–81.

1955

60. Deficiency motivation and growth motivation in M. R. Jones (Ed.), *Nebraska Symposium on Motivation: 1955* (Lincoln: University of Nebraska Press, 1955). Reprinted in *General Semantics Bulletin,* 1956, Nos. 18 and 19, 33–42. Reprinted in J. Coleman *Personality Dynamics & Effective Behavior* (Chicago: Scott, Foresman & Co., 1960). Reprinted in J. A. Dyal (Ed.), *Readings in Psychology: Understanding Human Behavior* (New York: McGraw-Hill Book Co., Inc., 1962). Reprinted in R. C. Teevan and R. C. Birney (Eds.), *Theories of Motivation in Personality and Social Psychology* (New York: D. Van Nostrand, 1964).

60a. Comments on Prof. McClelland's paper in M. R. Jones (Ed.), *Nebraska Symposium on Motivation, 1955* (Lincoln: University of Nebraska Press, 1955), pp. 65–69.

60b. Comments on Prof. Olds' paper in M. R. Jones (Ed.), *Nebraska Symposium on Motivation, 1955* (Lincoln: University of Nebraska Press, 1955), pp. 143–47.

1956

61. (With N. Mintz.) Effects of esthetic surroundings: I. Initial effects of three esthetic conditions upon perceiving "energy" and "well-being" in faces. *J. Psychol.,* 1956, *41,* 247–54.

62. Personality problems and personality growth in C. Moustakas (Ed.), *The Self* (New York: Harper & Row, 1956). Reprinted in J. Coleman, F. Libaw, and W. Martinson, *Success in College* (Chicago: Scott, Foresman & Co., 1961).

63. Defense and growth. *Merrill-Palmer Quarterly,* 1956, *3,* 36–47.

64. A philosophy of psychology, *Main Currents,* 1956, *13,* 27–32. Reprinted in *Etc.,* 1957, 14:10–22. Reprinted in J. Fairchild (Ed.), *Personal Problems and Psychological Frontiers* (New York: Sheridan House, 1957). Reprinted in *Manas,* 1958, *11,* Nos. 17 & 18. Reprinted in S. I. Hayakawa (Ed.), *Our Language and Our World* (New York: Harper & Row, 1959). Reprinted in L. Hamalian and E. Volpe (Eds.), *Essays of Our Times: II* (New York: McGraw-Hill Book Co., 1963). Reprinted in *Human Growth Institute Buzz Sheet,* 1964. Reprinted in F. Severin (Ed.), *Humanistic Viewpoints in Psychology* (New York: McGraw-Hill Book Co., Inc., 1965).

1957

65. Power relationships and patterns of personal development in A. Kornhauser (Ed.), *Problems of Power in American Democracy* (Detroit: Wayne University Press, 1957).

66. (With J. Bossom.) Security of judges as a factor in impressions of warmth in others. *J. Abn. Soc. Psychol.,* 1957, *55,* 147–8.

67. Two kinds of cognition and their integration. *General Semantics Bulletin,* 1957, Nos. 20 & 21, 17–22. Reprinted in *New Era in Home and School,* 1958, *39,* 202–5.

1958

68. Emotional Blocks to Creativity. *Journal of Individual Psychology,* 1958, *14,* 51–56. Reprinted in *Electro-Mechanical Design,* 1958, *2,* 66–72. Reprinted in *The Humanist,* 1958, *18,* 325–32. Reprinted in *Best Articles and Stories,* 1959, *3,* 23–35. Reprinted in S. Parnes and H. Harding (Eds.), *A Source Book for Creative Thinking* (New York: Chas. Scribner's Sons, 1962).

1959

69. Psychological data and human values in A. H. Maslow (Ed.), *New Knowledge in Human Values* (New York: Harper & Row, 1959).

70. Editor, *New Knowledge in Human Values* (New York: Harper & Row, 1959).

71. Creativity in self-actualizing people in H. H. Anderson (Ed.), *Creativity & Its Cultivation* (New York: Harper & Row, 1959). Reprinted in *Electro-Mechanical Design,* 1959 (Jan. and Aug.). Reprinted in *General Semantics Bulletin,* 1959, Nos. 24 and 25, 45–50.

72. Cognition of being in the peak experiences. *J. Genetic Psychol.,* 1959, *94,* 43–66. Reprinted in *Internat. Jour. Parapsychol.,* 1960, 2, 23–54. Reprinted in B. Stoodley (Ed.), *Society and Self: A Reader in Social Psychology* (Glencoe, Ill.: Free Press of Glencoe, 1962). Reprinted in W. Fullagar, H. Lewis and

C. Cumbee (Eds.), *Readings in Educational Psychology*, 2nd Edition (New York: Thomas Y. Crowell, 1964).

73. Mental health and religion in *Religion, Science and Mental Health*, Academy of Religion and Mental Health (New York: University Press, 1959).

74. Critique of self-actualization. I. Some dangers of Being-cognition, *J. Individual Psychol.*, 1959, *15*, 24–32. (Kurt Goldstein number.)

1960

75. Juvenile delinquency as a value disturbance (with R. Diaz-Guerrero) in J. Peatman & F. Hartley (Eds.), *Festschrift for Gardner Murphy* (New York: Harper & Row, 1960).

76. Remarks on existentialism and psychology. *Existentialist Inquiries*, 1960, *1*, 1–5. Reprinted in *Religious Inquiry*, 1960, No. 28, 4–7. Reprinted in Rollo May (Ed.), *Existential Psychology* (New York: Random House, 1961).

77. Resistance to being rubricized in B. Kaplan and S. Wapner (Eds.), *Perspectives in Psychological Theory* (New York: International Universities Press, 1960).

78. (With H. Rand and S. Newman.) Some parallels between the dominance and sexual behavior of monkeys and the fantasies of patients in psychotherapy. *Journal of Nervous and Mental Disease*, 1960, *131*, 202–212. Reprinted in M. DeMartino (Ed.), *Sexual Behavior and Personality Characteristics* (New York: Citadel Press, 1963).

1961

79. Health as transcendence of the environment. *Jour. Humanistic Psychology*, 1961, *1*, 1–7.

80. Peak-experiences as acute identity experiences. *Amer. Journ. Psychoanalysis*, 1961, *21*, 254–260. Reprinted in A. Combs (Ed.), *Personality Theory and Counseling Practice* (Gainesville, Fla.: University of Florida Press, 1961). Digested in *Digest of Neurology and Psychiatry*, 1961.

81. Eupsychia—The good society, *Journ. Humanistic Psychology*, 1961, *1*, 1–11.

82. Are our publications and conventions suitable for the Personal Sciences? *Amer. Psychologist*, 1961, *16*, 318–19. Reprinted as *WBSI Report* No. 8, 1962. Reprinted in *General Semantics Bulletin*, 1962, Nos. 28 and 29, 92–93.

83. Comments on Skinner's attitude to science. *Daedalus*, 1961, *90*, 572–73.

84. Some frontier problems in mental health. In A. Combs (Ed.), *Personality Theory and Counseling Practice* (Gainesville, Fla.: University of Florida Press, 1961).

84a. *Notes Toward a Psychology of Being. WBSI Report* No. 7, 1961 (includes 89, 98, and Appendix I in 102).

1962

85. Some basic propositions of a growth and self-actualization psychology. In A. Combs (Ed.), *Perceiving, Behaving, Becoming: A New Focus for Education*. 1962 Yearbook of Association for Supervision and Curriculum Development, Washington, D.C. Reprinted in C. Stacey and M. DeMartino (Eds.), *Understanding Human Motivation*, Revised Edition (Cleveland: Howard Allen, 1963). Reprinted in G. Lindzey and C. Hall (Eds.), *Theories of Personality: Primary Sources and Research* (New York: John Wiley & Sons, 1965).

86. *Toward a Psychology of Being* (Princeton, N.J.: D. Van Nostrand Co., 1962). Includes papers 60, 62, 63, 69, 71, 72, 74, 76, 77, 79, 80, 82, 85, 93. Japanese translation, 1964, by Y. Ueda (Tokyo: Charles Tuttle Co.).

87. Book review: John Schaar, *Escape from Authority. Humanist*, 1962, *22*, 34–35.

88. Lessons from the peak-experiences. *Journ. Humanistic Psychology*, 1962, *2*, 9–18. Reprinted as *WBSI Report* No. 6, 1962. Digested in *Digest of Neurology and Psychiatry*, 1962, p. 340.

89. Notes on Being-Psychology. *Journ. Humanistic Psychology*, 1962, 2, 47–71. Reprinted in *WBSI Report* No. 7, 1961. Reprinted in H. Ruitenbeek (Ed.), *Varieties of Personality Theory* (New York: E. P. Dutton, 1964).

90. Was Adler a disciple of Freud? A note. *Journ. Individual Psychology*, 1962, *18*, 125.

91. Summary Comments: Symposium on Human Values (L. Solomon, Ed.), *WBSI Report* No. 17, 1961, 41–44. Reprinted in *Journ. Humanistic Psychology*, 1962, *2*, 110–11.

92. *Summer Notes on Social Psychology of Industry and Management* (Delmar, Calif.: Non-Linear Systems, Inc., 1962). Includes papers 97, 100, 101, 104.

1963

93. The need to know and the fear of knowing. *Journ. General Psychol.*, 1963, *68*, 111–25.

94. The creative attitude. *The Structurist*, 1963, No. 3, 4–10. Reprinted as a separate by *Psychosynthesis Foundation*, 1963.

95. Fusions of facts and values. *Amer. Journ. Psychoanalysis*, 1963, *23*, 117–31.

96. Criteria for judging needs to be instinctoid. *Proceedings of 1963 International Congress of Psychology* (Amsterdam: North-Holland Publishers, 1964), 86–87.

Index